NOLO® Products & Services

⇨ ## Books & Software

Get in-depth information. Nolo publishes hundreds of great books and software programs for consumers and business owners. They're all available in print or as downloads at Nolo.com.

⇨ ## Legal Encyclopedia

Free at Nolo.com. Here are more than 1,400 free articles and answers to common questions about everyday legal issues including wills, bankruptcy, small business formation, divorce, patents, employment and much more.

⇨ ## Plain-English Legal Dictionary

Free at Nolo.com. Stumped by jargon? Look it up in America's most up-to-date source for definitions of legal terms.

⇨ ## Online Legal Documents

Create documents at your computer. Go online to make a will or living trust, form an LLC or corporation or obtain a trademark or provisional patent at Nolo.com. For simpler matters, download one of our hundreds of high-quality legal forms, including bills of sale, promissory notes, nondisclosure agreements and many more.

⇨ ## Lawyer Directory

Find an attorney at Nolo.com. Nolo's unique lawyer directory provides in-depth profiles of lawyers all over America. From fees and experience to legal philosophy, education and special expertise, you'll find all the information you need to pick a lawyer who's a good fit.

⇨ ## Free Legal Updates

Keep up to date. Check for free updates at Nolo.com. Under "Products," find this book and click "Legal Updates." You can also sign up for our free e-newsletters at Nolo.com/newsletters/index.html.

7th edition

101 Law Forms for Personal Use

**By Attorneys Ralph Warner & Robin Leonard
with the editors of Nolo**

SEVENTH EDITION	OCTOBER 2009
Editor	EMILY DOSKOW
Cover Design	SUSAN PUTNEY
Production	MARGARET LIVINGSTON
Proofreader	ANI DIMUSHEVA
CD-ROM Preparation	ELLEN BITTER
Index	THÉRÈSE SHERE
Printing	DELTA PRINTING SOLUTIONS, INC.

Warner, Ralph E.
    101 law forms for personal use / by Ralph Warner & Robin Leonard ; with the editors of Nolo. -- 7th ed.
        p. cm.
    Includes bibliographical references and index.
    ISBN-13: 978-1-4133-1066-5 (pbk.)
    ISBN-10: 1-4133-1066-4 (pbk.)
    1. Forms (Law)--United States--Popular works. I. Leonard, Robin. II.Nolo (Firm) III. Title.
IV. Title: One hundred one law forms for personal use. V. Title: One hundred and one law forms for personal use.
    KF170.L46 2009
    347.73'55--dc22

                               2009021417

Please note

We believe accurate, plain-English legal information should help you solve many of your own legal problems. But this text is not a substitute for personalized advice from a knowledgeable lawyer. If you want the help of a trained professional—and we'll always point out situations in which we think that's a good idea—consult an attorney licensed to practice in your state.

Acknowledgments

This book is a compilation and modification of some of the forms that exist in several other Nolo publications, plus several new ones. It couldn't have been written without the editorial assistance and support of Nolo's editorial department, particularly: Ilona Bray, Cathy Caputo, Amy DelPo, Emily Doskow, Steve Elias, Diana Fitzpatrick, Lisa Guerin, Ella Hirst, Shae Irving, Beth McKenna, Shannon Miehe, Janet Portman, Mary Randolph, Barbara Kate Repa, Alayna Schroeder, Betsy Simmons, Richard Stim, and Marcia Stewart. Thanks to Teresa Bruns for her research assistance. Terri Hearsh and Margaret Livingston labored long and hard to make the book both attractive and functional.

For the Fifth Edition, many thanks are due to John Lamb, whose work on Chapters 7, 8, 10, and 11 was invaluable. For the Seventh Edition as well as all previous editions, Nolo's Applications Development Department, represented by André Zivkovich and Ellen Bitter, did a great job making the forms in this book consistent and sensible.

Table of Contents

How to Use This Book

Filling in the Contracts and Forms..3

Editing the Forms 4

Describing People, Property, and Events...5

Signing the Forms..7

Resolving Disputes...8

Do You Need a Lawyer? 10

Delegating Authority to Care for Children, Pets, and Property

Form 1: Temporary Guardianship Authorization for Care of Minor............ 14

Form 2: Authorization for Minor's Medical Treatment................................... 15

Form 3: Authorization for Foreign Travel With Minor 16

Form 4: Housesitting Instructions... 16

Form 5: Children's Carpool Agreement.. 17

Form 6: Pet Care Agreement.. 18

Form 7: Authorization to Drive a Motor Vehicle....................................... 18

Form 8: Power of Attorney for Finances (Limited Power) 19

Form 9: Power of Attorney for Real Estate 23

Form 10: Notice of Revocation of Power of Attorney.............................. 27

Basic Estate Planning

Form 11: Property Worksheet.. 30

Form 12: Beneficiary Worksheet 31

Forms 13 and 14: Basic Wills... 32

Form 13: Will for Adult With No Children.. 34

Form 14: Will for Adult With Child(ren).. 34

Form 15: Will Codicil... 36

Things to Do After a Death: Documents for Executors

Form 16: Request for Death Certificate.. 38

Form 17: Notice to Creditor of Death 39

Form 18: Executor's Checklist... 40

Form 19: General Notice of Death 40

Form 20: Obituary Information Fact Sheet 41

Form 21: Notice to Deceased's Homeowners' Insurance Company 41

Form 22: Notice to Deceased's Vehicle Insurance Company 42

4 Renting a Place to Live

Form 23: Apartment-Finding Service Checklist 46

Form 24: Rental Application 47

Form 25: Fixed-Term Residential Lease and Form 26: Month-to-Month
Residential Rental Agreement 48

Form 27: Landlord-Tenant Agreement to Terminate Lease 50

Form 28: Consent to Assignment of Lease 51

Form 29: Landlord-Tenant Checklist 51

Form 30: Notice of Needed Repairs 52

Form 31: Tenant's Notice of Intent to Move Out 53

Form 32: Demand for Return of Security Deposit 53

5 Borrowing and Lending Money

Form 33: Loan Comparison Worksheet 56

Form 34: Authorization to Check Credit and Employment References 56

Form 35: Monthly Payment Record 58

Forms 36–40: Promissory Notes 58

Form 36: Promissory Note—Installment Payments With Interest 60

Form 37: Promissory Note—Installment Payments With Interest and
Balloon Payment 61

Form 38: Promissory Note—Installment Payments Without Interest 62

Form 39: Promissory Note—Lump Sum Payment With Interest 62

Form 40: Promissory Note—Lump Sum Payment Without Interest 63

Form 41: Cosigner Provision 63

Forms 42–45: Security Agreements 63

Form 42: Security Agreement Provision for Promissory Note 64

Form 43: Security Agreement 65

Form 44: U.C.C. Financing Statement 65

Form 45: Release of U.C.C. Financing Statement 66

Form 46: Agreement to Modify Promissory Note 66

Form 47: Overdue Payment Demand 67

Form 48: Demand to Make Good on Bad Check 67

6 Buying a House

Form 49: Ideal House Profile 70

Form 50: House Priorities Worksheet 71

Form 51: House Comparison Worksheet 72

Form 52: Family Financial Statement 72

Form 53: Monthly Carrying Costs Worksheet 75

Form 54: Mortgage Rates and Terms Worksheet 77

Form 55: Moving Checklist 80

7 Buying or Selling a Car, Dog, or Other Personal Property

Form 56: Motor Vehicle Bill of Sale 82

Form 57: Boat Bill of Sale 83

Form 58: Computer System Bill of Sale 84

Form 59: General Bill of Sale 84

Form 60: Bill of Sale for Dog 85

8 Renting Personal Property and Storing Goods

Form 61: Personal Property Rental Agreement 88

Form 62: Notice of Termination of Personal Property
        Rental Agreement 89

Form 63: Storage Contract 89

9 Home Repairs and Maintenance

Form 64: Home Maintenance Agreement 93

Form 65: Home Repairs Agreement 94

Form 66: Contractor Mid-Job Worksheet 94

10 Handling Personal Finances

Form 67: Daily Expenses 98

Form 68: Monthly Income 99

Form 69: Monthly Budget 99

Form 70: Statement of Assets and Liabilities 100

Form 71: Assignment of Rights 100

Form 72: Notice to Terminate Joint Account 101

Form 73: Notice to Stop Payment of Check 102

Form 74: Request for Credit Report 103

Form 75: Dispute Incorrect Credit Report Entry 104

Form 76: Dispute Credit Card Charge..105

Form 77: Demand Collection Agency Cease Contact.....................................106

11 Dealing With Junk Mail and Telemarketing Calls

Form 78: Notice to Remove Name From List...109

Form 79: Notice to Add or Retain Name but Not Sell or Trade It.............111

Form 80: Telemarketing Phone Call Log...111

Form 81: Notice to Put Name on Company's "Do Not Call" List................112

Form 82: Demand for Damages for Excessive Calls.......................................113

12 Hiring Child Care, Elder Care, or Household Help

Form 83: Child Care Agreement..118

Form 84: Child Care Instructions...120

Form 85: Elder Care Agreement..121

Form 86: Housekeeping Services Agreement..121

13 Living Together

Form 87: Agreement to Keep Property Separate...124

Form 88: Agreement for a Joint Purchase...125

Form 89: Agreement to Share Property..126

Form 90: Declaration of Legal Name Change...127

14 Settling Legal Disputes

Form 91: Demand Letter..130

Form 92: Online Auction Buyer Demand Letter...131

Form 93: Request for Refund or Repair of Goods Under Warranty..........132

Form 94: Accident Claim Worksheet..134

Forms 95–100: Releases...134

Form 95: General Release..136

Form 96: General Mutual Release...137

Form 97: Release for Damage to Real Estate..137

Form 98: Release for Property Damage in Auto Accident............................137

Form 99: Release for Personal Injury..137

Form 100: Mutual Release of Contract Claims..138

15 Miscellaneous Forms for Personal Use

Form 101: Complaint Letter 140

Form 102: Notice of Insurance Claim 141

Form 103: Notice to Cancel Certain Contracts.................................142

Form 104: Cancel Membership or Subscription Notice................143

Form 105: Request to Begin Special Education Process.............144

Form 106: Identity Theft Worksheet 145

Appendixes

A How to Use the CD-ROM

Installing the Files Onto Your Computer 150

Using the Word Processing Files to Create Documents................151

List of Files on the CD-ROM...153

B Tear-Out Forms...157

Index...359

How to Use This Book

Filling in the Contracts and Forms..3

Editing the Forms..4

    Selecting From Several Choices...4

    Deleting Clauses or Phrases..4

    Adding Clauses or Language...5

Describing People, Property, and Events...5

Signing the Forms..7

    Notarization...7

    Spouse's Signature 8

Resolving Disputes..8

Do You Need a Lawyer?...10

This book provides more than 100 ready-to-use forms and contracts for a variety of everyday legal and practical transactions that most Americans can safely handle themselves, without formal legal help. Among the forms are those necessary to write a simple will, settle minor legal disputes, prepare a power of attorney, lend or borrow money, rent a place to live, request your credit report, and sell a used car. Forms are also included to hire someone to do home repairs, to care for your children, and for a variety of other purposes.

Many of the forms in this book are primarily designed for your personal, individual use, such as the Apartment-Finding Service Checklist or Loan Comparison Worksheet. But other forms, such as the Elder Care Agreement, are contracts, designed to allow two or more parties to create a legally enforceable agreement.

Unlike commercial contracts used to buy a house or sign up with a health maintenance organization, which almost always consist of pages full of legalese, the contracts in this book are written in everyday (but legal) language. They are designed to describe and define a transaction, such as designating a temporary guardian for your child, with a reasonable level of specificity—without sacrificing clarity and simplicity.

Don't worry that because our contracts are jargon-free, they might be less valid than others. In general, as long as two parties—business entities or people—exchange promises to each do something of benefit for the other, a valid contract is formed. A contract will usually be enforced as long as all of the following requirements are met:

- **The terms are specific enough.** The contract must be clear and detailed enough so that an arbitrator or judge can sensibly decide who is right if there's a dispute later. For example, a house painting agreement that says "John the Painter shall paint Sally

The Importance of Getting Contracts in Writing

The most important rule when making any business agreement or transaction is this: Get it in writing. In a few situations—such as a contract to buy or sell real estate—you must have a written agreement for it to be legally enforceable. Similarly, a contract that can't be performed within one year of when it's made must be written.

But even when an oral contract is legal, there are many practical reasons why a written contract is preferable. Two years from now, you and the other people involved in any transaction might have significantly different recollections about what you agreed to. So putting your agreement into black and white is an important memory aid.

And a well-drafted contract has several other important benefits. For one, it serves as a framework for settling disputes. If this proves impossible and a court contest ensues, it will be far easier to prove the terms of a written contract than an oral one.

Another important benefit of drafting a written agreement is that the act of putting a contract together can help you and the other parties focus on all key legal and practical issues, some of which might otherwise be overlooked. By starting this process with a well-designed form—like those in this book—you increase your chances of creating a thorough and useful document.

the Homeowner's house" provides so little guidance that it is next to worthless and probably would not be enforced. At the very least, to be enforceable, the contract should state how much John is to be paid for his work. Of course, you'll want to create a contract that not only defines who and what is involved but also anticipates problems likely to arise under it. To be of real value, it should include key details such as the type and color of paint to be used, the work schedule, how and when payment is to be made, and what happens if John and Sally disagree about something.

- **The contract is for a legal purpose.** A contract formed to accomplish something illegal is not enforceable in a court. For instance, if two people who sign a contract to transfer an illegal gambling operation later have a falling out, the agreement will not be enforced by a judge.

- **Enforcement would not be grossly unfair.** The contracts you make using the forms in this book are unlikely to be challenged on the grounds of fairness. But in extreme situations, if a contract is both unfair and the result of one party's superior bargaining position (such as a one-sided premarital agreement between a millionaire and an unsophisticated recent immigrant), a court might not enforce it. If you keep in mind that the best contracts substantially benefit both parties, you will have no problems.

Filling in the Contracts and Forms

The forms in this book are designed to be used as needed; we don't expect you to read the book from start to finish. But we do ask one thing: Read this introduction, all of the introductory material at the beginning of any chapter containing a form that you will use, and the instructions for completing the form itself.

You can use the forms provided in this book in at least three ways:

1. **Use the Forms CD-ROM.** All the forms are contained on the accompanying disk. If you have access to a computer, the most efficient approach is to fill in and print a desired form using the computer's word-processing program, customizing the form as needed.

2. **Use the tear-out form.** You can also get the job done the old-fashioned way—by photocopying a form out of the book and filling it in with a typewriter or pen. *Don't,* however, use the original tear-out form from the book, or you'll be left without a clean copy. Although you'll be fine filling in some forms for your personal use by hand, such as the Property Worksheet, we suggest that you type the agreements whenever possible. While typing is not legally required, a printed document usually carries more weight than a hand-written one and is more legible. But if convenience or cost dictates that you fill in a contract or form by hand, do it neatly and you should be fine.

CAUTION

You must retype the tear-out will. As explained in Chapter 2, you cannot just tear out the will form, fill it in, and sign it. Instead, use the disk that comes with this book (or a typewriter if you don't have access to a computer) to prepare a fresh will that contains only the clauses you want. If you are writing a will, be sure to read the instructions in Chapter 2 carefully, including how wills must be signed and witnessed.

3. Use the forms in this book to evaluate similar forms and contracts. If someone drafts a contract and presents it to you to sign, you can use a corresponding form in this book as a checklist to make sure that the proposed contract has all the recommended ingredients. If it doesn't, use the form in this book as a model to suggest modifications or additions.

Editing the Forms

Many of the forms in this book may meet your needs perfectly. All you will need to do is fill in a few blanks and sign it. But for some forms, you'll want to make some changes—such as adding or deleting language or clauses. Here's how.

Selecting From Several Choices

Many of our forms require that you choose among several options, such as the method of payment for the work being performed under a Home Repairs Agreement or Child Care Agreement (see sample below). When you see a clause like this, simply check the correct box on the tear-out form and provide any requested additional information.

On several of our forms, you may encounter some slightly awkward language, such as ☐ Yes ☐ No or "his/hers." In either case, you can easily clean the form up by deleting words that don't apply or substituting more appropriate language (assuming you're using the forms on disk). If you're filling in a tear-out form, leaving the unneeded words in will not affect the validity of the contract. If you prefer, however, you can ink out the portion that does not apply.

Deleting Clauses or Phrases

Some individual clauses or phrases in our forms and agreements may not apply to your situation. If you are using the forms on the disk, making changes is easy—simply delete those clauses and renumber the remaining clauses as appropriate.

Example of Clause With Several Options (Clause 2 of Home Repairs Agreement)

---

2. **Payment**

   In exchange for the work specified in Clause 1, Homeowner agrees to pay Contractor as follows *[choose one and check appropriate boxes]*:

   ☐ $_____, payable upon completion of the specified work by ☐ cash ☐ check.

   ☐ $_____, payable by ☐ cash ☐ check as follows:

   _____% payable when the following occurs:_____

   _____% payable when the following occurs:_____

   _____% payable when the following occurs:_____ .

   ☐ $ _____ per hour for each hour of work performed, up to a maximum of $ _____ ,

   payable at the following times and in the following manner:_____

   _____ .

If you are using the tear-out forms, draw lines through the clause you want to delete and have all parties put their initials next to it. If you are deleting a complete clause, you'll need to renumber the clauses to avoid confusion. For example, if you do not want your lease to include a clause on extended absences of tenants (Clause 16 of Form 25, Fixed-Term Residential Lease), make the modifications as shown below.

Adding Clauses or Language

Adding extra terms to a contract is easy if you're using the forms on disk: Simply add the new language or clauses and renumber the remaining clauses as appropriate.

If you are using the tear-out forms and want to add words to a clause, use the space provided. If we didn't leave enough room, or if you want to add a new clause, you should prepare a separate addendum sheet or attachment. See "How to Prepare an Attachment Page," below, for details.

CAUTION

Be sure your changes are clear, easy to understand, and legal. If you add a list of property or work specifications to a contract, your contract should still be fine. But if you delete one of our clauses and substitute your own, make sure your language is easy to understand, free of ambiguity, and consistent with the rest of the contract. Also, if you have any doubt about the legal validity of language you want to add or delete—especially if significant amounts of money or property, or the personal rights of the other person are involved—have the changes checked by a lawyer.

Describing People, Property, and Events

Some forms ask you to name people or describe events or property. Here's the best way to do this.

People. Where you are asked to insert the name, address, and other identifying information for a person, use that person's legal name—the name on a driver's license—and home street

---

Example of How to Delete a Clause (Clause 16 of Form 25, Fixed-Term Residential Lease)

~~Clause 16. Extended Absences by Tenant.~~

MS ~~Tenant will notify Landlord in advance if Tenant will be away from the premises for _____ or~~ ~~consecutive days. During such absence, Landlord may enter the premises at times reasonably necessary~~ ~~maintain the property and inspect for needed repairs.~~

Clause ~~17~~. **16** Possession of the Premises

a. *Tenant's failure to take possession.*

If, after signing this Agreement, Tenant fails to take possession of the premises, Tenant will still be respo for paying rent and complying with all other terms of this Agreement.

How to Prepare an Attachment Page

If you need to add anything to a tear-out copy of one of the forms or agreements in this book, take the following steps.

1. If you want to add words to a clause and there is not enough space to insert the new language into the specific clause of the agreement, you can refer to it as an attachment by adding the words: "Clause *[number]* continued on Attachment A *[or B or C and so on]* of *[name of agreement or form]*."

   EXAMPLE: Clause 1 of the General Bill of Sale provides space for you to list the items you're selling. If there is not enough room to list all these items on the tear-out, write the words "Clause 1 continued on Attachment A of the General Bill of Sale."

   Similarly, if you want to add a new clause, insert the words "Agreement continued on Attachment A of *[name of agreement or form]*" after the last clause of the agreement and before the place where the agreement gets signed.

Use a separate attachment each time you need more room.

2. Make your own attachment form, using a sheet of blank white 8½" by 11" paper. At the top of the form, write "Attachment A *[or B or C and so on]* to *[name of agreement or form]* between *[insert names of all parties]*" for the first attachment, and so on. Then add the words "a continuation of *[number clause]*" if you're continuing a clause, or "an addition to *[number clause]*" if you're adding a new clause.

   EXAMPLE: "Attachment A to General Bill of Sale between Beth Spencer and Rich Portman. A continuation of Clause 1."

3. Type or print the additional information on the attachment.

4. Have both parties sign or initial the attachment at the bottom of each page.

5. Staple all attachments to the end of the main agreement or form.

address. If a person commonly uses two names (not including a nickname), include both, for example, "Alison Johnson, aka Alison Walker-Johnson."

Property. To identify property, such as a defective computer you're returning with a Request for Refund or Repair of Goods Under Warranty (Form 93), be as specific as you can. There are no magic words. Your goal is simply to identify the property clearly so that no misunderstanding will arise later. Normally, this means listing the make, model, type, color, identifying number if the item has one, and any

other identifying characteristics that come to mind. For instance, if you are requesting repair of a computer under warranty, you might say "Dell Inspiron 5500 laptop, ID # 445556, 30 GB hard disk."

Events. Take a similar approach when describing events, such as payment for a housecleaner (Form 86). As long as you identify the date, time (if appropriate), and location, and include a clear description of what happened or what is supposed to happen, your description should be adequate.

Signing the Forms

Each form has specific signing instructions, including who must sign, how many copies to make, whether notarization is required or recommended, and any requirements for a spouse to sign or for witnesses.

> **CAUTION**
>
> **Always keep your signed copy in a safe place, along with any related documents or correspondence.** You may need this at some point—for example, if you end up in court over a dispute concerning an agreement or contract.

Notarization

Whenever we suggest that you have the document notarized, we have included a notary certificate at the end of the form. Notarization means that a person authorized as a notary public certifies in writing that:

- you're the person you claim to be, and
- you've acknowledged under oath signing the document.

When you are having a form notarized, who has to visit the notary depends on the circumstances. If you're preparing a form that must be both witnessed and notarized (like the Power of Attorney forms in Chapter 1), you and your witnesses must appear together before the notary public so the witnesses can watch you sign the form. In other cases where more than one person signs the document, you can each visit the notary on your own, if you prefer. Each signer will get a separate notarization certificate and you'll attach all of them to the document.

Very few legal documents need to be notarized or witnessed. Notarization and witnessing are usually limited to documents, such as a power of attorney involving real estate, that are going to be recorded at a public office charged with keeping such records —for example, a county land records office or registrar of deeds. Occasionally—but very rarely—state laws require witnesses or notaries to sign other types of documents.

The notary will want proof of your identity, such as a driver's license that bears your photo and signature. The notary will watch each of you sign (or, in some circumstances, you can simply acknowledge that you signed the document already) and then will complete an acknowledgment, including a notarial seal. A few states have special requirements for notarization language. For example, Alaska uses the term "Judicial District" instead of "County," and Montana requires notaries to include their place of residence when they acknowledge a document. Notaries in your state will know the rules and can provide the appropriate certificate. A sample of typical notarization language (used in California and included on the power of attorney forms in Chapter 1) is shown below.

You can often find a notary at a bank, lawyer's office, real estate office, or title insurance office. Most charge under $20 for notarizing a document. In some states, if you are notarizing a document that relates to real estate, you will have to allow the notary to take your thumbprint.

> **TIP**
>
> **Notarization is always an option.** If there is no mention of notarization in the signing instructions for a form, that means it is not required or recommended. However, even if we don't suggest you have a form notarized, you may choose to— simply because it adds a measure of legal credibility.

Sample Notarization Language

Certificate of Acknowledgment of Notary Public

State of _____ $\Big\}$ ss

County of _____

On _____, _____, before me, _____ ,

personally appeared _____ , who proved to me on the basis of satisfactory

evidence to be the person(s) whose name(s) is/are subscribed to the within instrument and acknowledged to me that

he/she/they executed the same in his/her/their authorized capacity(ies) and that by his/her/their signature(s) on the

instrument, the person(s), or the entity upon behalf of which the person(s) acted, executed the instrument.

I certify under PENALTY OF PERJURY under the laws of the State of _____ that the

foregoing paragraph is true and correct.

WITNESS my hand and official seal.

_____

Notary Public for the State of _____

My commission expires _____

[NOTARY SEAL]

Spouse's Signature

If you'll be asked to sign a contract that makes you liable for a debt, such as a promissory note, the other person may ask that your spouse sign as well. This is most likely to happen, for example, if you're borrowing money to buy property that both spouses will use, or to help finance a new business venture. For more details, see the discussion of promissory notes in Chapter 5.

Resolving Disputes

It's sad but true—at some point you may have a legal dispute involving one of the forms or contracts in this book. For example, maybe your partner reneges on an agreement to share property (Form 89) when you split up, or you're upset because your dogsitter acted contrary to your pet care agreement (Form 6). One way to resolve a dispute is through a court fight. This is usually a bad way, given that lawsuits and trials are typically expensive, prolonged, and emotionally draining. It usually makes far more sense to attempt to resolve disputes through other means, including the following:

Informal negotiation. The parties to the dispute try to voluntarily work out their differences through open discussions, which often result in each compromising a little to put the matter to rest. It may make sense to have a trusted mutual friend informally negotiate an agreement.

Mediation. The parties try to achieve a voluntary settlement with the help of a neutral third party, a mediator. With mediation, the two of you get together to talk face to face about your disagreements, with the mediator working to help you communicate so that you can craft your own solution. No one has the power to impose a solution with mediation—rather, you must work out your own agreement voluntarily. Mediation is inexpensive, quick, confidential, and effective the majority of the time. Depending on your situation, you may want to contact a community mediation agency that offers mediation, usually by trained community volunteers.

Arbitration. If mediation fails to resolve a dispute, arbitration is the next best choice. With arbitration, the parties allow a neutral third party, an arbitrator, to arrive at a binding decision in order to resolve the dispute. Normally, the decision is solely up to the arbitrator, and the parties agree beforehand

Dispute Clause

Disputes

[choose one]

☐ **Litigation.** If a dispute arises, any party may take the matter to court.

☐ **Mediation and Possible Litigation.** If a dispute arises, the parties will try in good faith to settle it through mediation conducted by *[choose one]*:

    ☐ _____ *[name of mediator].*

    ☐ a mediator to be mutually selected.

    The parties will share the costs of the mediator equally. If the dispute is not resolved within 30 days after it is referred to the mediator, any party may take the matter to court.

☐ **Mediation and Possible Arbitration.** If a dispute arises, the parties will try in good faith to settle it through mediation conducted by *[choose one]*:

    ☐ _____ *[name of mediator].*

    ☐ a mediator to be mutually selected.

    The parties will share the costs of the mediator equally. If the dispute is not resolved within 30 days after it is referred to the mediator, it will be arbitrated by *[choose one]*.

    ☐ _____ *[name of arbitrator].*

    ☐ an arbitrator to be mutually selected.

The arbitrator's decision will be binding and judgment on the arbitration award may be entered in any court that has jurisdiction over the matter. Costs of arbitration, including lawyers' fees, will be allocated by the arbitrator.

---

to abide by the arbitrator's decision. In some situations, however, the parties establish certain rules in advance of the arbitration—for example, a limit on the amount of money that can be awarded. Where limits are set by the parties, the arbitrator is bound by them. Arbitration is almost always speedier and usually much less expensive than litigation.

Ideally, you'd like to be able to settle disputes informally. Unfortunately, however, even when everyone tries in good faith, they don't always reach a compromise. Therefore, a dispute resolution clause (see the one shown above) lets you agree in advance on a framework mandating mediation and arbitration for resolving disputes. This dispute resolution clause is already in several of the forms in this book. If it's not on a particular form and you want to add it, you can find it in the CD-ROM file **DISPUTE.** To add the dispute clause, simply follow the directions in "Editing the Forms," above, about adding a clause.

This dispute resolution clause allows the parties to make one of three choices:

- **Litigation.** You go to court and let a judge or jury resolve the dispute.

- **Mediation and possible litigation.** You agree to let a mediator help you try to reach a voluntary settlement of the dispute. If mediation doesn't accomplish this goal, either of you can take the dispute to court. You can name the mediator when you prepare the form or agree on one when the need arises.

- **Mediation and possible arbitration.** You start by submitting the dispute to mediation. If mediation doesn't lead to a settlement, you submit the dispute to arbitration. The arbitrator makes a final decision that will be enforced by a court, if necessary. You can name the arbitrator when you prepare the form or agree on one when the need arises.

RESOURCE

Information on mediation and other methods of resolving disputes is available online at www.nolo.com, under the heading "Rights & Disputes." An excellent source for more thorough information is *Mediate, Don't Litigate,* by Peter Lovenheim and Lisa Guerin, available as an eBook from www.nolo.com. If you do end up fighting a case in court, read *Represent Yourself in Court,* by Paul Bergman and Sara Berman-Barrett. If your case is worth less than a few thousand dollars, you may choose small claims court. In that case, see *Everybody's Guide to Small Claims Court,* by Ralph Warner or, if you live in California, *Everybody's Guide to Small Claims Court in California,* also by Ralph Warner. All titles are published by Nolo.

Do You Need a Lawyer?

Most of the contracts used in this book involve relatively straightforward transactions. Just as you routinely negotiate deals to lend money to a friend or hire someone to paint your kitchen without formal legal help, you can just as safely complete the basic legal paperwork needed to record your understanding.

But like most generalizations, this one isn't always true. Creating a solid written agreement—especially where a lot of money or property is at stake—will occasionally mean obtaining the advice of a lawyer. Fortunately, even when you seek a lawyer's help, the forms and information included here will let you keep a tight rein on legal fees. You'll have gotten a running start by learning about the legal issues and perhaps drawing up a rough draft of the needed document, allowing you and your lawyer to focus on the few points that may not be routine.

Ideally, you should find a lawyer who comes highly recommended from personal referrals. Look for someone who's willing to answer a few questions, or possibly to review a completed contract draft, but who respects your ability to prepare the routine paperwork. Adopting this approach should keep the lawyer's fee to a minimum. For more advice on finding and working with a lawyer, visit Nolo's Lawyer Directory at Nolo.com/lawyers/index.html ●

Delegating Authority to Care for Children, Pets, and Property

Form 1: Temporary Guardianship Authorization for Care of Minor................................ 14

Form 2: Authorization for Minor's Medical Treatment... 15

Form 3: Authorization for Foreign Travel With Minor... 16

Form 4: Housesitting Instructions... 16

Form 5: Children's Carpool Agreement.. 17

Form 6: Pet Care Agreement.. 18

Form 7: Authorization to Drive a Motor Vehicle.. 18

Form 8: Power of Attorney for Finances (Limited Power).................................... 19

Form 9: Power of Attorney for Real Estate... 23

Form 10: Notice of Revocation of Power of Attorney.. 27

Human beings can be distinguished from the rest of the animal kingdom in one fundamental way: the ability to reason or make decisions. Many of the key decisions adults make affect the care of their children, finances, and property. And sometimes, when we know we won't be available to make these decisions, we appoint a person we trust to do so. This chapter includes a temporary guardianship authorization, a power of attorney for finances, and several forms you can use to delegate decision making to others in a few common situations. It also includes forms where you can provide instructions for the care of your home and pets.

TIP

When it comes to care of your children, be sure you choose the right person. While it's important to prepare a sound agreement authorizing someone to care for your children when you can't, your children's interests aren't served if you don't choose a good caretaker. So be sure you pick someone you trust completely to follow your wishes for your child's care.

Form 1: Temporary Guardianship Authorization for Care of Minor

You may find it necessary to leave your child in the care of another adult for a few days, weeks, or months. If so, you should give the caretaker permission to authorize medical care and make other important decisions for your child. This includes school-related decisions—for example, if your child needs approval to go on a field trip, or becomes ill and needs to be picked up from school.

When you complete a temporary guardianship authorization, you are establishing what the law calls an "informal guardianship." By contrast, a formal guardianship requires court approval and is used most often when a child will be in a guardian's care for a long period of time—for example, when a young child moves in with her grandparents because her parents have died. A formal guardianship permits the guardian to make more extensive decisions for a child, such as taking the child out of one school and registering her at another.

An informal or temporary guardianship is most often used in these two situations:

- You will be traveling or otherwise unavailable for a relatively short period of time—for example, due to a hospital stay— and will leave your child in another adult's care.

- Your child lives with you and a stepparent who has not legally adopted your child. Because you travel frequently, the stepparent commonly functions as the primary caregiver.

If you have more than one child, you should prepare a separate temporary guardianship authorization for each child.

CROSS-REFERENCE

Authorizing medical care. When you make a temporary guardianship authorization, you should also consider making an Authorization for Minor's Medical Treatment, discussed below (Form 2). Although the temporary guardianship form gives the temporary guardian explicit permission to authorize medical examinations, X-rays, hospital care, and other necessary treatments, the medical treatment authorization form allows you to spell out your child's medical history and needs in more detail. The two forms work well together. Whichever form you complete, you should speak with the pediatrician's office so that they know that the person you name as temporary guardian has your permission to make health care decisions for your child.

Signing Instructions

The parent(s) and the temporary guardian must sign the Temporary Guardianship Authorization for Care of Minor before it will be valid. Print out two copies of the form (or enough copies to give each person who will be signing the form). The parent(s) and the temporary guardian should sign and date all copies of the authorization form. Give one of the signed documents to the temporary guardian. Keep the other signed document for your own records and store it in a safe place.

FORM
This form contains a space for the acknowledgment of a notary public. To have a form notarized, you must go to the notary before signing it. (See the introduction for general advice on having a form notarized.) Notarization will add a measure of legal credibility, but it isn't always necessary. For example, you probably don't need to have your temporary guardianship authorization form notarized if you will be leaving your child with a grandparent for a few days. But if you will be away from your child for a long time—especially if your child stays with a nonrelative—it's a good idea to visit a notary. Practically speaking, a notarized form is likely to be more readily accepted by others.

Form 2: Authorization for Minor's Medical Treatment

You can use a medical care authorization to permit an adult that you name to authorize necessary medical or dental care for your child.

This can help you rest easier when your child is participating in sports or other organized activity outside of your supervision. You should provide this authorization to any adult who will be caring for your child when you are away, including babysitters and temporary guardians. This form provides details on your child's doctor, dentist, insurance, allergies, and ongoing medical conditions such as diabetes or asthma, as well as information on how to reach you while your child is in another's care.

If your child is participating in a specified activity, such as a basketball league or dance lessons, the sponsoring organization may give you its own medical authorization to fill out. But if the organization doesn't give you a form, you should take the time to complete this one.

Signing Instructions

You (the parent[s]) must sign the Authorization for Minor's Medical Treatment document for it to be valid. Make two copies of the form and sign and date both. Give one of the signed documents to the person who has permission to authorize medical treatment for your child. Keep the other signed document for your own records and store it in a safe place.

FORM
This form contains a space for the acknowledgment of a notary public. To have a form notarized, you must go to the notary before signing it. (See the introduction for general advice on having a form notarized.) Notarization will add a measure of legal credibility, but it isn't always necessary. Practically speaking, a notarized form is likely to be more readily accepted by others.

Form 3: Authorization for Foreign Travel With Minor

Your child is unlikely to be permitted to travel outside the United States with someone other than a parent or legal guardian unless the travel companion has documentation showing the person's legal relationship to your child and his authority to travel with your child. If you are planning a trip for your child, you should prepare an authorization for foreign travel. This form provides necessary proof that you have given consent for your child to leave the country with another adult. It also provides information about the child's travel plans and contact information for you (the parents).

If you have more than one child who will be traveling outside the country with another adult, you should prepare a separate authorization form for each child.

In planning your child's trip, you should check travel rules carefully. Start by calling the embassy or consulate for the foreign country to which your child will be traveling. Ask whether the country has any rules or regulations governing adults traveling with an unrelated minor. Chances are good that the country does not, but it's always good to ask. If there are special requirements, you and the child's adult traveling companion can prepare for them in advance.

CROSS-REFERENCE

Authorizing medical care. This form does not permit the person traveling with your child to authorize medical care for the minor. To ensure that your child can receive any necessary medical treatment while traveling, you should also complete the Authorization for Minor's Medical Treatment (Form 2), discussed just above.

Signing Instructions

You (the parent[s]) must sign the Authorization for Foreign Travel With Minor for it to be valid. Make two copies of the form. You and your child's other parent (if any) should sign and date both copies of the document. If you and your child's other parent are divorced or separated, you must still obtain the signature of the second parent before authorizing your child to leave the country with another adult. This will eliminate the possibility that foreign authorities will detain the travelers, suspecting a violation of child custody laws.

Give one of the signed documents to the person who has permission to travel with your child. Keep the other signed document for your own records and store it in a safe place.

FORM

Your foreign travel authorization should be notarized. To have a form notarized, you must go to the notary before signing it. (See the introduction for general advice on having a form notarized.) The acknowledgment of a notary public will give the form a greater degree of legitimacy, especially in the eyes of a foreign government. This could help if problems arise during the trip.

Form 4: Housesitting Instructions

Many people arrange to have a relative, a friend, or even a friend of a friend housesit while they are away on vacation or for an extended period of time. Even if your housesitter is quite familiar with your home, it's always a good idea to provide written information about the care and maintenance of your house. Use this form to specify details such as what to do about mail, newspapers, garbage, and recycling; gardening and yard maintenance; operation of appliances, locks, and security systems; and where you keep supplies. Write down everything you think the housesitter should know, including the location of emergency gas and water shut-off valves, and any special house rules, such as no smoking. Your housesitting instructions should also provide details on how to reach you while you're away as well as the names and phone numbers of local contacts who can help with any problems or questions, such as a neighbor who has an extra key, your plumber, and your insurance agent. Preparing detailed housesitting instructions will greatly reduce the chances of problems and give you peace of mind while you're many miles from home.

CROSS-REFERENCE

Pets, cars, and kids. If your housesitter will be taking care of your pet or driving your car, be sure to complete the Pet Care Agreement (Form 6) and the Authorization to Drive a Motor Vehicle (Form 7). And if your child will be staying at home in this housesitter's care, complete Form 1, Temporary Guardianship Authorization for Care of Minor.

Signing Instructions

There are no signing instructions for the Housesitting Instructions. Simply fill it out and leave it with your housesitter. It's probably a good idea to give an extra copy to a friend or neighbor.

Form 5: Children's Carpool Agreement

It's a rare family these days that doesn't rely to some extent on carpooling. Whether it's a trip to school, lessons, clubs, or after-school jobs, carpools make it possible for parents to share transportation hassles and—no small matter—have some time for their own jobs, commitments, and even themselves.

But as any carpool-savvy parent can tell you, there are good arrangements and there are those that don't work. While we can't guarantee that using our form will result in smooth sailing, we can help all carpool members get off on the right foot by recording their agreements on issues that should be discussed and settled at the outset. In addition, our form gives you a place to record important information that may come in handy. Think about the following issues and talk them out; then record your conclusions on the form:

- Who will be the drivers, and are you all satisfied that the drivers are qualified to drive and that they'll do so safely? Is each vehicle that will be used adequately insured?
- How long will the carpool wait for children who aren't ready when the carpool arrives? What should the drive do in the event that there is no one home at the drop off site?
- Identify two people who can care for your child in an emergency, as you do when asked by your school for their records.
- Identify any special considerations, such as a child's dietary restrictions (watch those carpool snacks), items that must be brought along (don't forget to check that the trumpet comes home from the music lesson), and personal quirks (with small children, seating arrangements can assume monumental importance).

Signing Instructions

After you and the other parents have made your decisions about the issues raised in the Carpool Agreement, record your conclusions in the spaces provided. Then have each parent sign and date the document. Give a copy of the signed agreement to each parent and keep a copy for yourself.

> **CAUTION**
> Unlike many of the forms in this book, your Carpool Agreement is not a legally binding document. If a member doesn't live up to it, your only recourse is to talk it over and come to a consensus about what to do.

Form 6: Pet Care Agreement

If you're going on a trip or will be otherwise unable to care for your pet for a period of time, you might leave your animal in the care of a neighbor or friend. If you do, it's a good idea to make a written agreement describing the arrangement and setting out clear instructions for your pet's care.

With this form, you can specify your pet's needs (including food, medication, exercise, and grooming), veterinarian contact information, special instructions such as vaccination due dates, how you can be reached, how you will reimburse the caregiver for any expenses involved in caring for your pet, and more. Having an agreement will greatly reduce the chances of a misunderstanding that might hurt your pet—or your relationship with the caregiver.

If you do find yourselves involved in a dispute, this agreement states that you and the pet caregiver will select a mutually agreeable third party to help you mediate the dispute and that you will share equally any costs of mediation. Mediation and other dispute resolution procedures are discussed in the introduction.

> **TIP**
> **Payment for pet food and vet bills.**
> When a friend cares for your pet, you may think it unnecessary to pay for a few dollars' worth of pet food. Think again—you are already asking for a big favor, one that is likely to be extended again only if you are scrupulous about the details. Even if your friend has several animals already and ten bags of pet food in the garage, bring along more than enough chow to feed your pet while you will be away, plus some cash for unexpected expenses. Also, if your pet is prone to illness or is recovering from an illness or injury, arrange for payment of your vet bills in advance or ask to be billed. Otherwise, leave your credit card number with your vet in case your pet needs care while you are away. Finally, make sure you notify your vet, in writing, that your friend has the authority to make any necessary care decisions while you are away. Your vet may have an authorization form for you to fill out, or may ask you to write a simple letter authorizing the caregiver to make decisions.

Signing Instructions

You and the caregiver must sign the Pet Care Agreement for it to be valid. Make two copies of the agreement. You should each sign and date both copies. Give the caregiver one of the signed documents and keep the other one for your own records.

Form 7: Authorization to Drive a Motor Vehicle

Lending your vehicle to a friend or even a relative isn't always as simple as just handing over the keys. If the person who borrows your car is pulled over by the police or is involved in an accident, it will be important to be able to prove quickly that you agreed to lend out your car. If the borrower can't show that you gave permission, there may be a delay while police investigate whether the vehicle is stolen. Completing this authorization form provides the important legal proof that you've given someone else permission to drive your vehicle.

This form provides a place to list important information, such as your insurance policy number, that will help ensure that your guest driver (and car) are taken care of in the event of an accident or other mishap. If you want to set any restrictions on when or where the car may be used—for example, limiting driving to a specific geographic area—you can do so.

This motor vehicle authorization form is designed for a car, but it will work fine for a motorcycle, truck, or other motor vehicle, such as a motorboat.

Signing Instructions

You (the vehicle owner) must sign your Authorization to Drive a Motor Vehicle form to make it valid. Make two copies of the authorization document. Sign and date both copies. Give one of the signed originals to the person who will be driving your car or other vehicle. Keep the other for your own records.

Form 8: Power of Attorney for Finances (Limited Power)

A power of attorney is a legal document in which you give another person legal authority to act on your behalf. In legal jargon, you're called "the principal," and the person to whom you give this authority is called your "attorney-in-fact" or "agent." In this context, "attorney" refers to anyone authorized to act on another's behalf; it's most definitely not restricted to lawyers.

Your attorney-in-fact (including any alternates you choose to name) should be someone you trust completely to act in your best interests— such as a spouse, relative, or close friend—who has enough common sense and experience to carry out the tasks you assign.

A limited power of attorney for finances lets you appoint an attorney-in-fact to help you with one or more specific, clearly defined tasks involving your finances. For example, you may want to name a relative or close friend to monitor certain investments—and sell them, if necessary—while you are on vacation or in the hospital for a short period of time. Or you may need someone to sign business or legal papers for you while you are unavailable.

CAUTION

Don't use this power of attorney to give someone control over real estate transactions. If you need an attorney-in-fact to sell, buy, or manage real property for you, use Form 9, Power of Attorney for Real Estate.

To create your limited power of attorney, you'll enter some basic information about you (the "principal") and your attorney-in-fact, followed by the exact powers you want to grant—such as selling your car, signing loan papers while you're out of town, or monitoring your investments. Be as specific as possible—for example, if you want someone to sell your car for a minimum of $15,000 cash only, spell this out. Include relevant bank account numbers and complete descriptions of any property the attorney-in-fact may deal with.

The power of attorney form gives your attorney-in-fact the authority to act for you in all matters that you list. The attorney-in-fact, however, has a legal obligation to take only

When the Power of Attorney Begins and Ends

Your power of attorney takes effect on a date you specify in your document. It ends under the circumstances described below.

The termination date. When you prepare your document, you can specify the date on which it will expire. You can enter a specific day, such as the day you expect to return from a trip. Or, you can make an open-ended document. If you don't specify an ending date, your attorney-in-fact is legally permitted to act for you until you revoke the power of attorney in writing.

You revoke the power of attorney. You can revoke your power of attorney at any time, as long as you are of sound mind. (And if you aren't of sound mind, the document terminates automatically, so you don't have to worry about revoking it.) To revoke your document, all you need to do is fill out a simple form, sign it in front of a notary public, and give copies to the attorney-in-fact and to people or institutions the attorney-in-fact has been dealing with. Form 10 is a revocation form you can use.

After a divorce. In a number of states, if your spouse is your attorney-in-fact and you divorce, your ex-spouse's authority is immediately terminated. Regardless of state law, however, if you've named your spouse as attorney-in-fact and you get divorced, you should revoke your power of attorney and make a new one.

No attorney-in-fact is available. Your power of attorney will automatically end if your attorney-in-fact dies, resigns, or becomes unable to represent you for any other reason.

You become incapacitated or die. Your power of attorney states that it will automatically end if you become incapacitated or die. In most states, however, if the attorney-in-fact doesn't know of your incapacity or death and continues to act on your behalf, these actions are still valid.

those actions that are in your best interests, and to represent you honestly and carefully.

This power of attorney form includes language designed to reassure third parties that they can accept the document without risk of legal liability. This "indemnification" clause clearly states that a third party may rely on the document without worry—in other words, the third party may conduct business with your attorney-in-fact as you have instructed—unless the person knows that you have revoked the document.

Conventional Versus Durable Power of Attorney

This form is typically referred to as a "conventional" power of attorney. As you may know, there is another type of power of attorney, called a durable power of attorney, that remains in effect even if you become incapacitated and can no longer make decisions for yourself. Durable powers of attorney are commonly signed in advance of need by older and ill people who realize that at some point they may require help managing their affairs. In contrast, conventional powers of attorney like Form 8 are used when you want someone to handle specific transactions for you at a set time. Because state laws vary in this area, if you want a durable power of attorney, you will need more extensive information. One excellent resource is *Quicken Willmaker Plus* software, which lets you create a valid will, durable power of attorney for finances, health care directive, and final arrangements document, using your computer. If you live in California, you can use the book *Living Wills & Powers of Attorney for California*, by Shae Irving (Nolo). It contains all the forms and instructions California residents need to prepare a durable power of attorney for finances and health care directive.

TIP

Financial institutions may have their own power of attorney forms. If you're giving your attorney-in-fact authority to deal with a bank, brokerage firm, or other financial institution, find out whether it has its own power of attorney form. If it does, you'll probably want to use that form instead of this one. Doing so will reduce hassles for your attorney-in-fact, because a financial institution will know what powers its own form grants and will have no need to quibble with your document.

Signing Instructions

A Power of Attorney for Finances is a serious document. To make it legally valid and effective, you must observe certain formalities when you sign it. Specifically, you must have your power of attorney form notarized, and, in some states, you may need to sign your document in front of witnesses. (See "States That Require Witnesses for a Power of Attorney," below.)

In a few states, your attorney-in-fact must sign the power of attorney before taking action under the document. In other states, the attorney-in-fact's signature is not required, but it's a fine idea to include it anyway. The attorney-in-fact's signature acts as assurance that the attorney-in-fact has read and fully understands the document, and is willing to assume the responsibility of acting prudently and honestly on your behalf. For this reason this power of attorney form includes a blank for the attorney-in-fact to sign.

FORM

You must sign your power of attorney in the presence of a notary public for your state. In some states, notarization is required by law to make the power of attorney valid. But even where law doesn't require it, custom does. A power of attorney that isn't notarized may not be accepted by people your attorney-in-fact needs to deal with.

If you will have your form witnessed (see "States That Require Witnesses for a Power of Attorney," below), everyone who has to sign the form must appear together in front of the notary. After watching each of you sign, the notary will complete an acknowledgment, including a notarial seal.

For more information on finding and using a notary, see the introduction.

Give the original, signed, and notarized document to the person you authorized. Your attorney-in-fact will need it as proof of authority to act on your behalf. Make a copy

States That Require Witnesses for a Power of Attorney

Most states don't require a power of attorney to be signed in front of witnesses. The few states that do and the number of witnesses required are listed below. Witness requirements normally consist of the following:

- Witnesses must be present when you sign the document in front of the notary.

- Witnesses must be mentally competent adults.

- The person who will serve as your attorney-in-fact can't be a witness.

Choose witnesses who will be easily available if they are ever needed. It's obviously a good idea to choose witnesses who live nearby and will be easy to contact.

State	Number of Witnesses	Other Requirements	State	Number of Witnesses	Other Requirements
Arizona	1	Witness may not be your attorney-in-fact, the spouse or child of your attorney-in-fact, or the notary public who acknowledges your document.	New York	2	Witnesses may not be your attorney-in-fact or anyone who stands to personally benefit from your power of attorney document.
Connecticut	2	Neither witness may be your attorney-in-fact.	Oklahoma	2	Witnesses may not be your attorney-in-fact or anyone who is related by blood or marriage to you or your attorney-in-fact.
District of Columbia	2	Witnesses are necessary only if your power of attorney is to be recorded. Neither witness may be your attorney-in-fact.	Pennsylvania	2	Witnesses are necessary only if the power of attorney is finalized with a mark (rather than a signature) or if you direct another person to sign on your behalf. Witnesses may not be your attorney-in-fact or the person who signs your document for you.
Florida	2	Neither witness may be your attorney-in-fact.	South Carolina	2	Neither witness may be your attorney-in-fact.
Georgia	2	Neither witness may be your attorney-in-fact. In addition, one of your witnesses may not be your spouse or blood relative.	Vermont	1	Witness may not be your attorney-in-fact or the notary public who acknowledges your document.
Illinois	1	Witness may not be your attorney-in-fact.	Wisconsin	2	Witnesses may not be your attorney-in-fact, anyone who is related to you by blood or marriage, or anyone entitled to inherit a portion of your estate under your will.
Michigan	2	Witnesses are necessary only if your power of attorney is to be recorded. Neither witness may be your attorney-in-fact.			

for yourself and store it in a safe place. If you wish, you can give copies of your power of attorney to the people your attorney-in-fact will need to deal with—for example, banks or government offices. If your financial power of attorney is already in their records, it may eliminate hassles for your attorney-in-fact later. Be sure to keep a list of everyone to whom you give a copy.

> **CAUTION**
>
> **Revoking a power of attorney.** If you later revoke your power of attorney, you must notify each institution of the revocation. We include a formal notice of revocation form below (Form 10).

Form 9: Power of Attorney for Real Estate

A power of attorney for real estate allows you to give someone the authority to buy or sell a piece of real estate for you, or to conduct any other business concerning real estate that you own. A power of attorney for real estate is a "conventional" power of attorney, meaning that it automatically expires if you become incapacitated or die. (If you want a document that will stay in effect even if you become incapacitated, you need a "durable" power of attorney—see "Conventional Versus Durable Power of Attorney," above.)

A power of attorney for real estate may be useful in a number of situations. Here are a few common ones:

- You will be out of town or otherwise unavailable when important real estate documents need to be signed.

- You will not be available to look after your real estate for a limited period of time.

- You live far away from property that you own and you want to authorize someone to manage it in your absence.

EXAMPLE 1:

Alan is purchasing a condominium. Escrow has been opened at a title company, but the closing is delayed for several weeks. Because of the delay, the closing is now scheduled for the middle of Alan's long-planned trip to Greece. To solve this problem, Alan prepares a power of attorney for real estate, authorizing his sister Jennifer to sign any documents necessary to complete the closing and to withdraw any amounts of money (from an identified bank account) necessary to pay expenses and costs incurred because of the closing. Alan specifies that Jennifer's authority expires on the date he is to return from Greece.

Alan discusses his plans with his bank and the title company before he leaves, to be sure they'll accept the power of attorney and the authority of his attorney-in-fact. Both organizations assure him they'll accept a valid power of attorney for real estate. He has copies of his power of attorney placed in the bank's records and in his file at the title company. He leaves the original document with Jennifer, his attorney-in-fact.

EXAMPLE 2:

Ann owns a summer cottage. Her friend June lives in the next cottage as her permanent home. Ann and June agree that because June is on the spot she'll take care of renting Ann's cottage, collecting rent, and paying all house bills and costs. Ann prepares a power of attorney for real estate giving June authority to represent Ann for all transactions concerning her property at 20 Heron Lake Road. Ann specifies that the power of attorney will continue indefinitely. She also provides that June has no authority to sell the cottage nor to represent her in any transaction that doesn't concern the cottage.

TIP

Make sure your power of attorney will be accepted. The most important thing you can do to ensure that financial institutions, such as your mortgage lender or title company, will accept your power of attorney is talk with them in advance. Be sure that they're willing to accept the document and the authority of your attorney-in-fact. Your financial institution may ask you to include certain language in your form or even to use its own power of attorney form. If so, you should comply with its wishes. (If you're working with more than one financial institution, you may end up using more than one form.) Even though you can make a perfectly valid, legal document with this form, your financial institution may balk at accepting any form other than its own. Following your financial institution's recommendations will save time and trouble for you and your attorney-in-fact.

Instructions for Preparing Your Power of Attorney for Real Estate

Here are instructions for filling in the Power of Attorney for Real Estate form.

Step 1. Principal and Attorney-in-Fact

In the first four blanks on the form, fill in your name and the city, county, and state where you live. Enter your name as it appears on official documents such as your driver's license, bank accounts, and real estate deeds. This may or may not be the name on your birth certificate.

EXAMPLE:

Your birth certificate lists your name as Rose Mary Green. But you've always gone by Mary, and always sign documents as Mary McNee, your married name. You would use Mary McNee on your power of attorney.

Be sure to enter all names in which you hold bank accounts or other property your attorney-in-fact will be dealing with. This will make his or her job far easier. If you're including more than one name, enter your full legal name first, followed by "aka" (also known as). Then enter your other names.

If during the course of a year you live in more than one state, use the address in the state where you vote, register vehicles, own valuable property, have bank accounts, or run a business. If you've made your will, health care directives, or a living trust, be consistent: Use the address in the state you declared as your residence in those documents.

Next, type in the name of the person who has agreed to serve as your attorney-in-fact. Then enter the city, county, and state where your attorney-in-fact lives.

Step 2. Description of Your Real Property

There is a large blank space following the first paragraph of the form. In it, you should type a description of the real estate your power of attorney will govern. Enter the exact street address, if your property has one. Then, attach a copy of the deed to your power of attorney form to avoid the trouble of retyping the lengthy and often confusing legal description contained in the deed.

EXAMPLE:

9 Lotus Lane, Danville, CA 94558, Contra Costa County, California, as further described in the attached deed.

If you're up for it, you can type in the legal description instead. But be sure to type the entire description, exactly as it appears on the deed.

EXAMPLE:

LOT 195, as shown upon that certain map entitled, "Map of Greenbrae Sub. No. One, Marin Co. Calif.," filed May 2, 1946, in Book 6 of Maps, at Page 7, Marin County Records.

Step 3. Limiting the Powers Granted to the Attorney-in-Fact

Read through the powers described in the second paragraph of the document. If you don't want to grant one or more of the numbered powers, you can delete or type a string of x's through those that you don't need. If you just want to limit the numbered powers in some way, include your instructions in the blank space following the list of powers. For example, you might want to forbid your attorney-in-fact from selling your property; you can type that limitation in the blank space.

If you don't want to limit the powers in any way, delete or type a string of x's through the phrase "However, my attorney-in-fact shall not have the power to:"

Step 4. Additional Powers

In the fourth paragraph of the form, you can authorize your attorney-in-fact to carry out any additional powers related to the real estate powers you've granted. For example, you may

want to authorize your attorney-in-fact to withdraw funds from a named bank account to cover any costs that arise in relation to his or her duties.

SAMPLE CLAUSE:

I further grant to my attorney-in-fact full authority to act in any manner both proper and necessary to the exercise of the foregoing powers, including <u>withdrawing funds from my checking account, #4482 478 880, Anderson Valley Savings and Loan, Booneville, CA,</u> and I ratify every act that my attorney-in-fact may lawfully perform in exercising those powers.

If you don't want to add any powers to the document, delete or type a string of x's through the word "including."

Step 5. Termination Date

In the last paragraph of the form, you can type in a specific date on which you want the power of attorney to expire. See "When the Power of Attorney Begins and Ends," in the instructions for Form 8, above.

If you want the power of attorney to continue indefinitely, delete or type a string of x's through "or until _____, whichever comes first." If you do so, and you later want to terminate the power of attorney, you must revoke it in writing.

Signing Instructions

A power of attorney is a serious document, and to make it effective you must observe certain formalities when you sign it. Fortunately, these requirements aren't difficult to meet.

You must sign your power of attorney in the presence of a notary public for your state. See the introduction for instructions on having a document notarized.

Witnesses

Most states don't require the power of attorney to be signed in front of witnesses. (See "States That Require Witnesses for a Power of Attorney," in the instructions for Form 8, above.) Nevertheless, it doesn't hurt to have a witness or two watch you sign, and sign the document themselves. Witnesses' signatures may make the power of attorney more acceptable to lawyers, banks, insurance companies, and other entities the attorney-in-fact may have to deal with.

If you're giving your attorney-in-fact authority to handle real estate in a state other than the state where you live, be sure the document has at least the number of witnesses required by the state where the real property is located. Otherwise, you may not be able to record the power of attorney in that state.

SKIP AHEAD

If you will be using the CD-ROM to create your Power of Attorney for Real Estate, you don't need to read the cautionary instructions that follow. You can skip to the section on the attorney-in-fact's signature just below. The form on the CD-ROM contains instructions to help you print the right number of signature lines.

CAUTION

The Power of Attorney for Real Estate tear-out form in the back of the book has multiple last pages that may, at first glance, appear to be duplicates. Each of these pages is slightly different, however. Choose only the last page that has room for the number of witnesses your state requires—none, one, or two. (You can find the number of witnesses required by your state in "States that Require Witnesses for a Power of Attorney," in the instructions for Form 8, above.) Then, check the page numbers of your document to make sure everything's in proper order and you aren't missing pages or including any extras.

The Attorney-in-Fact's Signature

In a few states, your attorney-in-fact must sign the power of attorney before taking action under the document. In other states, the attorney-in-fact's signature is not required, but it's a fine idea to include it anyway. The attorney-in-fact's signature acts as assurance that the attorney-in-fact has read and fully understands the document, and is willing to assume the responsibility of acting prudently and honestly on your behalf. For this reason, the form includes a blank for the attorney-in-fact to sign.

Putting Your Power of Attorney on Public Record

You must put a copy of your power of attorney on file in the county land records office, called the county recorder's or land registry office in most states. This is called "recording" or "registration" in some states. If you don't record the power of attorney, your attorney-in-fact may not be permitted to handle real estate transactions for you.

Recording makes it clear to all interested parties that the attorney-in-fact has power over the property at issue. County land records are checked whenever real estate changes hands or is mortgaged. If, for example, your attorney-in-fact is supposed to sell or mortgage a piece of property for you, there must be something in the public records that proves he or she has authority to do so.

If you put your power of attorney on public record and then later revoke it in writing, you must also record the notice of revocation, Form 10.

Where to Record Your Power of Attorney

In most states, each county has its own county recorder's (or registry of deeds) office. Take the power of attorney to the office in the county where the real estate is located. If you are granting your attorney-in-fact authority over more than one parcel of real estate, record the power of attorney in each county where you own property.

How to Record a Document

Recording a document is easy. You may even be able to do it by mail, but it's safer to go in person. The clerk will make a copy for the public records. It will be assigned a reference number, often called an "instrument number." It shouldn't cost more than $20 to record your document.

What to Do With the Signed Document

Give the original, signed, and notarized document to the attorney-in-fact, who will need it as proof of authority to act on your behalf.

Making and Distributing Copies

You should give copies of your power of attorney to the people your attorney-in-fact will need to deal with—banks or title companies, for example. If your power of attorney is in their records, it may eliminate hassles for your attorney-in-fact later.

Be sure to keep a list of everyone to whom you give a copy. If you later revoke your power of attorney, notify each institution of the revocation.

Keeping Your Document Up to Date

If you've made a power of attorney without a specific termination date, you should redo it every year or so. Banks and other financial institutions may be reluctant to accept a power of attorney that's more than a couple of years old, even though the document is still technically valid. You should destroy any copies

of the old power of attorney document and notify the people and institutions with copies of the former document that you have revoked your old power of attorney and made a new one.

Form 10: Notice of Revocation of Power of Attorney

You can use a Notice of Revocation of Power of Attorney form in two situations:

- You want to revoke your power of attorney before the termination date set out in the document.

- Your power of attorney has ended as specified in the document, but you want to be absolutely sure that all institutions (such as banks, stockbrokers, and insurance companies) and people (such as your attorney or accountant) who have received it know that it is no longer in force.

Signing Instructions

Sign and date the Notice of Revocation in front of a notary public for your state as explained in the discussion of Form 8, Power of Attorney for Finances (Limited Power).

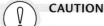 **CAUTION**

If you recorded your power of attorney, record the Notice of Revocation. If you put your power of attorney on file in the public records office and it hasn't expired on its own, you should also record your Notice of Revocation. Otherwise, people who don't actually know of your revocation are entitled to continue to deal with your attorney-in-fact on your behalf.

Basic Estate Planning

Form 11: Property Worksheet 30

Form 12: Beneficiary Worksheet 31

Forms 13 and 14: Basic Wills.. 32

Form 13: Will for Adult With No Children 34

Form 14: Will for Adult With Child(ren) 34

Form 15: Will Codicil 36

Making arrangements for what will happen to your property after you die is called estate planning. Generally, if you die without a will or other legal means for transferring property, your property will be distributed to certain close relatives—your spouse or domestic partner, children, parents, or siblings—under state "intestacy" laws.

Making a will is an important part of estate planning. For many people, a will, coupled with naming beneficiaries for retirement plans, insurance policies, and other investments, is the only estate plan they need. Whether that is true for you or not depends on your circumstances. Generally speaking, the more wealth you possess, the more you'll want to consider legal issues beyond the scope of a will, such as avoiding probate—the court-supervised process of gathering and distributing a deceased person's assets—and reducing estate taxes. And, depending on your situation, you may want to provide for a disabled child, establish a fund for grandchildren, or make charitable gifts.

This chapter introduces the concept of estate planning and provides some useful worksheets and some basic will forms. Resources listed here explain where to go for more detailed information.

Form 11: Property Worksheet

Before you write a will or other estate planning document, you may find it helpful to make an inventory of your property, including real estate, cash, securities, cars, household goods, and business personal property, such as a company you own or the right to receive royalties. Filling out the Property Worksheet can jog your memory to make sure you don't overlook important items.

Describe each asset on the Property Worksheet under the appropriate section of the "Property" column. If an asset such as a house or car is jointly owned, specify the percentage you own.

Even if you haven't made a will, you may have already named someone to get some of your property at your death. For example, if you have an IRA, 401(k) retirement plan, or insurance policy, you have probably named a beneficiary and alternate beneficiary on a form provided by the account custodian company. If you own real estate, you may hold it in joint tenancy with right of survivorship, meaning that the other joint owner will automatically inherit your share at your death. If you've already named someone to inherit an asset after your death, write down the beneficiary's name on the Property Worksheet under "Name of Any Existing Beneficiary."

Signing Instructions

You don't need to sign the Property Worksheet. Simply fill it out and use it when preparing your will or other estate planning document.

RESOURCE

Organize your personal information. *Get It Together: Organize Your Records So Your Family Won't Have To*, by Melanie Cullen and Shae Irving, helps you leave survivors a clear record of your important documents and information, including secured places and passwords, retirement accounts, insurance policies, real estate records, and much more. It also provides a road map to the arrangements you have made for after your death.

Form 12: Beneficiary Worksheet

Like the Property Worksheet, the Beneficiary Worksheet is a tool that can help you get ready to draft estate planning documents. On the Beneficiary Worksheet, list each item of property and then list the people or organizations to whom you want to leave the property. If you name more than one beneficiary to share a specific gift, state the percentage share each is to receive.

It is also highly advisable to name an alternate beneficiary or beneficiaries for each gift, in case your first choice dies before you do.

You can also list people who owe you money, if you want to forgive these debts at your death. For example, if you loaned your best friend $10,000 and he pays you back with interest $100 a month, it will take him many years to pay off the debt. If he still owes you money when you die, you can forgive or waive the balance due. This means that your heirs cannot go after your friend for the rest.

Finally, list a "residuary" beneficiary or beneficiaries. This is one or more people or organizations who will get everything that's left after your specific gifts are distributed. Do this even if you are sure you have identified all your property and named a beneficiary to receive it; there is always a chance that you'll acquire additional property between the date you make your will and your death.

Common Property That May Already Have Beneficiaries

You may have already planned the eventual disposition of much of your property before you prepare a will. Here are some examples of property for which you may have already named a beneficiary:

- bank accounts, naming a payable-on-death beneficiary (on a form provided by the bank)
- real estate, holding it with someone else in joint tenancy, in tenancy by the entirety, or (in community property states) as community property with right of survivorship with your spouse
- securities, registering them in transfer-on-death form if your state law allows it
- retirement accounts, naming a beneficiary (on a form provided by the account custodian) to take whatever is still in the account at your death, and
- life insurance policies, naming a beneficiary (on a form provided by the company) to receive the proceeds at your death.

 TIP

Do you need to use the Beneficiary Worksheet? If you plan to leave all your property to one or a very few people (for example, "all property to my spouse, or if she predeceases me, to my children in equal shares"), there is no need to complete the Beneficiary Worksheet. You already know who will get your property at your death, and you can turn to the will forms that follow.

Signing Instructions

You don't need to sign the Beneficiary Worksheet. Simply fill it out and use it when preparing your will or other estate planning documents.

Nolo Resources on Estate Planning

Nolo publishes several books and software products containing more sophisticated—but still easy-to-use—information on wills and living trusts. A living trust is the document used most often to avoid probate, the process of distributing a person's property under court supervision.

- *Plan Your Estate,* by Denis Clifford, is a comprehensive estate planning book, covering everything from basic estate planning (wills and living trusts) to sophisticated tax-saving strategies (AB trusts and much more). If you haven't yet decided how to approach your estate planning tasks, this is Nolo's best resource.

- *The Busy Family's Guide to Estate Planning,* by Liza Weiman Hanks, outlines ten simple steps to plan your estate with confidence. Just tackle one step every month and you'll be able to cross estate planning off your to-do list—and have peace of mind knowing you've looked after your family.

- *Quicken WillMaker Plus* interactive software lets you make a more sophisticated will than those offered here. For example, you can choose among three ways to provide property management for children should you die before they are competent to handle property

themselves. In addition, with *Quicken WillMaker Plus* you can create a separate document to express your wishes for your funeral and burial. It also contains a health care directive (living will), a durable power of attorney for finances, and many other useful forms.

- *Nolo's Simple Will Book,* by Denis Clifford, provides step-by-step instructions and forms to create a detailed will. Its will is similar in scope to the will that's included in *Quicken WillMaker Plus.* The book comes with a CD-ROM, which you can use with any standard word-processing program to make drafting and printing out the will easy.

- *8 Ways to Avoid Probate,* by Mary Randolph, explains important and often overlooked ways to avoid probate. It is now possible to avoid probate for many kinds of property without creating a living trust. If you vaguely know you should be paying attention to probate avoidance, but dread thinking about it, start with this small but thorough book.

- *Special Needs Trusts: Protect Your Child's Financial Future,* by Stephen Elias, explains how you can leave money to a loved one who has a disability, without interfering with eligibility for SSI or Medicaid benefits.

Forms 13 and 14: Basic Wills

A basic will is easy to make. It's also easy to change or revoke; you won't be stuck with it if you change your mind later. With the will forms in this book, you can:

- leave your property to anyone you wish

- name a guardian to raise young children if you can't, and

- appoint an executor to carry out your will's terms.

This section gives an overview of making a basic will. Next come two bare-bones forms, which can be used by residents of all states except Louisiana.

These wills are a good choice if you want a will quickly on the eve of a long trip or don't want to spend much time on estate planning right now. You'll probably want to draft a more extensive will for the long term. Precisely because these forms are short, simple, and easy to use, they do not include a lot of options. For example, they do not let you create a trust to hold property that may be left to children or young adults.

If you have children, use Form 14, the Will for Adult With Child(ren). Otherwise, use Form 13, the Will for Adult With No Children.

Anyone who is of legal age (18 years old in most states) and of sound mind can make a valid will. You have to be very far gone before your will can be invalidated on the grounds that you were mentally incompetent. If you're reading and understanding this book, your mind is sound enough to make a will.

> **CAUTION**
>
> **Do not just fill in and sign a will form. You must retype it.** Unlike the forms in the rest of this book, will forms cannot just be torn out, filled in, and signed. A will cannot contain a mix of handwritten and machine-printed material. To prepare a legally valid will, you must use the CD-ROM that comes with this book (or a typewriter if you don't have access to a computer) to print out a typed will that eliminates all the clauses you don't need. Then sign this will in front of witnesses following the instructions below. If you simply fill in the blanks and sign it, your will won't be valid.

Leaving specific items. If you want to list specific items of property you're leaving through your will, you'll use the "Specific Gifts" section (Clause 3 of Form 13, Clause 4 of Form 14). When you list items, describe them so that your executor—and anyone else—will know exactly what you meant. There is no need to use formal legal descriptions unless they are really necessary to identify the property. Here are some examples of good property descriptions:

- "my house at 435 76th Avenue, Chicago, Illinois"
- "all household furnishings and possessions in my house at 435 76th Avenue, Chicago, Illinois," and

- "$10,000 from my savings account, No. 44444, at First National Bank, Chicago, Illinois."

Then you'll need to say what you want to happen to the rest of your property, which is called your "residuary." For example, say you make a few small specific gifts and want everything else to go to your three children. You would use Clause 3 (Form 13) or Clause 4 (Form 14) to make your specific gifts and the "Residuary Estate" clause (Clause 4 of Form 13, Clause 5 of Form 14) to leave everything else to your children.

Leaving Everything. If you want to leave everything to just one beneficiary, or a group of them—your spouse or your three children, for example—don't use the "Specific Gifts" part of the will. Instead, use the "Residuary Estate" clause (Clause 4 of Form 13, Clause 5 of Form 14). Since "residuary" simply refers to the rest of your estate and you have made no specific gifts, everything will go to the person or persons you name as your residuary beneficiary(ies).

Property with debt. When you leave property, any encumbrances on it—for example, a mortgage—pass with the property. In other words, the beneficiary takes the debt as well as the property.

Naming your executor. In your will, you must name someone to be in charge of winding up your affairs after your death. This person is called your executor (the term "personal representative" is used in some states). The executor must shepherd your property through probate—the court process of distributing the property of a deceased person—if it's necessary, and must see that your property is distributed according to the wishes expressed in your will.

Many people name their spouse or a grown child as executor. The executor usually doesn't need special financial or legal expertise. The important thing is that the person you choose is completely trustworthy and will deal fairly with other beneficiaries.

Typing up your will. After you've created a rough draft of your will using the forms in this book, you must use either the will documents on the CD-ROM or a typewriter to create your final draft.

Remove any clauses that you do not need— for example, remove the specific bequest clauses if you're leaving everything to your spouse or partner. Then renumber the remaining clauses. When you're done, read your will carefully to make sure you understand and agree with every word.

If you do not agree with something in the will, do not reword the will language yourself, or you'll risk your will's validity. Instead, you may need to use a more complex will that can be more carefully tailored to your situation. See "Nolo Resources on Estate Planning," above.

Signing Instructions

Your signature on your will must be witnessed. When you are ready to sign it, gather together two adults who aren't beneficiaries of your will. Your witnesses do not need to read your will. You simply tell them, "This is my will." Then you sign and date your will while the witnesses watch. Finally, each witness signs while the other witness watches. You do not need to have your will notarized. Be sure to store your will in a safe place.

CAUTION

If you're married or in a registered domestic partnership, your spouse may be able to claim a share of your estate. In most states (all except Arizona, California, Idaho, Louisiana, Nevada, New Mexico, Texas, Washington, and Wisconsin, which follow the community property system), a surviving spouse has the right to reject what the will says and instead claim a share of the deceased spouse's entire estate. In many states, that share is about one-third of the estate. The details get tricky fast. As long as you plan to leave your spouse or partner at least half of your property, you don't need to worry about it. But if you plan to leave less than half of your property to your spouse or partner, see a lawyer and don't try to use the forms in this book.

Form 13: Will for Adult With No Children

This is the will to use if you don't have children. If you have children, use Form 14. Remember, these forms can be used by residents of all states except Louisiana.

Read the introduction to Basic Wills (above) for brief but important instructions on filling out the form correctly, so that you will create a legally valid will that accomplishes what you want.

Form 14: Will for Adult With Child(ren)

First, read the material on Basic Wills, above, for brief but important instructions on filling out the form correctly, so that you will create a legally valid will that accomplishes what you want. Because you have children, you have some special issues to consider before you make your will.

Heading off claims. You should mention each of your children in your will, even if you don't leave them any property through the will. That's because, although children are not usually entitled to claim any property from a parent's estate, they do have certain rights if it appears that they were unintentionally overlooked. By listing all of your children, including those you have legally adopted, you head off any argument that you forgot any of them.

Custody of minor children. If you have children under age 18, use Clause 8 to name the person you want to raise the children if you die and the other parent is unavailable to raise them. This person is called their "personal guardian." It is also wise to nominate an alternate personal guardian, in case the first choice can't serve.

If a guardian is ever needed, a judge will review your choice. If no one objects, the person you name will most likely be appointed. But in an unusual situation, a judge who is convinced that naming a different personal guardian is in the best interests of the child has the authority to do so.

CAUTION

With this will form, you cannot name different guardians for different kids. This will form requires that you name the same personal guardian for all of your minor children. If for some reason you want to name different people as guardians for different children, use *Nolo's Simple Will Book* or *Quicken WillMaker Plus* software.

Property left to children. Minors cannot legally own property outright, free of supervision, beyond a minimal amount—$2,500 to $5,000, depending on the state. By law, an adult must be legally responsible for managing any significant amount of property owned by a minor child. So if your children might inherit property through your will—even if they're only alternate beneficiaries—you should arrange for an adult to supervise it. You can do this easily in your will.

Form 14 gives you two ways to provide for adult supervision for gifts to your children:

- **Name a custodian for each child.** The custodian will manage any property slated for the child until the child turns 21 (in most states). A custodian is authorized under your state's Uniform Transfers to Minors

Act (UTMA). (See below and see Clause 10 of the will.)

- **Name a property guardian.** You should always name a property guardian and successor property guardian in your will, even if you appoint a custodian under the Uniform Transfers to Minors Act. The property guardian will be formally appointed by a court and will manage any property not left through your will (and so not covered by the UTMA custodianship)—for example, property the minor gets from someone else.

Uniform Transfers to Minors Act. All states except South Carolina and Vermont have adopted the Uniform Transfers to Minors Act (UTMA). This law authorizes you to appoint an adult custodian and successor custodian in your will to supervise property you leave to a minor. The custodianship ends, and any remaining property must be turned over to the child outright, at the age the UTMA specifies. In most states, this is 21, but a few (for example, California and Alaska) allow you to choose up to age 25. Our form sets the ending age at the oldest age allowed in your state, which in the majority of states is 21.

Because the custodian has almost complete discretion over management of the property, it is essential that you name someone who is totally honest and has good financial management skills. The custodian also has a legal duty to act prudently in the best interests of the child. Normally, no court supervision is required.

You can name UTMA custodians for as many children as you wish. In addition, you can name a different custodian for each child. When preparing your will, you'll first list all gifts you leave, including gifts to your minor or young adult children. Then you'll complete a separate UTMA clause for each child.

Other Property Management Options

The Will for Adult With Child(ren) does not offer two other fairly common—but legally more complicated—ways to arrange for a minor's property to be managed by an adult:

- A family pot trust that will hold property left to all your minor children, allowing the trustee you name to spend it as needed. For example, if one child had an expensive medical problem, the trustee could spend more for that child and less for others.

- A trust for each child. This option is primarily of value for people with larger estates who do not want adult children to take control of money outright until they are in their middle or late twenties. It gets around the fact that in most states a custodianship under the terms of the Uniform Transfers to Minors Act ends at age 21.

These options are available in *Quicken WillMaker Plus* software and in *Nolo's Simple Will Book*.

Form 15: Will Codicil

A codicil is sort of a legal "P.S." to a will. In a codicil, you can revoke a clause in your will and then substitute a new clause. Or you can simply add a new provision, such as a new gift of an item of property.

A codicil must be signed and witnessed just like a will. The form must be retyped or computer printed (start with "First Codicil to the Will of _____," leaving off our title), then dated and signed by you in front of two witnesses. You don't have to use the same witnesses who signed your will, but in many states the witnesses cannot be people named as beneficiaries in your will or codicil.

Today, codicils are less commonly used than they were in the days when wills were laboriously copied by hand or typed on a typewriter. With almost universal access to computers, it's usually easier—and less likely to confuse—to prepare a whole new will, revoking the previous one. Nevertheless, codicils can still be sensibly used to make limited changes to a will—for example, when you want to change who receives one item.

Things to Do After a Death: Documents for Executors

Form 16: Request for Death Certificate 38

Form 17: Notice to Creditor of Death 39

Form 18: Executor's Checklist 40

Form 19: General Notice of Death 40

Form 20: Obituary Information Fact Sheet 41

Form 21: Notice to Deceased's Homeowners' Insurance Company 41

Form 22: Notice to Deceased's Vehicle Insurance Company 42

After a death, someone must step in and wind up the deceased person's affairs. An executor—sometimes called personal representative or administrator—is the person named in the will, or appointed by the probate court, who has legal responsibility for safeguarding and handling the deceased person's property, seeing that debts and taxes are paid, and distributing what is left to beneficiaries as directed by the will. This chapter contains a number of simple forms and letters you can use if you are named as someone's executor, as well as a checklist to help you be sure you are taking care of all that needs to be done.

RESOURCE

Nolo has books that can help you. *How to Probate an Estate in California*, by Julia Nissley, gives California residents step-by-step instructions for handling an estate. *The Executor's Guide: Settling a Loved One's Estate or Trust*, by Mary Randolph, covers the legal and financial matters that crop up after a death, helping the surviving family through what is often a difficult and confusing time.

CAUTION

These forms are not applicable in all situations. The forms in this chapter cannot be used to claim benefits under an insurance policy or retirement plan. You will need to contact the appropriate companies and complete their forms.

Form 16: Request for Death Certificate

As an executor or personal representative, you will need to handle many tasks, such as terminating leases and credit cards, notifying banks and the post office, and so forth. If you will be contacting agencies, businesses, or organizations about the death, you will need

certified copies—probably about ten—of the death certificate. Typically, the mortuary you deal with will get copies of a death certificate (and add the cost to the bill).

If you need to order copies yourself, there are two ways to do it. In many states, you can use the form in this book to request copies of a death certificate by mail. These days, however, it's often easiest to order online. Many county websites offer request forms that you can print out and send; others allow you to submit your request electronically and pay by credit card. To find out your options for ordering online, go to the official website of the county where the death occurred. You can usually find it by using this formula, substituting the county name and the state postal abbreviation in www.co.[county name].[XX].us.

EXAMPLE:

You can find the website for King County, Washington, at www.co.king.wa.us.

If you want to use the form in this book to order copies of a death certificate, follow the rest of the instructions in this section.

CAUTION

Check state rules on providing death certificates. Because of concerns about identity theft, some states restrict access to death records to those who are related to the deceased, or to people who have a legal role in the deceased's affairs, such as the executor. If you are requesting the death certificate for any reason other than taking care of a deceased's estate—for example, genealogical research—do not use this form. There may be other requirements as well. For example, several states now require you to send in a photocopy of your driver's license or other photo identification with the request. Before you mail in your request, check with your state's office of vital statistics about any special rules you must follow.

Where to send the request for death certificate form. Before you send in a request, call the local vital statistics office or county health department in the county where the decedent died and ask where to send your request. Also find out the cost of a certified copy of a death certificate.

If at least several weeks have passed since the death, you can also obtain copies by writing to your state's vital statistics office. To find out where to write in your state and how much the copies cost (about $5 to $15 each, depending on the state), go to the website of the National Center for Health Certificates at www.cdc.gov/nchs and click "Find a birth, death, marriage, or divorce certificate."

Information to include in your request. You will need the name of the deceased and place of death. The deceased person's place of birth and Social Security number are optional, but they can be very helpful for identification purposes. Be sure to state your relationship to the deceased person whose death certificate you are requesting, such as a spouse.

Reason for the request. Most states now require you to include the reason you are requesting the death certificate. This form tells the vital records office that you need the death certificate in order to wind up the affairs of the deceased's estate. Be sure to indicate the number of copies you want. Most executors need at least ten copies.

Signing Instructions

Sign and date your Request for Death Certificate. Mail it to the appropriate agency, along with a check for the proper amount and a stamped self-addressed envelope (use a business-size envelope). Keep a copy of the form for your records.

Form 17: Notice to Creditor of Death

After someone dies, the executor needs to notify creditors of the death and close the deceased person's credit accounts. That's the purpose of this form. You can send it to credit card issuers, department stores, banks, mortgage companies, and other businesses the deceased bought on credit from or had an account with (such as a local pharmacy or furniture store).

You will need to put the date of death and the appropriate account number on this notice. You may also need to attach a document showing your appointment as executor or administrator.

CAUTION

If a formal probate court proceeding is conducted, you'll also have to follow special rules for notifying creditors, for example, mailing a notice to creditors you know about and publishing a notice in a local newspaper to alert those you're not aware of. Check with the lawyer who is handling the probate proceedings, or, if you are handling probate on your own, ask the probate clerk at the county courthouse for the rules.

Signing Instructions

Sign the notice and mail two copies to each of the deceased's creditors. The creditor who receives this notice should sign and date it—and mail a copy to you in the stamped, self-addressed envelope you enclose. Keep the completed copy you receive for your records. You may later need it as proof that you notified the creditor of the death.

TIP

Reconcile the deceased person's records. This notice asks the creditor to forward information to you about any remaining balance owed by the deceased. Once you hear back from the creditor, check the information sent by the creditor against the deceased person's records.

Form 18: Executor's Checklist

The executor of an estate has many small and large tasks. The Executor's Checklist contains a list of tasks that an executor must typically complete when winding up the affairs of someone who has died. Keep in mind, however, that an executor's specific duties depend on the needs of the estate and the requirements of state law. These vary based on the size of the estate, the kind of assets in the estate, and other, more personal factors, such as the needs and expectations of the family. Use the Executor's Checklist as a guide, tailoring it to your situation.

One of the tasks in the Executor's Checklist is to decide whether or not you want to work with a lawyer. You can hire a lawyer to act as a "coach," answering your legal questions as they come up and possibly doing research for you or looking over documents before you file them. Or, you can hire a lawyer to do everything. To find a competent lawyer who charges a reasonable fee, talk to friends who have small businesses to see if they have a good relationship with a lawyer. That lawyer can probably recommend an attorney who has estate planning and probate experience. In addition, local senior centers often have a list of recommended estate planning lawyers. And Nolo's lawyer directory (www.lawyers.nolo. com) has detailed profiles of attorneys who practice estate planning and probate.

Signing Instructions

There's no need to sign or fill in any part of the Executor's Checklist. Simply use it as a guide to ensure that you are taking care of all the tasks required of you as the executor of an estate.

Form 19: General Notice of Death

You may want to notify businesses and organizations that aren't creditors—that is, they aren't owed any money—of the death. For example, you might want to send a simple notice communicating the fact that someone has died to charities to which the deceased person has donated regularly, magazine publishers, and mail-order businesses that frequently send catalogs.

CROSS-REFERENCE

If you want to get the deceased's name deleted from junk mail lists, use Form 78, Notice to Remove Name From List.

It's easier to send a form than to write individual letters to each organization or business. You can also send this form to individuals who need to be notified of the death—unless they are friends or relatives who merit a personal call or note.

CAUTION

Do not use this general notice of death form for creditors and government agencies. Many need specific information about the deceased, such as the accounts owing or type of benefits received.

CAUTION

To notify creditors, use Form 17, above. To stop Social Security payments, follow the tip just below. For other government agencies, it's a good idea to call and find out what type of notice they require.

TIP

How to stop Social Security payments after a death. If a deceased person was receiving Social Security benefits, the executor or personal representative must notify the Social Security Administration (SSA) of the death. There is no form for this purpose. To stop payments, call the SSA at 800-772-1213 or 800-325-0778 (TTY).

Signing Instructions

Sign and date your General Notice of Death and mail it to the business or organization you wish to notify. Keep a copy of the notice for your records or, if you are sending many copies, keep a record of everyone on your mailing list, rather than copies of every notice sent.

Form 20: Obituary Information Fact Sheet

When a family member or friend dies, it's always a challenge to focus on the many details that need your attention. This form will help you with one of those tasks: organizing information for your loved one's obituary.

Most of the time, local newspapers obtain obituary information from the funeral home. On some occasions, the newspaper may obtain this information directly from the family—for example, when the death occurred away from home or when a funeral home is not handling arrangements.

Regardless of who speaks to the newspaper's obituary writer, there's less chance of error if you complete a fact sheet providing relevant information. Be sure to spell all names accurately, and include any business or personal information of interest. For example, "He founded the Carverville Barbershop Quartet" or "She was widely traveled and a frequent visitor to Nairobi and the Serengeti." When

listing survivors, include surviving spouses and children of previous marriages.

The amount of detail that's included in a newspaper obituary and the placement of the obituary in the newspaper (some obituaries are published in the news section, not the obituary section) depend on the prominence of the deceased in the community. It's possible that space limitations will preclude the newspaper from including some or all of the information that you submit.

Signing Instructions

You don't need to sign the Obituary Information Fact Sheet form. Simply fill it out and mail it to local newspapers you think will be likely to publish the obituary. The mortuary will have a list of contacts for local obituary columns.

Form 21: Notice to Deceased's Homeowners' Insurance Company

Use this form if the deceased person owned a home and insured it. The form notifies the insurance company of the death and asks that you, the executor, be added as a "named insured" to the homeowners' insurance policy.

CAUTION

If you are a co-owner of the home, do not use this form. Instead, call the insurance company to report the death.

As the executor, you will want to be added as a named insured to that policy as soon as possible. This status will give you all the protections and rights that the deceased person had under the policy. This means that you will be covered if you or anyone is injured on the premises due to your carelessness. And you will be able to make claims for property damage, if necessary. As a named insured, you also have the right to increase coverage or change policy limitations. For example, if you discover that the home and its contents are underinsured, you can make changes in the coverage. Finally, if the insurance company makes a payment after a claim has been made under the policy—for example, paying for the results of a wind-damaged roof—you will be a co-payee on the check. This is important because these payments are part of the estate, and you will need to receive and account for them.

After you are added as a named insured, you'll want to discuss with the insurance agent or broker how best to continue insurance coverage for the deceased's home. You may want to add coverage or increase coverage limits, particularly if you discover that the home was underinsured. You may also want to add riders for jewelry or other special items.

To complete this form, you will need the following information:

- the deceased person's full name (if the deceased's name is different on the insurance policy, be sure to note that)
- the date of death
- the name of the insurance company that issued the policy and the complete address of its home office
- the homeowners' policy number, and
- a certified copy of the death certificate (see Form 16 to request a death certificate).

Signing Instructions

Sign and date the Notice to Deceased's Home-owner's Insurance Company. Make two copies of the signed notice. Mail the original and one copy to the insurance company office, along with a stamped, self-addressed envelope and a certified copy of the death certificate. Keep the second copy of the notice for your records.

Form 22: Notice to Deceased's Vehicle Insurance Company

Use this form if the deceased person owned and insured any automobiles, trucks, motorcycles, motor homes, or trailers. The notice informs the insurance company of the death of the insured person and asks them to add you, the executor, to the insurance policy.

You will want to be added as a "named insured" to that policy so you will have all the protections and rights that the deceased person had under the policy. Most important, you will be permitted to add or delete coverage or adjust policy limits, if appropriate. Also, you will be named as a co-payee (along with others insured under the policy) in any payment from the company. Since these payments are part of the estate, you must receive and account for them.

Many people own more than one vehicle, and they may be insured under separate policies. Even if the deceased person used the same company for multiple policies, you should send a separate notice for each policy.

After you are added as a named insured, talk to the insurance agent or broker about how best to continue insurance coverage for the deceased's vehicles. You may want to add coverage or increase coverage limits; and if the deceased was rated a poor risk, you may even want to ask for a reduction in premiums.

Even if you do not expect that the vehicle will be used, you must insure it in case of a fire or other calamity. A parked car in a home garage, for example, will not be covered by the homeowner's policy if there is a fire—you need an auto policy or other insurance coverage. When the vehicle is distributed or sold and is no longer part of the estate, you can easily cancel the insurance you have purchased.

To complete this form, you will need the following information:

- the deceased person's full name (if the deceased's name is different on the insurance policy, be sure to note that)
- the date of death (if you don't know it, look on the death certificate)
- vehicle year, make, and model
- the name of the insurance company that issued the policy and the complete address of its home office
- the vehicle insurance policy number
- the latest billing statement from the insurance company
- a certified death certificate for the person who has died (see Form 16 to request a death certificate), and
- in some cases, a certified copy of your driving record (available from your state's department of motor vehicles).

 TIP

Document your role as executor. The insurance company may require proof of your status as the executor. Be prepared to send a copy of the court order (often called "letters testamentary" or "letters of administration") that names you as the executor. If you do not have a court order by the time the insurance company calls you, ask what other proof it will accept.

Signing Instructions

Sign and date the Notice to Deceased's Vehicle Insurance Company. Make two copies of the signed notice. Mail the original and one copy to the insurance company office, along with a stamped, self-addressed envelope. Remember to enclose a certified copy of the death certificate. Keep the second copy of the notice for your records.

Renting a Place to Live

Form 23: Apartment-Finding Service Checklist 46

Form 24: Rental Application 47

Form 25: Fixed-Term Residential Lease and Form 26: Month-to-Month
           Residential Rental Agreement 48

Form 27: Landlord-Tenant Agreement to Terminate Lease 50

Form 28: Consent to Assignment of Lease 51

Form 29: Landlord-Tenant Checklist 51

Form 30: Notice of Needed Repairs 52

Form 31: Tenant's Notice of Intent to Move Out 53

Form 32: Demand for Return of Security Deposit 53

Whether you rent or own property, you probably understand just how bad a failed landlord-tenant relationship can be. But there is an excellent way to get any landlord-tenant relationship off to a good start and minimize the possibility of future misunderstandings and legal problems: Put all agreements in writing. This chapter includes a rental agreement, a lease, and the principal forms you'll need to do this, plus a few forms that will be helpful at move-out time.

RESOURCE

To learn more details of landlord-tenant law, see the following Nolo books and software:

From the landlord's point of view:

- *Every Landlord's Legal Guide*, by Marcia Stewart, Ralph Warner, and Janet Portman. This 50-state book provides extensive legal and practical information on leases, tenant screening, rent, security deposits, privacy, repairs, property managers, discrimination, roommates, liability, tenancy termination, and much more. It includes more than 30 legal forms and agreements as tear-outs and on CD-ROM.

- *Every Landlord's Guide to Finding Great Tenants*, by Janet Portman (Nolo). This book provides an in-depth process for finding tenants, from advertising to dealing with current residents, to evaluating applications, credit reports, and more. Over 40 forms on CD-ROM, complete with essential 50-state legal tables with the law landlords need to know.

From the tenant's point of view:

- *Every Tenant's Legal Guide*, by Janet Portman and Marcia Stewart. This book gives tenants in all 50 states the legal and practical information they need to deal with their landlords and protect their rights when things go wrong. It covers all important issues of renting, including signing a lease, getting a landlord to make needed repairs, fighting illegal discrimination, protecting privacy rights, dealing with roommates, getting the security deposit returned fairly, moving out, and much more.

Form 23: Apartment-Finding Service Checklist

Many landlords list their rental property with a homefinders' service that provides a centralized listing of rental units for a particular geographic area. Using one of these services, many of which are online, can be an efficient way for a tenant to search for a place to live, especially in metropolitan areas. Prices of "brick and mortar" apartment-finding services vary, but typically tenants pay a flat fee, often between $50 and $100, for a one-month membership. In some tight rental markets, you may also have to pay the service a percentage of your monthly rent if you find an apartment through them. Online services such as craigslist or Rent.com are typically free. Check newspaper ads or look in the yellow pages under "Apartment Finding and Rental Services." To find an online service (national or regional), type "apartment finding" into your brower's Search box.

TIP

Do a little investigating. Many home-finding services do a good job of helping people find a place to rent, but some are sloppy and a few are actually crooked. Unscrupulous companies have been caught selling either outdated rental lists—most or all of the apartments have already been rented—or lists no different from what is in a newspaper. So before you sign up with and pay an apartment-finding service, check with the Better Business Bureau and local consumer organizations to be sure the service is reputable and worth the money. Also, especially in urban areas, pay close attention to the geographical scope of any service you are considering. Some may be excellent in one area but not others.

Form 23, the Apartment-Finding Service Checklist, offers you a good way to organize and collect the information you need before pulling out your checkbook and signing up with a service. Use it to jot down the type, number, and locations of listings typically available, the membership costs, and additional services such as roommate referrals.

Signing Instructions

There are no signing instructions for the Apartment-Finding Service Checklist. Simply fill one out each time you start collecting information on a different homefinding service. Keep a copy and make it the first entry in your rental file, where you'll put all important papers relating to your rental.

Form 24: Rental Application

Landlords routinely use rental applications to screen potential tenants and select those who are likely to pay the rent on time, keep the unit in good condition, and not cause problems. Form 24 calls for a wide variety of information, including the applicant's rental, employment, and credit history, and personal references. Conscientious landlords will insist on verifying this information before signing a lease or rental agreement.

If you own or manage rental property, you can use this rental application to help screen potential tenants. Be sure to ask all serious applicants to fill out an application, not just those who you think need special scrutiny. Ask all applicants to sign the rental application authorizing you to verify the information and references and to run a credit check. Also, use the "Notes" section at the end of the application to write down legal reasons for refusing an individual—for example, negative credit history, insufficient income, or your inability to verify information. You will want this kind of record in order to survive a fair housing challenge if a disappointed applicant files a discrimination complaint.

> **CAUTION**
> **Make sure you understand how discrimination laws work.** Many types of discrimination are illegal, including race, religion, national origin, sex, familial status, disability, and, in some states, sexual orientation or marital status. For more information on legal and illegal reasons to reject a tenant, see the resources listed at the beginning of this chapter.

Savvy tenants will also find Form 24 useful when looking for a new place to live. If you're a tenant, we suggest you complete this rental application in advance of apartment-hunting—providing information about your employment, income, credit background, and rental housing history. Take a copy of the completed application with you when you see a potential rental unit. This is almost guaranteed to impress a landlord or rental agent.

Signing Instructions

There are no signing instructions for the Rental Application. If you're a landlord, give a copy to each tenant applying for your rental property. Be sure the tenant fills it in completely and signs it before you call references or run a credit check.

If you're a tenant, complete the application in advance of apartment-hunting. You can either give your application to prospective landlords or use the information you've pulled together on Form 24 to complete the landlord's application.

Form 25: Fixed-Term Residential Lease and Form 26: Month-to-Month Residential Rental Agreement

Leases and rental agreements often look so similar they can be hard to tell apart. That's because both cover nitty-gritty issues such as the amount of rent and deposits tenants must pay, and the number of people who can live in the rental unit. The big difference is the length of the tenancy. A rental agreement typically lasts only from one month to the next (although week-to-week agreements are possible). The agreement automatically self-renews unless terminated by either the landlord or tenant, by giving the proper amount of written notice (typically 30 days). By contrast, a lease almost always covers a longer, fixed term, such as one year. With a lease, the landlord can't raise the rent or change other terms of the tenancy until the lease runs out (unless the lease itself allows future changes or the tenant agrees in writing). In addition, a landlord can't terminate the tenancy before the lease expires, unless the tenant fails to pay the rent or violates another significant term of the lease or the law.

Form 25 is a fixed-term lease. Form 26 is a month-to-month rental agreement. We believe both are fair and balanced from both landlord and tenant viewpoints. Each clause is important, but there are three that merit mention here:

Clause 4, Rental Agreement. Every state has specified how much notice you and your tenant must give each other to terminate the month-to-month rental agreement. You'll need to check your state laws to learn the rule in your state.

Clause 8, Security Deposit. The laws of several states require that landlords give tenants written information on various aspects of the security deposit, including where the deposit is being held, interest payments, and the terms and conditions under which the security deposit may be withheld. Check with your state consumer protection agency or research the law to find out whether this is required.

Clause 15, Landlord's Right to Access. This provision tries to balance the tenant's right of privacy against the landlord's right to enter the rental unit to make repairs or for other legitimate reasons. A landlord always has the right to enter a rental unit in case of a genuine emergency, such as fire. But to show the unit to prospective tenants or to make repairs, many states require 24 hours' written notice. Some states have no notice requirements or simply require the landlord to give the tenant "reasonable notice." Others require two days, 24 hours, or other specified times. As with the security deposit details, you'll want to find out what your state requires before filling in this clause.

Clause 19, Payment of Court Costs and Attorney Fees in a Lawsuit. Our clause provides that if the landlord and tenant have a dispute about the meaning or implementation of the lease or rental agreement, and if the disagreement results in a lawsuit that involves lawyers, the winning party will be entitled to have the loser pay the winner's attorney fees and court costs. Unlike many fees-and-costs clauses that would compensate only a victorious landlord, ours is even-handed (in many states, a one-sided clause will be interpreted by a judge to run both ways anyway).

For tenants, an attorney fees clause often makes it easier to find a lawyer willing to take a case that does not have the potential for a hefty money judgment. That's because with an attorney fees clause, a winning tenant's lawyer will get paid by the landlord, rather than having to rely on the tenant's pocketbook. On the other hand, tenants who are confident about representing themselves may prefer not to have an attorney fees clause, reasoning that a landlord who can't recover attorney fees in a lawsuit may be more willing to compromise, rather than go to court.

Landlords usually prefer to include an attorney fees clause unless they intend to do all or most of their own legal work in any potential eviction or other lawsuit concerning the meaning or implementation of the rental agreement or lease. When there's no costs-and-fees clause, the landlord and tenant each pay their own expenses regardless of who wins.

Signing Instructions

Print out two copies of the lease (or rental agreement)—one for the landlord and one for the tenant(s). The landlord and every tenant should sign and date both originals in the spaces indicated. The landlord should keep one signed original and the tenant(s) the other. (Co-tenants, if any, may make their own copies of the tenants' signed document.) Store your document in a safe place.

State Laws Vary Concerning Any Key Issues

All states have laws regulating residential landlord-tenant relationships. Typically, these laws include establishing the maximum amount allowed for a security deposit and the deadline for returning it, the amount of notice required to change or end a month-to-month tenancy, tenants' privacy rights, late rent charges, a tenant's right to install locks, and disclosures regarding the condition of property. For details, see the Nolo resources listed at the beginning of the chapter.

Some states require that leases include certain language. Many states require land-lords to give tenants written information on various aspects of the security deposit, such as where it is held, interest payments, and when the deposit may be withheld. Even if it's not required, you may want to provide details on security deposits in the space provided in Clause 8 of Forms 25 and 26.

Also, local rent control ordinances may require that your lease include specific language, such as the address of the local rent control board. Check your local ordinance for more information.

Federal law requires landlords to disclose known lead-based paint hazards in the rental premises. In addition, some states require landlords to make other disclosures about the property, such as flood hazards, before a new tenant signs a lease or rental agreement. Clause 20 is the place to make these kinds of disclosures.

Form 27: Landlord-Tenant Agreement to Terminate Lease

If you're a tenant with a long-term lease, ideally you'll have a lease for just the amount of time you need the rental. But despite your best efforts to plan ahead, you may want to move before your lease is up.

One option is simply to move out early. Leaving before a fixed-term lease expires, without paying the remainder of the rent due under the lease, is called breaking the lease. With a little luck, it may not cost you much—in most states, the landlord is required to take reasonable steps to re-rent the property. If the landlord does so (and doesn't attempt to hide the fact that there's now a new rent-paying tenant), your financial liability will be limited to paying the rent for the brief time the unit was vacant.

Nevertheless, if you plan to leave early, you don't just have to move out and hope your landlord plays fair and gets a new tenant quickly. For a variety of reasons, the landlord may procrastinate, claim an inability to find a new tenant, or rent the unit to a tenant who pays less rent than you did—meaning you're liable for the difference. Fortunately, there are steps you can take to minimize your financial responsibility—as well as help avoid a bad reference from the landlord next time you're apartment hunting.

First, consider simply asking the landlord to cancel the lease, using Form 27. If you and the landlord both sign and date this form, your obligations for rent beyond the termination date end. (You are still responsible for unpaid back rent and any damage you've caused beyond normal wear and tear.) Why would a landlord voluntarily agree to let you off the hook? If you have been a steady and considerate tenant, it's possible that you'll be treated in kind, especially if the market is tight or the landlord has a new tenant standing by who will pay a higher rent. If the landlord initially balks at canceling the lease, you might prevail by offering to pay an extra month's rent in exchange for the lease cancellation.

In some states, landlords must allow early termination of a lease under certain conditions. For example, in Delaware you need give only 30 days' notice to end a long-term lease if you must move because your present employer has relocated or because of health problems—yours or a family member's. In New Jersey, a tenant who has suffered a disabling illness or accident can break a lease and leave after 40 days' notice. Federal law allows military and other personnel to terminate a lease early when called to active duty, and some states, such as Georgia, allow members of the military to break a lease because of a change in orders. If you have a good reason for a sudden move, check your state's law.

If you can't get the landlord to cancel the lease outright, your best approach is usually to find a new tenant who will be ready to move in as soon as you leave and who will sign a new lease at the same or higher rent. If you follow this approach, you should owe nothing additional since the landlord won't be able to argue that a suitable replacement tenant couldn't be found.

 TIP

When the landlord won't accept the tenant you find. Keep careful records of all prospective tenants you find, especially their credit histories—you can use the Rental Application (Form 24). If the landlord sues you for back rent, present these records to the judge as proof the landlord failed to limit (mitigate) damages by refusing to accept a suitable replacement tenant.

If the landlord accepts the new tenant, you and the landlord should cancel your lease by completing Form 27. The landlord and the new tenant can sign their own lease, and you will no longer be in the picture.

Signing Instructions

Print out two copies of the Landlord-Tenant Agreement to Terminate Lease form—one for the landlord and one for the tenant(s). The landlord and every tenant should sign and date both originals. The landlord should keep one signed original and the tenant(s) the other. (Co-tenants, if any, may make their own copies of the tenants' signed document.)

Form 28: Consent to Assignment of Lease

If you are a tenant who wants to move out permanently, but the landlord won't cancel your lease or sign a new lease with a tenant you find, your next best option may be to "assign" your lease to a new tenant (called an "assignee") who is acceptable to the landlord. With an assignment, you turn over the remainder of your lease to someone else. You can do this with Form 28. Unless the landlord agrees otherwise, you remain in the picture as a guarantor of rent payments in case the new occupant (the assignee) fails to pay. Having a second source for the rent is one reason a savvy landlord might agree to an assignment but not a cancellation.

Landlords can voluntarily waive their rights to look to you as the guarantor of the assignee's rent, something that is not uncommon when the new tenant has excellent credit. Clause 4 of Form 28 releases you from this worrisome obligation, essentially putting you in the position of someone who has terminated the lease. If the landlord balks at the release, and

you are reasonably sure of your replacement's ability to pay the rent, you may not be risking much if you cross out Clause 4 and remain theoretically responsible for the rent.

Signing Instructions

Print out three copies of the Consent to Assignment of Lease form—one for the landlord, one for the tenant, and one for the assignee. Each person should sign and date all originals in the spaces indicated. The landlord should keep one signed original and the tenant and assignee the others.

Form 29: Landlord-Tenant Checklist

Legal disputes between tenants and landlords have justly gained a reputation for having the potential to be almost as nasty as a bad divorce. And like a failed marriage, disputes often continue after the legal relationship is over. This is most likely to occur when a landlord keeps all or part of a tenant's security deposit, claiming the place was left excessively dirty or damaged.

Fortunately, using Form 29, a landlord and tenant can work together to minimize deposit-related disputes by inspecting the rental unit together at both the start and end of the tenancy. The idea is to identify damage, dirt, mildew, and obvious wear and tear before the tenant moves in (use column 1) and inspect the unit again in the company of the landlord or property manager just before the tenant moves out (use columns 2 and 3).

In the "additional explanation" section at the end of the form, note any areas of disagreement between the landlord and the tenant. (Incidentally, to avoid a court battle over security deposit deductions, many wise landlords and tenants try to compromise any disputed damage claims when doing the final inspection.) Tenants should read and check the box on the bottom of the third page of the form regarding smoke detectors and fire extinguishers.

Signing Instructions

After completing the Landlord-Tenant Checklist at move-in time, make two copies. The landlord and tenant should sign and date both originals and each keep one original. Review the checklist again at move-out time.

> **TIP**
>
> **Take photos or a video at move-in and move-out to avoid disputes.** Having photos lets you compare "before" and "after" pictures, rather than dealing with competing versions of the condition of the property. If you end up in court fighting over the security deposit, photos will be invaluable visual proof. Tenants should consider taking along a friend or colleague as a potential witness to the condition of the rental unit at move-in and move-out time—someone who will be available to testify in court on your behalf if necessary.

Form 30: Notice of Needed Repairs

Landlords are legally required to provide tenants livable premises when they offer a unit for rent, and to maintain the rental property in decent condition throughout the rental term. In most states, the legal jargon used to describe this obligation is the "landlord's legal duty to fulfill the implied warranty of habitability."

Tenants have the right to a decent place to live even if they move into a place that's clearly substandard (below reasonable habitability standards), or even if the lease comes right out and says that the landlord doesn't have to provide a habitable unit. Or put another way,

all courts have rejected the sleazy argument that tenants waive the right to a livable place when they accept a substandard rental unit.

If there's a problem with the physical condition of your rental unit, you'll want to notify your landlord or manager as soon as possible so that it can be promptly fixed. The best approach is to put every repair and maintenance request in writing, using Form 30, keeping a copy for yourself. You may find it easier to call your landlord first, particularly in urgent cases, but be sure to follow up with a written repair request.

Be as specific as possible regarding the problem —whether it's plumbing, heating, security, weatherproofing, or other defects. Note the effects of the problem on you, what you want done, and when. For example, if the thermostat on your heater is always finicky and sometimes doesn't function at all, explain how long you've been without heat and how low the temperature has dipped—don't simply say "the heater needs to be fixed." Be sure to note the date of the request and how many requests, if any, have preceded this one. Keep records of all repair requests.

If you are a landlord, it's a good idea to give tenants copies of Form 30 and encourage them to immediately report plumbing, heating, weatherproofing, or other defects or safety problems. Be sure to note details as to how and when the problem was fixed, including reasons for any delay, on the bottom of the tenant's repair request form. Keep copies of all completed forms in your tenant files.

Signing Instructions

There are no specific signing instructions for the Notice of Needed Repairs form. Tenants should simply sign the document and keep a copy for their records. If your landlord has an on-site office or a resident manager, deliver the repair request personally. If you mail it, consider sending it certified mail (return receipt requested) or use a delivery service that will give you a proof of delivery. Besides keeping a copy of every written repair request, keep notes of oral communications, too.

> **TIP**
> **If your landlord ignores your requests and your rental is unlivable, you'll have to undertake stronger measures.** These might include calling state or local building or health inspectors, moving out, withholding the rent, or repairing the problem yourself. These remedies, available only in certain situations according to your state's laws, are thoroughly discussed in the Nolo books listed at the beginning of this chapter.

Form 31: Tenant's Notice of Intent to Move Out

If you have a month-to-month tenancy, in most states and for most rentals you must provide 30 days' notice to your landlord if you want to move out. In some states, if you pay rent weekly or twice a month, you can give written notice to terminate that matches your rent payment interval. For example, if you pay rent every two weeks, you may need to give only 14 days' notice.

In most states, you can give notice at any time during the month. For example, if you pay rent on the first of the month but give notice on the tenth, you will be obliged to pay for only ten days' rent for the next month, even if you move out earlier. To calculate the amount, prorate the monthly rent using 30 days.

Check the Nolo resources listed at the beginning of the chapter for specific require-ments as to how and when to give notice.

Signing Instructions

Tenants should sign and date the Tenant's Notice of Intent to Move Out form and give or mail it to the landlord. Be sure to check your state rules to make sure you are meeting any specific notice requirements.

> **TIP**
> **If you give oral notice, follow up in writing with this form.** If you know your landlord or manager well, you may wish to convey your moving plans in a face-to-face or phone conversation. Fine, but immediately follow up with written con-firmation. The law almost always requires written notice. You can use Form 31 for this purpose.

Form 32: Demand for Return of Security Deposit

Getting cleaning and security deposits returned can be a problem for tenants. To avoid trouble, or to successfully deal with a landlord who unfairly retains your deposit, use Form 29, the Landlord-Tenant Checklist, to make a written and photographic record of what the place looks like when you move in and when you move out. Be sure you leave the rental in good condition, give proper notice, and are paid up in rent when you leave. And don't forget to give the landlord your new address.

Depending on the law of your state, you should normally receive your deposits back within 14 to 30 days of moving out. If you don't, send a written request using the Demand for Return of Security Deposit form. If this doesn't work, you may need to sue the landlord in small claims court. (Some state security deposit statutes require tenants to make a written request; and in some states, small claims court rules require you to send a demand letter before you can sue.)

Your demand letter should state the date you moved out of the rental and lay out the reasons your landlord owes you deposit money. Refer to any statutory deadlines and tangible evidence supporting your demand, such as photos or a before-and-after Landlord-Tenant Checklist. In Form 32, you make it clear that if the landlord does not promptly return your deposit by a specified date (we suggest seven to ten days), you plan to go to small claims court.

In many states, if a landlord withholds a deposit without giving the tenant a good written reason for doing so (for example, to cover specific damage or unpaid rent) within the required time, the tenant has some powerful options. Tenants can sue for the amount of the wrongly withheld deposit, plus an extra amount for punitive damages if the landlord intentionally failed to return the deposit on time. Check your state law for specifics and refer to them in any correspondence with your landlord. For example, California landlords have three weeks to return the security deposit with an itemized statement of deductions and copies of receipts or invoices for needed cleaning or repairs.

Signing Instructions

Sign your Demand for Return of Security Deposit letter and send it certified mail (return receipt requested) to the landlord, or use a delivery service that will give you a proof of delivery. Keep a copy of your letter and all related correspondence. You'll need this if you end up in a court dispute over your security deposit.

Going to Small Claims Court

Hopefully, your Demand for Return of Security Deposit letter will spur action on the landlord's part and you'll get your deposit back. If it doesn't, you may need to file in small claims court. These courts will handle disputes worth up to a certain amount—typical limits are $5,000, $7,500, and up to $10,000 (each state sets its own limit). Most security deposit disputes will fit within the court's limit. You can sue your landlord for your security deposit and for interest (if it's required in your state or city). In many states you can also sue for extra punitive damages if the landlord intentionally failed to return the deposit on time.

It is inexpensive (usually $10 to $50) to file a case in small claims court, you don't need a lawyer, and disputes usually go before a judge (there are no juries) within 30 to 60 days. Small claims courts are informal places, intended to be used by regular folks presenting their own cases.

RESOURCE

For detailed advice on filing (or defending) a case in small claims court, see *Everybody's Guide to Small Claims Court*, or, if you live in California, *Everybody's Guide to Small Claims Court in California*, both by Ralph Warner (Nolo).

Borrowing and Lending Money

Form 33: Loan Comparison Worksheet 56

Form 34: Authorization to Check Credit and Employment References 56

Form 35: Monthly Payment Record 58

Forms 36–40: Promissory Notes 58

Form 36: Promissory Note—Installment Payments With Interest 60

Form 37: Promissory Note—Installment Payments With Interest and
        Balloon Payment 61

Form 38: Promissory Note—Installment Payments Without Interest 62

Form 39: Promissory Note—Lump Sum Payment With Interest 62

Form 40: Promissory Note—Lump Sum Payment Without Interest 63

Form 41: Cosigner Provision 63

Forms 42–45: Security Agreements 63

Form 42: Security Agreement Provision for Promissory Note 64

Form 43: Security Agreement 65

Form 44: U.C.C. Financing Statement 65

Form 45: Release of U.C.C. Financing Statement 66

Form 46: Agreement to Modify Promissory Note 66

Form 47: Overdue Payment Demand 67

Form 48: Demand to Make Good on Bad Check 67

This chapter contains several promissory notes you can use when you borrow money from or lend money to a friend, relative, or someone else who isn't a commercial customer. (Banks and other institutional lenders follow many legal rules and must use forms with far more fine print.) This chapter also includes a loan comparison worksheet to keep track of information you collect on different loans (whether from a personal or commercial lender), a form to authorize a lender to check the borrower's credit, and "demand" letters to use when trying to collect an overdue payment or bad check.

Form 33: Loan Comparison Worksheet

A good consumer shops around before making a significant purchase. There is no reason to do otherwise when you are looking to borrow money. A loan from one bank may come with very different terms than a loan from a credit union or finance company—or even from a different bank across town. And a loan from your former college roommate or your Aunt Charlotte may be very different still.

The cost of a loan doesn't depend only on how much interest you pay. Long-term loans carry a higher rate of interest than short-term loans (the lender runs the risk that inflation will erode the real value of the interest it receives for a longer period, so it passes some of this risk on to you in the form of a higher interest rate). But short-term loans are not necessarily cheaper. You need to consider application fees and other up-front fees, which can vary considerably from one lender to the next, when computing the cost of a loan. Fortunately, this isn't true of all short-term loans, so be sure to shop around. When you apply for a commercial loan, the lender must tell you the annual cost of the loan. This is stated as the annual percentage rate, or APR. You can use that figure to compare the annual cost of different loans.

APR isn't the entire story, especially for adjustable rate loans or loans with a balloon payment or other features. For a full comparison of loans, use this worksheet to record the terms of any loans you are considering, whether to buy a car or computer system or pay down your credit cards. See "Basic Loan Terms Explained," below, before you start collecting information on different loans.

Because mortgage loans involve far more considerations than the loans discussed in this chapter, use Form 54 (Mortgage Rates and Terms Worksheet) in Chapter 6 when shopping around for a mortgage.

Signing Instructions

There are no signing instructions for the Loan Comparison Worksheet. Simply fill one out each time you start collecting information on different loans.

Form 34: Authorization to Check Credit and Employment References

Commercial lenders—banks, credit unions, and finance companies—will always check a loan applicant's credit before agreeing to lend money. If you're thinking of lending someone money, it makes good sense to check the borrower's credit and employment references. You'll need the borrower's signed authorization to do this. Most employers, financial institutions, and credit sources require this kind of signed authorization before providing information on the borrower. That's the purpose of Form 34. The borrower should complete all sections, including details on employment and credit history.

Basic Loan Terms Explained

To understand your loan agreement, you'll need to know the meaning of a few terms.

Adjustable rate. An interest rate that changes over time. It is set initially by the lender, usually fairly low, and then fluctuates (usually meaning it increases) every several months.

Balloon payment. A lump sum payment made at the end of a loan to cover the remaining balance. For example, you borrow $10,000 for five years at 6% interest. The monthly payments are $193.33. You can afford to pay only about half that amount, so the lender lets you pay $100 a month. At the end of five years, however, you owe a balloon payment of $6,511.53. Balloon payments are usually bad deals. Borrowers often get into trouble by focusing on the low monthly payments rather than the large and often unaffordable sum due at the end of the loan term.

Cap. On an adjustable rate loan, the cap refers both to the maximum amount the interest rate can increase each year and the ultimate maximum an interest rate can reach. For example, an adjustable rate loan that begins at 4% may have an annual cap of 0.5% and a lifetime cap of 7%. This means that at the beginning of the second year, the rate will be 4.5%. If the loan continues to increase 0.5% each year, it will reach its lifetime cap of 7% in six years.

Collateral. Property a borrower pledges as security for repayment of a loan. Sometimes it's the item being purchased, such as a car. Other times the collateral is property the borrower already owns. If the borrower defaults, a lender can take the collateral without first suing the borrower and obtaining a judgment.

Cosigner. A credit-worthy person who agrees to be fully liable for repayment of a loan if the borrower defaults.

Credit check. A lender getting a copy of the borrower's credit report from a credit reporting agency in order to verify the borrower's credit-worthiness.

Credit insurance. Insurance coverage offered by some lenders to ensure payment of a loan in the event the borrower becomes disabled or dies.

Fixed rate. An interest rate that is established by the lender at the outset and will never change.

Grace period. The number of days a borrower has after a loan payment is due to make the payment without being charged a late fee. For example, if your loan payments are due on the 1st of the month, you may have a grace period until the 10th, meaning that the lender will accept your payment until that date without penalizing you.

Late fee. The fee a lender charges when a borrower pays late. See "Grace period."

Loan application fee. Fees charged by lenders for the work involved in lending money. These include credit checks, appraisals on collateral, and loan processing fees.

Loan discounts. Incentives offered by a lender that reduce a loan's interest rate. For example, you might be offered a 0.5% discount if you set up direct payment from your checking account or if you maintain a checking account with the lender with a minimum balance requirement.

Points. Real estate loans usually come with points, an amount of money equal to a percentage of your loan. This money is paid to the lender simply for the privilege of borrowing money.

Prepayment penalty. A penalty imposed on a borrower for paying off a loan early. It's usually expressed as a flat fee or a percentage of the interest the lender lost as a result of your prepaying.

Doing a credit and reference check will give you an idea whether the borrower is likely to repay you in full and on time, and put you in a good position to say "no" to someone with poor credit. Checking a person's credit references and saying "no" is likely to put a strain on a personal relationship, but making a loan to someone who can't handle the payments is more likely to cause long-term problems.

Signing Instructions

The person borrowing money should sign and date the Authorization to Check Credit and Personal References. The lender should keep the original and give the borrower a copy. The lender should also send copies of the signed authorization form to the credit and employment references that will be checked. It may be helpful to enclose a stamped, self-addressed envelope.

Form 35: Monthly Payment Record

If a loan will be repaid over many months or years, it's easy to forget whether and when every payment has been made. This is especially likely if the debtor misses several payments because of an emergency and then makes them up a little at a time. In this case, the amounts will be different each month. Use Form 35, Monthly Payment Record, to keep track of payments made under installment notes, such as the promissory notes (Forms 36-40) included in this chapter.

Signing Instructions

There are no signing instructions for the Monthly Payment Record. The lender simply records payments due and made every month.

Forms 36–40: Promissory Notes

A promissory note is a written agreement to pay money to someone. As with all legal documents, promissory notes often contain loads of unnecessary legalese. Because the notes in this chapter are designed to be used primarily between family and friends, we prefer to keep the language simple.

The primary function of a promissory note is to document the amount of a debt and the terms under which it will be repaid, including the interest rate (if any). A promissory note is typically signed when. a person borrows money or buys something on credit. Here are several important reasons why all promissory notes should be put in writing:

- You are assured that the borrower and lender have agreed to the same terms, including the repayment schedule and interest rate.

- You specify exactly what those terms are.

- Both parties have a written document to refresh their memories.

This chapter contains five promissory notes, each designed to deal with a somewhat different repayment scenario:

- Form 36: Promissory Note—Installment Payments With Interest

- Form 37: Promissory Note—Installment Payments With Interest and Balloon Payment

- Form 38: Promissory Note—Installment Payments Without Interest

- Form 39: Promissory Note—Lump Sum Payment With Interest

- Form 40: Promissory Note—Lump Sum Payment Without Interest.

All of these notes are for unsecured loans—meaning that the borrower does not pledge any property, such as a car, as collateral to guarantee repayment. This means if the borrower doesn't repay the loan, the lender must sue in court to get a judgment, which then makes the lender eligible to use wage garnishment or property attachments to collect on the note. You can add a security provision to your note using Form 42, which gives the lender the right to force the sale of personal property pledged as collateral if the borrower doesn't repay. Form 43 is the actual security agreement you will use when property is pledged.

Signing Instructions for Promissory Notes

The borrower(s) must sign the Promissory Note for it to be valid. (There may be two borrowers—for example, if a husband and wife are jointly borrowing money. See "Does a Borrower's Spouse Need to Sign a Promissory Note?") Print out one copy of the form. The borrower(s) should sign and date only one copy of the document in the space provided. This signed original should be given to the lender. The borrower(s) should keep a copy of the signed document for their own records.

FORM

The promissory note forms contain a space for the acknowledgment of a notary public. You may want to have the borrower sign the promissory note in front of a notary public. This may be required in some states; even if it is not, notarization adds a measure of legal credibility to your promissory note. (See "Signing the Forms," in the introduction, for general advice on having a form notarized.)

Does a Borrower's Spouse Need to Sign a Promissory Note?

A promissory note is a contract that makes a borrower liable for a debt. The lender may ask that the borrower's spouse sign as well. This is likely to happen, for example, if someone is borrowing money to buy property that both spouses will use or to help finance a new business venture. Keep in mind that a lender may not require a borrower's spouse to sign if the borrower is the only one applying for the loan and no jointly held or community property is involved.

By having the borrower's spouse sign, a second person becomes legally liable for repaying the debt. Normally, if only the borrower signed the contract and didn't repay it, the other party to the agreement could get a judgment against the borrower but not the borrower's spouse. This means that the creditor would be able to seize property that the borrower owns as sole owner, but not property that the borrower and a spouse own in both of their names or that the spouse owns solely, unless the borrower lives in a community property state such as California. (See "Who Pays the Debts in Community Property States?" for more details.) But if the borrower and spouse both sign a contract and then default, the other party can sue and get a judgment against both. That judgment can be enforced by seizing the couple's joint bank account, putting a lien on jointly owned real estate, seizing property in the borrower's name alone, and seizing property in the spouse's name alone.

Who Pays the Debts in Community Property States?

Arizona, California, Idaho, Louisiana, Nevada, New Mexico, Texas, Washington, and Wisconsin follow the community property system. (In Alaska, a couple can choose to have their property treated as community property by preparing a written agreement.) In these states, property acquired during a marriage is generally considered community (joint) regardless of whose name it's in or who paid for it. In addition, all debts incurred during the marriage—even if only one spouse signed the loan papers—are considered community (joint) debts unless a creditor was explicitly told that only one spouse would be liable for the debt.

In most situations, the rights of creditors to seize property after getting a judgment for nonpayment of a debt depend on whether the property is considered community or separate.

- **Community Property.** Usually, property earned or acquired by either spouse during the marriage—except property acquired by gift or inheritance or defined as separate under a premarital agreement—is considered community property. A creditor can go after all community property to pay for either a community debt or a separate debt of one spouse.

- **Separate Property.** This is property a spouse owned before getting married, acquired during the marriage by gift or inheritance, or agreed in writing to be kept separate. It's also property acquired using separate assets. For example, if a woman owned a house when she got married, then sold it and used the proceeds to buy stock held in her name, the stock is clearly her separate property. For community debts, a creditor can seek reimbursement from either spouse's separate property. For example, for debt the wife accumulates while married, a creditor can go after her separate property and all community property, including her husband's share.

TIP

If the borrower's credit is questionable, consider requiring a cosigner. You can add a cosigner clause to your promissory note by using Form 41.

Form 36: Promissory Note—Installment Payments With Interest

Form 36 allows the borrower to repay the note in installments rather than all at once, and charges interest. Charging a friend or family member interest strikes some people as being ungenerous. In our opinion, this view is based on a misconception about the function of interest, which is to compensate the lender for the use of the money. Think of it this way. Suppose Joan lends Harry $5,000 for a year, interest free. If Joan had put the money in a certificate of deposit, she would have earned the going rate of interest. By giving Harry the money interest free, Joan ends up paying for the privilege of lending the money to Harry.

Interest charged on money lent to friends and relatives tends to run between 5% and 10%. If you wish to charge a higher rate of interest, check your state law to see if the rate is legal; it may constitute the crime of usury. How much interest is appropriate? In an effort to be generous to a relative or friend, many lenders charge interest at somewhat less than the market rate, sometimes as little as—or just slightly more than—they would receive if they purchased a bank certificate of deposit for the same time period. This is a great deal for the borrower; after all, even if Harry qualified to borrow from a bank or other commercial lender, he would have to pay a much higher rate of interest than Joan would receive if she put the money in a CD.

Charging interest does add a level of complication when it comes to figuring out the amount of the monthly payments. For this, you will need an amortization calculator or software program. You can find one at www.nolo.com. You plug in the loan amount, interest rate, and number of months the borrower will take to repay the loan. The calculator gives you the monthly payment amount.

If the borrower decides to pay off the principal sooner than the promissory note calls for under the installment plan, you will have to recalculate the payments based on the new outstanding balance. This is easy to do with an amortization calculator.

Form 37: Promissory Note—Installment Payments With Interest and Balloon Payment

Form 37 is similar to Form 36 in that the loan must be repaid in installments with interest. But there's an additional twist: Individual payments are lower than they otherwise would be, with the shortfall made up by one large balloon payment at the end of the loan term. To see how this works, let's take a look at an example. You lend a friend $10,000 at 7% interest and want the money paid back in three years. Using an amortization calculator, you

Legal Terminology of Promissory Notes

Here we translate some legal terms into plain English.

Acceleration. Our promissory notes accelerate the borrower's responsibility to make all necessary loan payments, meaning that if the borrower misses one or more regularly scheduled payments, the entire loan amount is immediately due. You specify the number of days—typically 30 or 60—the borrower has to pay before you exercise this option. Without this provision you can't sue for loan installments not yet due, even though the borrower has missed several payments and obviously has no plans to repay.

Attorney fees. Our promissory notes include a clause providing that the borrower has to pay the lender's attorney fees and court costs in a legal dispute if the lender wins. Under the laws of some states, this type of clause will be read by a court to go both ways. This means that if the borrower wins, she or he will be entitled to attorney fees and court costs, even if the loan papers don't specifically say so.

Buyer in due course. This is a person who buys or otherwise legally receives a promissory note from a lender. The borrower's obligation to repay the note doesn't change just because the lender sells the note to someone else.

Joint and several liability. This means that if there is more than one borrower, all borrowers are liable for repaying 100% of the loan. If Chuck and Laura borrow $5,000 from Miguel and then default, Miguel can go after either Chuck or Laura for the full $5,000. They can't claim that each person is liable for only $2,500.

discover that your friend would have to pay you $308.78 each month to pay it back over that time.

Your friend can't afford to pay that amount each month now, but expects to receive some money in about three years when a trust matures. So you propose the following: Your friend can borrow $10,000 from you at 7% and repay it over three years. But to make the payments affordable now, you agree to amortize the loan as though it were to be paid off in ten years, meaning your friend's monthly payments are only $116.11, far less than $308.78. You agree to take these low payments for 36 months and at the end, your friend will make you one large payment, called a balloon payment, of the remaining principal. That amount is $7,693.

Form 38: Promissory Note— Installment Payments Without Interest

Use Form 38 if the borrower will repay you in installments, but you won't charge interest. When the parties involved in the transaction are family members or close friends, the amount borrowed is relatively small, and the probability of repayment is high, lenders sometimes prefer to use an interest-free installment note.

Be aware that if the IRS learns of an interest-free loan, it can impute interest. This means that the lender will be assumed to have earned interest and will be required to report that interest as income on that year's tax return. For most personal loans, this won't be a problem because uncharged interest can be treated as a tax-free gift, as long as the total amount given and imputed to the borrower in a calendar year is $13,000 or less ($12,00 for gifts made between 2006 and 2008).

Form 39: Promissory Note— Lump Sum Payment With Interest

This note is normally used when the borrower won't be able to repay the loan for a period of months or years. For example, you might borrow money from a friend to help you open a small business. You aren't likely to have the cash flow for at least six months or a year to repay the loan. In such a situation, your friend might agree to be repaid in a lump sum in two years.

The easiest way to determine the amount of annual interest that will be due on the loan is to use simple, not compound, interest. Multiply the amount of the loan by the annual interest rate. For instance, if the loan is for $4,000 and your annual interest rate is 10%, the annual amount of interest on the loan is $400. To determine the total amount of interest due, multiply the annual interest amount by the time period of the loan. In our example, if the loan is for two years, the interest due would be $800.

If you need to compute the interest for a period of months rather than years, compute the interest for one year, divide by 12, and then multiply the result by the number of months. For example, assume the $4,000 loan is for an 18-month period. Take the annual interest amount ($400), divide by 12 ($33.33) and multiply by 18 ($600).

If the loan is paid back before it is due, Clause 2 gives the lender two choices:

- Charge the full interest. This is not unreasonable, given that you committed yourself to being without the amount of the entire loan for the time indicated.

- Prorate the interest to correspond to the actual period of time the loan was out-standing. Returning to the $4,000 loan example, if you originally figured interest at

10% for two years ($800) but the loan was paid back in 18 months, simply charge the 18-month figure ($600) instead.

Form 40: Promissory Note— Lump Sum Payment Without Interest

This promissory note, which calls for a lump sum loan repayment and no interest, is about as basic as you can get. This sort of note is normally used by people with a close personal relationship when the person lending the money is primarily interested in helping out the borrower and expects nothing in return except, eventually, the return of the amount borrowed.

If the IRS learns of the loan, it can impute interest. This means that the lender will be assumed to have earned interest and will be required to report that interest as income on that year's tax return. For most personal loans, this won't be a problem because uncharged interest can be treated as a tax-free gift, as long as the total given to the borrower by the lender and imputed by the IRS is $13,000 or less in a calendar year.

Form 41: Cosigner Provision

A cosigner is someone who promises to repay a loan if the primary debtor defaults. If you'll be lending money to someone with a questionable (or no) credit history or a background of sporadic employment, you might require one or more cosigners, such as a parent or friend. (Each cosigner is 100% liable to repay the note if the borrower fails to.)

Federal law requires that commercial lenders give cosigners a notice of their potential liability when they agree to cosign a debt. Although this is not required for personal loans between friends and relatives, we believe full disclosure of the risks of cosigning is a good idea and so we incorporate much of that notice language in Form 41.

Signing Instructions

After filling in the top of the Cosigner Provision, staple it to your promissory note and then have the cosigner complete, sign, and date it. The lender should keep the original and give each cosigner a copy, along with a copy of the promissory note.

Forms 42–45: Security Agreements

If you lend money to someone who does not repay it, your only recourse usually is to sue the person, get a court judgment, and then take money or property that can legally be seized to satisfy a debt.

There is an easier way: You can attach a security agreement to the promissory note. In a security agreement, you specify certain property belonging to the borrower, such as a car or computer, as collateral for repayment of the loan. If the borrower doesn't repay the loan, you can take the property, sell it, and use the proceeds to satisfy what you are owed. You don't have to go to court. However, you do have to follow proper procedures when you take back (repossess) the property.

Sometimes, a dishonest borrower will try to use the same piece of collateral to secure more than one debt. If that happens and the unscrupulous borrower later defaults on these secured loans, the lenders will find themselves competing to sell the collateral and use the proceeds to satisfy all their debts. How can secured creditors protect themselves? It's very simple: They must be the first to file evidence of their claim with the correct recording agency.

This chapter includes four different forms relating to security interests:

- Form 42: Security Agreement Provision for Promissory Note
- Form 43: Security Agreement
- Form 44: Uniform Commercial Code (U.C.C.) Financing Statement
- Form 45: Release of U.C.C. Financing Statement

Creating a security interest is a multistep process. First you must add Form 42 to your promissory note. Second, you must complete a Security Agreement (Form 43) and attach it to your promissory note. Third, a U.C.C. Financing Statement (Form 44) will usually need to be filed with the appropriate state agency (this is typically done by the lender).

Note that the forms in this book are intended to be used only when the borrower is securing a loan with tangible personal property, such as a computer or car. If you are considering using real property, such as a house, as collateral for a loan, you should seek the assistance of a real estate lawyer. Title to real estate is a highly technical matter beyond the scope of this book. Similarly, if you are considering using intangible personal property (bank accounts, stock in a corporation) or intellectual property (copyright, trademark, patent) as collateral for the loan, you should consult an attorney.

Using Your House as Collateral

Think twice before you pledge real estate, and especially your home, as collateral for a loan. If you are unable to make loan payments, you could lose a large investment, not to mention a roof over your head.

When you pledge your home or other real estate as security for a loan, a security agreement is not adequate to protect the lender. The borrower generally needs to sign a mortgage or a deed or trust, which can then be recorded (filed) at a county office to establish the lender's security interest in the real estate. Then, if the borrower defaults, the lender has the right to sell the property to recover the amount due under the promissory note. This sort of transaction is complicated—you should seek the advice of a real estate lawyer before signing a mortgage or deed of trust.

Form 42: Security Agreement Provision for Promissory Note

You can use Form 42 to identify the security interest, such as a car or valuable personal property, as a part of your contract. Choose the sample language on the form that is most appropriate for your situation and delete the others.

Signing Instructions

There are two ways to use the Security Agreement Provision. You can either copy the security language that's appropriate into your promissory note itself, or you can complete the security agreement form and staple it to your promissory note. If you use the form separately, the borrower (owner of the collateral) should sign and date the form. The lender should keep the original and give the borrower a copy, along with a copy of the promissory note. Otherwise, if the security provision becomes part of the note, the signing instructions for the note apply.

Form 43: Security Agreement

Use the Security Agreement to state the terms of the lender's security interest in the property that will be used as collateral for the loan, and to describe the property.

CAUTION

Do not use this agreement if the collateral is real property, such as a house. In that case, you will need to file a mortgage or deed of trust with the county land records office. See a real estate lawyer for assistance with this transaction.

When describing the property that will be used as collateral, be sure that you describe it in enough detail that the property can be easily identified. For example, you would describe a vehicle as a "1998 Toyota Tacoma, license plate number 9876543, Vehicle Identification Number ABC1234567" instead of simply "my red truck."

In paragraph 1 of the agreement, you'll need to insert information from the promissory note (the date, amount, and annual percentage rate). In paragraphs 5 and 9, insert the state where the property is located and the state whose laws will govern the agreement—usually the state where the parties live.

The agreement states that the lender will file a U.C.C. Financing Statement (Form 44) and that the borrower will sign any additional documents needed to protect the lender's security interest. Signing additional documents may be necessary in some situations, such as when the secured property includes certain kinds of assets (particularly cars and boats) that

may require the lender to be added to the asset's certificate of title instead of filing a Financing Statement. See the discussion of Form 44 for more information.

Be sure that you read and understand the entire agreement—it contains many important clauses, including requiring the borrower to take care of the secured property, stating when the borrower will be considered in default, and describing what the lender can do if the borrower defaults.

Signing Instructions

After completing the Security Agreement, both parties should sign and date the last page. The lender will keep the original and will attach it to the original promissory note. Because the Security Agreement is an important part of the promissory note, be sure to also attach a copy of the signed agreement to the borrower's copy of the promissory note.

Form 44: U.C.C. Financing Statement

Use the U.C.C. Financing Statement to record your security interest in personal property.

Once you have completed the security agreement (Form 43), contact the appropriate state agency to find out your state's rules for documenting the lender's security interest in the property. If the collateral is a car, boat, or similar vehicle, you will most likely need to contact the motor vehicles department. Some kinds of assets (often those that are licensed by the state, such as cars and boats) require the lender to take a security interest in the property by listing its name on the certificate of title instead of filing a Financing Statement. For most other property, such as electronics equipment or a computer system, contact the

Secretary of State's office. Ask for a copy of your state's rules for filing a U.C.C. Financing Statement, and find out whether your state has any special form you must use. If it does, use the state form (not this one). Otherwise, use Form 44.

> **TIP**
>
> **What is a "buyer in due course"?** Forms 43, 44, 45, and 46 all contain a phrase that says that "the term Lender refers to any person who legally holds this note, including a buyer in due course." This phrase refers to any person who buys goods from another person. In the context of these forms, it refers to anyone who might purchase the promissory note from the original lender, and says that such a purchaser would hold the same rights as the original lender to collect the money from the borrower.

Signing Instructions

The borrower(s) should sign and date the U.C.C. Financing Statement. The lender should keep the original and give the borrower a copy. The lender should attach the promissory note and the security agreement to the U.C.C. Financing Statement and file these with the appropriate state office, such as the secretary of state. Leave the section at the bottom of the form blank; the filing officer will complete this.

Form 45: Release of U.C.C. Financing Statement

Once a loan is paid off, the borrower will want the public record to reflect that the property is no longer encumbered (being used as collateral) in favor of the lender. To do this, you will need to file Form 45 with the public agency, such as the Secretary of State's office, where you filed the U.C.C. Financing Statement. That will let prospective lawyers, creditors, and credit rating agencies know that the lender no longer claims an interest in the borrower's collateral.

This form should correspond to your original U.C.C. Financing Statement. Therefore, make sure the description of property listed as collateral is identical and the other information makes clear which U.C.C. Financing Statement is being released.

Signing Instructions

The borrower(s) should sign and date the Release of U.C.C. Financing Statement. The lender should keep the original and give the borrower a copy. The lender should file this release with the appropriate state office, such as the Secretary of State. Leave the section at the bottom of the form blank; the filing officer will complete this.

Note: Make sure your state does not have special U.C.C. form requirements before using this form.

Form 46: Agreement to Modify Promissory Note

If someone who borrows money from you falls behind on repayment, give a call to find out what's wrong. Offer whatever help you can to get the borrower back on track. Sometimes this will require no more than being willing to extend the repayment period for a few months. In other instances, you might take interest-only payments or rewrite the loan at a lower interest rate. Whatever you agree on, you must put it in writing. You can use Form 46 for that purpose.

Signing Instructions

The borrower(s) who signed the promissory note should sign and date the Agreement to Modify Promissory Note, and indicate the location (city or county) where this agreement is being signed. The lender should keep the original signed document and give a copy to the borrower(s).

Form 47: Overdue Payment Demand

If someone who owes you money under a promissory note falls behind on repayment despite your efforts to work out a new repayment plan, your next step is to send the borrower a formal demand letter. You can use Form 47 in such a situation. It serves as a formal notice to the borrower that you are demanding repayment. It states that if you do not hear from the borrower within 15 days, you will enforce your rights under the promissory note, including possibly filing a lawsuit to collect the debt.

> **CAUTION**
>
> **Be careful not to make any threats that you don't intend to follow up.** Although the federal and state fair debt law probably don't apply to you, it's still a good idea to be fair, yet firm, in trying to persuade the borrower to pay you back.

Signing Instructions

Sign the Overdue Payment Demand and send it to all borrowers and all cosigners by certified mail (return receipt requested). Keep a copy for your records. You may later need this if you end up suing the borrower to collect the money owed.

> **CROSS-REFERENCE**
>
> If you are writing a demand letter to request the return of a security deposit, use Form 32 in Chapter 4.

Form 48: Demand to Make Good on Bad Check

This form is similar to Form 47 in that it's used when someone who owes you money is not meeting the obligation to pay you and has ignored all your efforts to resolve the problem informally. The difference is that this form is used when the person who owes you money writes you a bad check, a slightly more complicated legal situation. Use Form 48 to make a formal written demand for payment on a bad check.

Although writing a bad check is a crime in every state, prosecutions for writing bad checks are rare. Even in the unlikely event that a district attorney is willing to bring charges, there's a good chance the person would avoid a trial by agreeing to attend a diversion program for bad-check writers and making restitution—that is, paying up.

In most states, you'll want to deal with a bad check through civil, not criminal, remedies. The person who receives a bad check can usually sue for extra damages (above and beyond the amount of the check) if not paid within 30 days of making a formal written demand for payment.

A clause is included in the Demand to Make Good on Bad Check stating that if you sue over the bad check, you may ask for the maximum monetary damages allowed under state law. This is often two or three times the amount of the check. You can find the maximum damages permitted by your state online at the Bilateral Credit Corporation website, www.bilateral.com.

Signing Instructions

Sign the Demand to Make Good on Bad Check form and deliver it personally to the person who wrote you the bad check. Have the person acknowledge receipt by signing and dating an extra copy. Alternatively, send the form by certified mail (return receipt requested) or use a delivery service that will give you a receipt establishing delivery. Some states (California, for example) require that the demand be sent by certified mail (return receipt requested) in order for the lender to recover statutory damages. Keep copies of the demand and the return receipt. You may later need this if you end up filing a lawsuit to collect payment.

Buying a House

Form 49: Ideal House Profile... 70

Form 50: House Priorities Worksheet... 71

Form 51: House Comparison Worksheet.. 72

Form 52: Family Financial Statement... 72

Form 53: Monthly Carrying Costs Worksheet... 75

Form 54: Mortgage Rates and Terms Worksheet.. 77

Form 55: Moving Checklist... 80

No doubt about it—a house is one of the most important investments you'll ever make. Careful planning and organization are key to getting the best house for your money. The forms in this chapter help you:

- identify house features most important to you and keep a record of relevant information about each house you see (Forms 49 to 51)

- determine how much you are able to spend on the down payment and monthly mortgage payments (Forms 52 and 53), and

- keep track of information you collect on different loans and compare features such as interest rates and loan costs (Form 54).

This chapter also includes a handy checklist (Form 55) to help plan your move.

Real Estate on the Web

You can find a wide range of house-buying resources in the "Buy/Sell Houses" area of the "Property and Money" section of Nolo's website (www.nolo.com), which has information on:

- comparing interest rates and applying for a mortgage

- mortgage calculators

- screening houses that meet your needs

- gathering information on neighborhood schools, crime, and more

- checking sales prices of comparable properties to make a realistic offer

- arranging house inspections, and

- finding a real estate agent, home inspector, or other professional.

RESOURCE

For an excellent resource on all aspects of home buying, check out *Nolo's Essential Guide to Buying Your First Home*, by Ilona Bray, Alayna Schroeder, and Marcia Stewart. It covers the entire process, from deciding whether you're ready to buy to settling in to your new home.

Form 49: Ideal House Profile

When you're looking for a house, it's easy to become overwhelmed by the huge array of choices, from size to style to floor plan. Then there's the issue of location—houses come in all sorts of neighborhoods, school districts, and potential hazard zones (fire, earthquake, and flood, to name a few). And, of course, price and purchase terms are crucial considerations for most homebuyers. To cope with all these and at least a dozen other relevant variables, it's essential to establish your priorities in advance and stick to them.

The Ideal House Profile lists all major house features such as upper price limit, number and type of rooms, and location. Use it to identify the essential characteristics you're looking for in a house.

Price is an obvious consideration for most people, so fill in the top section first. For example, under "Upper price limit," you might note $600,000, with a maximum down payment of $60,000. And if you have two kids, you might note that three bedrooms and excellent public schools are also "must haves."

In most cases, it will be obvious where to note your priorities. For example, if extreme quiet is important (you don't want to be near a freeway off-ramp) or you want walking access to a park, list these under "Desired neighborhood features." If you're not sure where to list a particular must have, such as a hot and dry climate, ocean view, or garage parking, put it in the "Other desired features" category on the Ideal House Profile.

Once you've compiled your list of "must haves," jot down features that you'd like but that aren't crucial to your decision of whether to buy. For example, under *Type of yard and grounds*, you might note "patio and flat backyard" in the *Hope to Have* column. Or under *Number and type of rooms*, you might list "a finished basement" or "master bedroom with bath."

Be sure to list your *Absolute no ways* (you will not buy a house that has any of these features) at the bottom of the form. Avoiding things you'll always hate, such as a house in a flood zone or in a poor school district, or one that's too far from where you work, can be even more important than finding a house that contains all your mandatory priorities.

If you're buying with another person, prepare your list of priorities together, so that each person's strong likes and dislikes are respected.

 TIP

Can any of your priority items be added after you move in? A new kitchen, deck, patio, and sometimes even an extra room, can be added a few years down the road. Of course, replacing a small dark yard with a large sunny one can't be done.

Signing Instructions

You don't need to sign the Ideal House Profile. Simply fill it out and use it to help narrow your house search.

TIP

Getting more neighborhood information. If you're moving to a new area, you may not have a good sense of what particular cities and neighborhoods are like. Before finalizing a decision to buy, you'll want to get more information. For example, if under your *Must Have* column you've written "excellent public schools," you need in-depth information about the school system in each community you are

considering. It's fine to ask a real estate agent. Also, take the time to talk to people in the area whose kids currently attend its schools, or ask for help from a reference librarian at an area public library. And don't forget to check the wealth of community and neighborhood information available online. (See "Real Estate on the Web," above.)

Form 50: House Priorities Worksheet

Now it's time to use the information collected in Form 49 to create a House Priorities Worksheet, which will help you see how each house you visit stacks up with your priorities.

First, copy your "must haves," "hope to haves," and "absolute no ways" onto a master copy of Form 50. Then, make several copies of this worksheet, to allow for mistakes or the eventual scaling back of your priority list if it turns out you can't afford all the features you would like.

Once you have completed your House Priorities Worksheet to your satisfaction, make several copies. Take one with you each time you visit a house. For each house you see, fill in the top of the worksheet. Enter the address, asking price, name and phone number of the contact person (listing agent, or seller if it's for sale by owner), and the date you saw the house.

As you walk around each house and talk to the owner or agent, enter a checkmark if the house has a desirable or undesirable feature. Also make notes next to a particular feature if it can be changed to meet your needs (an okay kitchen could be modernized for $25,000). Add comments at the bottom, such as "potential undeveloped lot next door" or "neighbors seem very friendly." If you look at a lot of houses, these notes will ensure you don't forget important information.

You should seriously consider only those houses with all or most of your "must haves" and none of your "no ways."

Signing Instructions

You don't need to sign the House Priorities Worksheet. Simply fill it out and use it to help narrow your house search.

> **TIP**
>
> **Set up a good filing system.** As the list of houses you look at grows, keep track of the information you collect. Failing to adopt a good system may lead to revisiting houses you've already seen and rejected or making decisions based on half-remembered facts. For each house that seems promising, make a file that includes a completed House Priorities Worksheet, the information sheets provided at the open house, the Multiple Listing Service information, ads, and your notes. You can also use your computer to set up a simple database with key details on each house you see.

Form 51: House Comparison Worksheet

If, like many people, you look at a considerable number of houses over an extended period of time, you may soon have trouble distinguishing or comparing their features. That's where Form 51, the House Comparison Worksheet, comes in.

Across the top of the form, list the addresses of the three or four houses you like best. In the left column, fill in your list of priorities and "absolute no ways" from your Ideal House Profile and House Priorities Worksheet. Then put a check mark on the line under each house that has that feature, to allow for a quick comparison.

Signing Instructions

You don't need to sign the House Comparison Worksheet. Simply fill it out and use it to help focus your house search.

Form 52: Family Financial Statement

When planning to buy a house, one of your most important tasks is to determine how much you can afford to pay. Begin by preparing a thorough family financial statement that includes:

- your monthly income
- your monthly expenses, and
- your net worth (your assets minus your debts or liabilities).

We use the word "family" as shorthand for the economic unit that will buy a house. For these purposes, an unmarried couple or a single person is just as much a family as is a married couple with three kids.

Preparing a family financial statement begins the process of learning how much house you can afford—in terms of both the down payment and monthly mortgage payments. And if you haven't been preapproved for a mortgage loan when you make a purchase offer, a financial statement can be extremely helpful to convince the seller that you're a serious bidder. This may be crucial, especially if there's more than one prospective buyer. The person who can best convince the seller of the financial ability to swing the deal with no glitches often prevails, even without the highest offer.

CAUTION

This statement is for you, not your lender. No matter how much debt a lender ultimately says you can handle, the purpose of this statement is to help you develop your own realistic picture of what this debt will mean for your monthly cash flow. The information you collect will help you fill out your loan application, but you won't give this statement directly to the lender. That means that now is not the time to exaggerate your income or underestimate your expenses—you'll only be fooling yourself.

Directions for Completing the Family Financial Statement

Top. Indicate the name(s), address(es), email address(es), home phone number(s), employer's name(s) and address(es) and work phone number(s) for yourself and any coborrower. A coborrower includes anyone with whom you are purchasing the house.

Worksheet 1: Income and Expenses

This worksheet shows you how much disposable income you have each month, a key fact in determining how much you can afford to spend on a house. In the first two columns, you and any coborrower each list your monthly income and expenses. Total them in the third column.

IA. Monthly gross income. List your monthly gross income from all sources. Gross income means total income before amounts such as taxes, Social Security, or retirement contributions are withheld.

  1. Employment. This is your base salary or wages plus any bonuses, tips, commissions, or overtime you regularly receive. If your income is irregular, take the average of the past 24 months. If you have more than one job, include your combined total.

  2. Public benefits. Include income from Social Security, disability, Temporary Assistance for Needy Families (TANF), Supplemental Security Income (SSI), and other public programs.

  3. Dividends. Include all dividends from stocks, bonds, and similar investments.

  4. Royalties. If you have continuing income from the sale (licensing) of books, music, software, inventions, or the like, list it here.

  5. Interest and other investment income. Include interest received on savings or money market accounts, or as payments on rental property. If the source of the income has costs associated with it (such as the costs of owning rental property), include the net monthly profit received.

  6. Other. Include payments from pensions, child or spousal support, or separate private maintenance income. Specify the source.

IB. Total monthly gross income. Total items 1–6. (This is the figure that lenders use to qualify you for mortgages.)

IIA. Monthly nonhousing expenses. List what you spend each month on items such as child care and clothing. These won't interest the lender as much as they are important to you in evaluating how much house you can afford. Here are some notes clarifying specific items. Also, see Form 67, Daily Expenses, for advice on computing average monthly expenses.

  3. Food. Include eating at restaurants, as well as at home.

  4. Insurance. List the monthly cost of your auto, life, and medical and dental insurance. If you pay any of these costs yearly, divide the annual amount by 12 and include here.

5. **Other medical.** List uninsured medical expenses.

6. **Personal.** Include costs for both personal care (haircuts, shoe repairs, and toiletries) and personal fun (attending movies, buying CDs and lottery tickets, subscribing to newspapers). Also, include any regular personal loan payments.

7. **Education.** Include monthly payments for education loans here, plus educational payments, such as your child's private school tuition.

9. **Transportation.** Include costs for both motor vehicles (include monthly car loan payments, but exclude insurance) and public transit. Include monthly upkeep for a vehicle and a reasonable amount for repairs.

10. **Other.** Specify such expenses as regular monthly credit card payments, charitable or religious donations, savings deposits, and child or spousal support payments.

IIB. Current housing expenses. If you currently own a home, list the monthly mortgage payments, taxes, insurance, and utilities (including gas, electricity, water, sewage, garbage, telephone, and cable service). If you rent, include your monthly rent and renter's insurance (if any).

IIC. Total monthly expenses. Here, total your nonhousing and housing expenses. Then subtract line C from line B to see how much disposable income you have available to put toward a monthly mortgage payment. Of course, you can also add in whatever amount you currently spend on your mortgage payment or rent.

Worksheet 2: Assets and Liabilities

I. **Assets.** In the first two columns, you and any coborrower write down the cash or market value of the assets listed. Total them up in the third column.

A. **Cash and cash equivalents.** List your cash and items easily converted into cash. Deposits include checking accounts, savings accounts, money market accounts, and certificates of deposit (even if there is a withdrawal penalty).

B. **Marketable securities.** Here you list items like stocks and bonds that are regularly traded and that you can normally turn into cash fairly readily. List the cash surrender value of any life insurance policy. Include items such as a short-term loan you made to a friend under the category "Other."

C. **Total cash and marketable securities.** Add up items A and B.

D. **Nonliquid assets.** These are items not easily converted into cash.

1. **Real estate.** List the market value—the amount the property would sell for.

2. **Retirement funds.** Include public or private pensions and self-directed accounts (IRAs, Keoghs, or 401(k) plans). List the amount vested in the plan.

3. **Business.** If you own a business, list your equity in it (market value less the debts on the business). Many small businesses are difficult to sell, and therefore difficult to value, but do your best.

4. **Motor vehicles.** List the current market value of any car, truck, RV, or motorcycle, even if you're still making payments. Check used car guides for the information; you can check the Kelly Blue Book online at www.kb.com.

5. Other. Include nontangible assets such as copyrights, patents, and trademarks. Yes, it is hard to value these types of assets, but it can be done, especially if you've been receiving income and it promises to continue. Depending on your field, professional organizations that serve authors, inventors, musicians, or software writers may be able to help. In the "Other" category, also include the current value of long-term loans you've made to others, and any really valuable personal property such as expensive jewelry or electronic gear.

E. Total nonliquid assets. Total up items D1–5.

F. Total all assets. Total up items IC and IE.

IIA. Liabilities—Debts. In columns 1 and 2, you and any coborrower write the total balances remaining for your outstanding loans under their respective categories.

Under "Other," don't include monthly insurance payments or medical (noninsurance) payments, as these go on Worksheet 1, Section IIA, Monthly Expenses—Nonhousing. Do include stock pledges, lawyer's and accountant's bills, and the like.

IIB. Total liabilities. Total the monthly payments and balances remaining for items 1–7.

III. Net worth. Total of all assets minus total liabilities.

Now that you understand what assets you have available, you can estimate how much money you'll have to put toward a down payment.

Signing Instructions

You don't need to sign the Family Financial Statement. Simply fill it out and use it to help evaluate how much house you can afford.

Form 53: Monthly Carrying Costs Worksheet

Your next step is to understand how much money a lender will allow you to borrow. This will be based on your income, your debts, and the monthly expenses—called "carrying costs"—associated with buying your home. To make this calculation, complete Form 53, the Monthly Carrying Costs Worksheet. You will need to provide the following information:

Line 1: Estimated purchase price. How much money you'll need to spend on a house likely to have at least most of the "must have" features listed on your Ideal House Profile (Form 49).

Line 2: Down payment. Enter the down payment you plan to make.

Line 3: Subtract your anticipated down payment (line 2) from your estimated purchase price (line 1). The result is the amount you'll need to borrow.

Line 4: Interest rate. Estimate the mortgage interest rate you'll pay based on the rates listed in tables printed in the Sunday newspaper real estate section and online websites featuring mortgage information. (You'll know what rate you'll pay more precisely when you start shopping for a mortgage using Form 54, Mortgage Rates and Terms Worksheet.)

Line 5: Principal and mortgage interest payment factor per $1,000 over the length of the loan. You can find this using the amortization chart below.

Line 6: Monthly mortgage payment. Divide line 3 by $1,000, then multiply that amount by the factor from the amortization chart (line 5). For example, if you estimate the house you want to buy will cost $260,000, a 20% down payment of $52,000 leaves you with a $208,000 mortgage loan. Divide $208,000 by $1,000 to get $208. Your research shows you can get a 6%

Amortization Chart

Mortgage Principal & Interest Payment Factors (Per $1,000)

Interest rates (%)	15-year mortgage	30-year mortgage
5.00	7.91	5.37
5.25	8.04	5.52
5.50	8.17	5.68
5.75	8.30	5.84
6.00	8.44	6.00
6.25	8.57	6.16
6.50	8.71	6.32
6.75	8.85	6.49
7.00	8.99	6.65
7.25	9.13	6.82
7.50	9.27	6.99
7.75	9.41	7.16
8.00	9.56	7.34
8.25	9.70	7.51
8.50	9.85	7.69
8.75	9.99	7.87
9.00	10.14	8.05
9.25	10.29	8.23
9.50	10.44	8.41
9.75	10.59	8.59
10.00	10.75	8.78
10.25	10.90	8.96
10.50	11.05	9.15
10.75	11.21	9.33
11.00	11.37	9.52

interest rate for a fixed-rate loan. The monthly factor per $1,000 for a 30-year loan at a 6% rate is 6. So your monthly mortgage payments will be $208 x 6, or $1,248.

Line 7: Homeowner's insurance. You can get exact quotes in advance from insurance agents. Very roughly, expect to spend $300–$650 yearly per $100,000 of house value, depending on where you live and other factors.

Line 8: Property taxes. These vary tremendously depending on where you live. You'll need to get an estimate from a local tax assessor's office.

Line 9: Now add up your mortgage payment (line 6), insurance (line 7), and taxes (line 8). This is your monthly carrying cost (also called PITI—principal, interest, taxes, and insurance).

Line 10: Other monthly debts. These are items such as monthly payments on a car or student loan. Exclude any debts that will be paid off within ten months.

Line 11: Private mortgage insurance (PMI). Your lender may require this if you're making a down payment of less than 20% and aren't taking out a second mortgage. PMI is often about .5% of the loan.

Line 12: Homeowners' association fee. You may have to pay this monthly fee if you're looking at a condo or a house in a development.

Line 13: Add lines 9–12 for the sum of your total monthly carrying costs and long-term debts.

Line 14: Lender qualifying ratio. Other things being equal (which they rarely are), lenders normally want you to pay monthly carrying costs (mortgage payment, property taxes and homeowner's insurance) with 28%–36% of your monthly gross income. Whether you qualify at the bottom or top of this range depends on the amount of your down payment, the interest rate on the type of mortgage you want, your credit score (a numerical measure that reflects how you've managed credit in the past), and the level of your other long-term debts.

Line 15: Divide line 13 by line 14 to determine the monthly income needed to qualify.

Line 16: Multiply line 15 by 12 to calculate the yearly income to qualify.

Signing Instructions

You don't need to sign the Monthly Carrying Costs Worksheet. Simply fill it out and use it to help evaluate how much house you can afford.

Form 54: Mortgage Rates and Terms Worksheet

As with any other consumer product, you can save money by carefully shopping for a mortgage. But because of the wide variety of mortgages on the market and the fact that fine-print terms can significantly influence how much you'll really have to pay, it's essential that you carefully compare the total cost of different deals.

You can use the Mortgage Rates and Terms Worksheet to keep track of information you collect on different loans. It is helpful whether you'll be working with a loan broker (a person who specializes in matching house buyers and appropriate mortgage lenders) or shopping for a mortgage on your own.

This form is important for three primary reasons:

- Filling it out all but requires you to really understand the fine-print details of every loan you consider.

- Having this information will aid your memory days or weeks later when you can't remember what you've been offered.

- Assuming you get information about more than one loan, you can efficiently compare features.

Instructions for Completing the Mortgage Rates and Terms Worksheet

Heading

At the top of the table, enter the lender's name (such as Bank of Richmond), the name of the loan agent you met or spoke with, the agent's phone number, and the date of your meeting or telephone conversation.

Section 1: General Information

Enter the type of loan: fixed or adjustable; the rate, if it's a fixed mortgage; whether it qualifies for government financing (if that's a need you have); the minimum down payment required; whether private mortgage insurance (PMI) is required and, if so, whether you'll need to set up an impound account; the term (number of years of the loan); whether it's assumable; whether it has a prepayment penalty; and whether it has negative amortization and, if so, whether it lets you (and for how much) lock in at a certain rate. See the table below for a brief description of key mortgage terms. For more information, check the "Property and Money" section of Nolo's website at www.nolo.com.

Section 2: Debt-to-Income Ratios Information

Here you need to indicate the percentage of your income each lender allows for the monthly carrying costs to obtain the mortgage, and for monthly carrying costs plus monthly payments on other long-term debts. Then, based on these debt-to-income ratios, enter the maximum loan each lender will make.

Section 3: Loan Costs

If possible, enter the costs associated with getting the loan—the number of points and their cost, PMI, additional loan fee, credit report, application fee, appraisal fee, and other miscellaneous costs. Then total them up. Your estimate will have to be rough, because most lenders won't estimate closing costs until they start processing your loan (you may also be able to negotiate with the lender to eliminate or reduce some of these costs). Even then, the costs are still estimates. You won't know the actual total of loan costs until you review the final papers at the close of escrow.

Section 4: Time Limits

You want to know how long it will take for the lender to process your loan application and, if it's approved, come up with the money (called "funding the loan"), enabling you to close the deal. Enter this information in the fourth section. Also, pay attention to the following items:

- the date each month your payment will be due (the first of the month is standard, although some portfolio lenders set the 15th of the month or allow you to choose a date)
- how many "grace" days you have (after which the payment is considered late—15 days is standard), and
- the fee for late mortgage payments.

Section 5: Other Features

If the loan has any special features, such as discounted points if you have a savings account with the bank, indicate them.

Section 6: Fixed Rate Two-Step Loans

If you look at any fixed rate loans that step up to a higher rate after several years, indicate the initial annual percentage rate, and for how many years it stays in effect.

Section 7: Fixed Rate Balloon Payment Loans

If you are considering a fixed rate loan for a short period (often three, five, or seven years)

that ends with one large balloon payment, indicate the interest rate and monthly payment, the term of the loan and the amount of the balloon payment.

Section 8: Adjustable Rate Mortgages (ARMs)

First, enter the adjustable loan criteria—what index it's tied to and the amount of the margin.

Next, write down interest rate information—the initial rate, how long it lasts, the periodic interest rate cap, the adjustment period, and the life-of-the-loan cap (see the table below for definitions of all these terms). Be sure you understand whether the periodic cap is a true cap (limiting how much your interest rate can change at each adjustment period) or just a payment cap (limiting how much your payment can increase even if the interest rate goes up). The down side of a payment cap is that it may result in negative amortization, as explained in "Key Mortgage Terms," below.

Finally, enter the payment information—the initial payment, cap, and payment cap period. Also calculate your worst-case scenario: the highest interest rate and monthly payments possible with the adjustable rate loan offered for different time periods.

Section 9: Hybrid Loans

If you are interested in an ARM that has a fixed rate for the first few years and then becomes adjustable, enter the information here. Pay particular attention to how much the interest rate can jump at the first adjustment period.

Signing Instructions

You don't need to sign the Mortgage Rates and Terms Worksheet. Simply fill it out and use it to help compare various loan options and packages.

Key Mortgage Terms

Fixed rate mortgage. The interest rate and the amount you pay each month remain the same over the entire mortgage term, which is traditionally 15 or 30 years.

Adjustable rate mortgage (ARM). The interest rates on these mortgages fluctuate according to interest rates in the economy. Initial interest rates are typically offered for a set period (sometimes as short as one month). This discounted interest rate is lower than the going rate for fixed rate mortgages. When the initial discount period ends, the interest rate adjusts according to current market rates. The amount of the adjustment is tied to a market-sensitive number called the "index." A "margin" is the factor or percentage a lender adds to the index to arrive at the interest rate you pay over the market rate. Though your interest rate can increase based on the index plus the margin, there usually is a maximum limit, called the "life-of-the-loan cap" (usually, five or six percentage points above the initial rate). A periodic cap limits the amount your interest rate can go up or down at each adjustment period, such as going up 2% annually, with your payments increasing accordingly.

Negative amortization. Sometimes called "deferred interest" or "interest advances," negative amortization happens when you have a payment cap, which limits only the amount your monthly payment can go up (not the total you owe, which is not capped). If your interest rate increases and your monthly payment doesn't cover the interest owed that month, the extra money is simply added onto the mortgage total you owe, often with the result that you'll owe larger payments in the future or a large balloon payment at the end of the mortgage.

PMI and impound account. Lenders may require private mortgage insurance (PMI) if you're making a down payment of less than 20%. PMI insures the lender if you don't pay the mortgage. Some lenders require that you set up an impound account at the time you close the house purchase, where you deposit up to a year's payments of PMI. In addition, you make monthly payments into the impound account for property taxes and homeowner's insurance, which in turn are paid by the lender or company that services the loan. To avoid PMI, you can take out a second mortgage to cover the difference between the amount of money you have for your down payment and the 80% first mortgage.

Assumable loan. A loan that a creditworthy buyer can take over (assume) from a seller. Most fixed-rate loans are not assumable.

Prepayment penalty. A charge for paying off your mortgage early. Most high-quality commercial mortgages don't charge a prepayment penalty.

Rate lock-in. A lender's guarantee to make a loan at a particular interest rate, even if the market changes. The lock-in is usually for a specific time period, such as three to six weeks.

Debt-to-income ratio. The ratio of your monthly mortgage payments (including insurance and property taxes) plus long-term debts to your income; also called lender qualification.

Monthly carrying costs. The sum of your monthly payments for your mortgage principal and interest, homeowner's insurance, and property taxes.

Key Mortgage Terms (continued)

Points and loan costs. The fees associated with getting a mortgage, which usually add up to 2%–5% of the cost of the mortgage. Points make up the largest part of lender fees, with one point equaling 1% of the loan principal. Not all loans have points, but often, loans charging points have a slightly lower interest rate. If you will own a house for many years, paying relatively high points to get a lower fixed rate of interest is usually a good idea—the cost of points is more than paid for by the reduction in interest payments over the life of the loan. But the reverse is also true—if you will move in three to five years or fewer, try to pay as few points as possible, even if you pay a little more interest, because it takes several years for the monthly interest savings to offset the initial high cost of points.

Form 55: Moving Checklist

Congratulations! If you are looking at this form, chances are you found a good house, closed escrow, and are getting ready to move in. Use the Moving Checklist to help you plan your move.

Signing Instructions

You don't need to sign the Moving Checklist. Simply fill it out and use it to keep track of moving tasks.

Buying or Selling a Car, Dog, or Personal Property

Form 56: Motor Vehicle Bill of Sale 82

Form 57: Boat Bill of Sale 83

Form 58: Computer System Bill of Sale 84

Form 59: General Bill of Sale 84

Form 60: Bill of Sale for Dog 85

This chapter contains forms for use when you sell used personal property, such as a car, boat, appliance, furniture, or computer. It also includes a bill of sale for a dog. Use these simple agreements to record the terms of sale of all types of property (with the exception of real estate and securities, which are closely regulated by law).

A bill of sale is a written document that, at a minimum, includes:

- the names of the seller(s) and buyer(s) (there may be two sellers—for example, if the goods are co-owned as joint property by a husband and wife)

- a statement that a sale has taken place

- a description of the item(s) sold

- the amount paid, and

- the signature of the person selling the property and the date of the signing.

In addition, the bills of sale in this chapter often include:

- a promise that the seller owns or otherwise has the right to sell the item, and details of any liens or encumbrances giving someone else ownership in the goods being sold

- a written warranty or guarantee that the item is in good condition and will be repaired or replaced if it fails within a certain period

- disclosures of any major defects known to the seller, and

- a statement that the item has been inspected by an expert and that the expert's report is attached, if appropriate.

TIP

Use a well-drafted bill of sale to head off future legal trouble. When used cars, boats, and other items of property are sold without a written bill of sale, the chances of future legal problems—maybe even a court battle—go way up. Far better to define in advance all key terms of the sale, including the condition of the goods being sold and whether the sale includes any seller's warranty (for example, 30 days on parts and labor) or is made "as is."

In some states, a bill of sale must have a notary clause. Although this isn't common, we've included a Certificate of Acknowledgment of Notary Public on each bill of sale form in this chapter. If your state doesn't require notarization, you don't need to use it—but it can never hurt. See the Introduction to this book for more about notarization.

Form 56: Motor Vehicle Bill of Sale

Use this bill of sale when you buy or sell a vehicle that must be registered with your state's motor vehicles department. This typically includes cars, trucks, motorcycles, recreational vehicles, and motor homes. It does not include stationary nonregistered mobile homes that are designed to be used semipermanently at a fixed location, such as a mobile home park. Such homes are commonly treated as real property—just as if they were houses—and are covered by special transfer, financing, and recording rules not discussed here. This category of motor vehicle also doesn't include off-road farm machinery— for that, use Form 59 (General Bill of Sale)— unless it can be registered in your state as a motor vehicle.

Describe the vehicle in detail on the bill of sale, including the vehicle identification number, or VIN (this is typically found on the driver's side of the dashboard, close to the windshield), and indicate the price paid. (Your state motor vehicles department needs the price to compute the sales tax.) List any personal property included in the sale, such as a bicycle rack.

CAUTION

Double check ownership interest in the vehicle. If you are buying a motor vehicle and you don't know the seller, check with the motor vehicles department where the vehicle is registered to be sure that the seller is the owner, and that no one else claims an ownership interest (lien) in the vehicle. (If the seller hadn't yet repaid a purchase loan, for example, the lender migiht have an ownership claim). You can get additional useful information about the vehicle's ownership history from services such as Carfax Vehicle Reports (www.carfax.com) or Autocheck (www.autocheck.com) if you have the VIN. For example, you can learn whether the car was ever severely damaged and "salvaged" or whether the odometer has been rolled back.

Clauses 4 and 5 disclose any mechanical problems with the vehicle. These provisions will help the seller avoid future legal problems. If the vehicle is inspected by a mechanic who prepares a written report that is given to the buyer, and the seller conscientiously lists all known defects, it's highly unlikely that an unsatisfied buyer can later get a judge to agree that the seller was guilty of misrepresentation.

The seller can add a short warranty covering parts, labor, or both to Clause 8 if desired.

Be sure to contact your state motor vehicles department for any special requirements when selling a motor vehicle. For example, the vehicle may have to qualify for a smog certificate. If these exist, include them in Clause 8.

If the seller hasn't fully repaid a loan on the vehicle, the seller should ask the lender if its permission is required in order to sell the vehicle. If the vehicle is leased, the seller should ask the lessor what it requires before the vehicle can be transferred or sold.

Signing Instructions

The buyer(s) and seller(s) must sign the Motor Vehicle Bill of Sale for it to be valid. Print out two copies of the form (or enough for everyone who signs the form to have a separate copy). Each person should sign and date all copies of the form and keep a signed document with all original signatures.

Be sure to check with your state motor vehicles department regarding any official signing requirements that must be met. For example, the seller's signature on the vehicle's title probably must be notarized. And in some states, the bill of sale itself needs to be notarized. (If so, see the instructions about notarization in the Introduction to this book.) In addition, the seller may need to file an official form to avoid liability if the buyer hits someone with the vehicle after the sale, and the buyer may have to file an official form to register the vehicle in his or her name.

Form 57: Boat Bill of Sale

This form is similar in content to the Motor Vehicle Bill of Sale (Form 56), but it covers boats of all kinds. The form contains details about the boat, as well as any engines, electronics, and other equipment that are to be sold along with it.

Carefully read the discussion that accompanies Form 56, Motor Vehicle Bill of Sale, especially the advice about arranging for an inspection by a third party and having the seller list (disclose) all defects. These provisions make it difficult for a lawyer to claim later that the condition of the boat was misrepresented.

This bill of sale includes a number of entries unique to boat sales. Fill in the details key to your sale, such as a thorough list of all personal property items included in the sale or the maintenance history of the boat.

If the seller hasn't fully repaid a purchase loan on the boat, the seller should ask the lender whether its permission is required in order to sell the boat.

Signing Instructions

The buyer(s) and seller(s) must sign the Boat Bill of Sale for it to be valid. Print out two copies of the form (or enough for each person signing the form to have a separate copy). Each person should sign and date all copies of the form and keep a signed document with all original signatures.

Be sure to check with your state motor vehicles department (or the department in your state that registers boats) regarding any official signing requirements that must be met. For example, the seller's signature on the boat's title probably must be notarized. In addition, the seller may need to file an official form to avoid liability if the buyer hits someone with the boat after the sale, and the buyer may have to file an official form to register the boat in his or her name.

Form 58: Computer System Bill of Sale

This bill of sale should be used for computers, computer peripherals, and software, especially if a whole system is being sold. If only one or two components are being sold, use Form 59, General Bill of Sale. Before using this form, review the material that precedes the Motor Vehicle Bill of Sale (Form 56). It discusses a number of the key clauses in this agreement.

Signing Instructions

The buyer(s) and seller(s) must sign the Computer System Bill of Sale for it to be valid. Print out two copies of the form (or enough for each person signing the form to have a separate copy). Each person should sign and date all copies of the form and keep a signed document with all original signatures.

Form 59: General Bill of Sale

Form 59, General Bill of Sale, should be used for the sale of personal property such as jewelry, artwork, sports equipment, rare books, furniture, collections, appliances, tools, photographic equipment, and electronic items. Do not use this form if you are selling a car or other motor vehicle, boat, or computer system (these categories are specifically covered above). Before using this form, read the brief discussion that precedes the Motor Vehicle Bill of Sale (Form 56), which discusses key clauses in a bill of sale.

Signing Instructions

The buyer(s) and seller(s) must sign the General Bill of Sale for it to be valid. Print out two copies of the form (or enough for each person signing the form to have a separate copy). Each person should sign and date all copies of the form and keep a signed document with all original signatures.

Form 60: Bill of Sale for Dog

Use this bill of sale when you buy or sell a dog in a transaction with a private party or a breeder. It spells out exactly what terms the seller is promising, including price, how and when the dog will be turned over to the buyer, and who will pay shipping costs (if any). Form 60 provides basic information on the dog, including birth date, medication information such as vaccination history, health, name of breeder, special training (if any), and registration with the American Kennel Club or other entity. Most of the form is self-explanatory. You can add any items of special concern—for example, if the seller wants the buyer to have the dog spayed or neutered.

Clause 6 gives the buyer two options if a veterinarian certifies, in writing, that the dog has a disease or a congenital defect that was present when the buyer bought the dog. Within 14 days, the buyer may either return the dog to the seller and be reimbursed for the purchase price and for reasonable veterinary bills already paid, or keep the dog and also receive reimbursement for reasonable veterinary bills, up to the amount of the purchase price.

If you're buying a dog from a pet store: You may have other legal rights in addition to those set out in this bill of sale. Because consumers have had so many problems with dogs bought in pet stores, many states impose special requirements on pet retailers that don't apply to breeders who raise and sell dogs themselves. You may be entitled to a disclosure sheet, stating where the animal came from (it may have been shipped across the country at a young age), and its health and vaccination history. You may also have a right to return or exchange an unhealthy dog, or get reimbursement for veterinary bills, that is different from the right this bill of sale gives you. You can check your state's law on Nolo's website at www.nolo.com/legal-research; select "State Laws," then the name of your state to search for applicable laws.

Signing Instructions

The buyer(s) and seller(s) must sign this Bill of Sale for Dog for it to be valid. Print out two copies of the form (or enough for each person signing the form to have a separate copy). Each person should sign and date all copies of the form and keep a signed document with all original signatures.

Renting Personal Property and Storing Goods

Form 61: Personal Property Rental Agreement 88

Form 62: Notice of Termination of Personal Property Rental Agreement 89

Form 63: Storage Contract 89

People frequently rent tools, equipment, and other personal property. While equipment is often rented from commercial companies that have their own forms, it is also not uncommon to rent items from a neighbor or friend as an informal way of helping your friend or neighbor with the purchase cost.

Many rented items are used to perform a particular task, as would be the case if you rented a rototiller and weight drum to lay sod, or a power saw and sander to do a small remodeling job around your home. In other situations, you might rent property for a recreational purpose—for example, if you're assigned to bring a volleyball net and badminton set to the family reunion.

This chapter includes a form for renting personal property. You can tailor the form based on the type of property you're renting, its value, and how long you need to rent it for. The chapter also includes a notice to end this type of rental agreement.

In addition to borrowing or renting tools, equipment, and other items, people often turn to friends or neighbors to store their personal property, such as furniture, for an extended period of time. This chapter includes a storage contract for use in these situations.

Whether or not a rental or storage fee is paid, it makes sense to write down your understanding of key issues, such as the length of the rental or storage period and who will be responsible if the rented or stored property is damaged. Having a written agreement is especially important if valuable property is to be rented or stored for an extended period. If any problem comes up, having a simple written contract will help you arrive at a fair settlement and preserve relations between the parties.

Form 61: Personal Property Rental Agreement

You can use Form 61 for a short-term rental (30 days or fewer) of personal (non-real estate) property. It is primarily geared toward renting relatively inexpensive personal property from a neighbor or friend. It is not intended to be used for rental of a motor vehicle, motorcycle, ATV, boat, personal watercraft, or the like. Because not much is at stake, this rental agreement doesn't deal with the many potentially complex issues that can arise when expensive property is rented for an extended period. But this personal property rental agreement covers all the basics, including the names of the parties (owner and renter), a description of the property and its condition, the amount of rent (if any), length of the rental period, and delivery arrangements. It includes a dispute resolution clause that provides for negotiation, mediation, and/or arbitration as a means for the parties to resolve any disputes that may arise over the agreement. (See the Introduction for more on dispute resolution procedures.)

Signing Instructions

The owner and the renter must both sign this Personal Property Rental Agreement for it to be valid. Print out two copies of the form (or enough for each person who will be signing the form to have a separate copy). Each person should sign and date all copies of the form and keep a signed document with all original signatures.

Form 62: Notice of Termination of Personal Property Rental Agreement

This form can be used by either the owner or the renter to end any personal property rental agreement that is not made for a specific period. You do not need to give a reason (unless this is required by your rental agreement—not the case with Form 61).

> ! **CAUTION**
> **Do not use this termination notice if you have rented personal property for a specific rental period.** In that case, you cannot terminate the agreement unless both parties agree.

Signing Instructions

Simply sign the Notice of Termination of Personal Property Rental Agreement and give it to the other party. Keep a copy for your records, and note on your copy the date and time you delivered the notice.

Form 63: Storage Contract

It is common to store property with friends and relatives—everything from bikes, beds, and books to washing machines, weights, and walking sticks. Sometimes this amounts to nothing more than leaving a few small objects for a short time. On other occasions, however, it means storing a household- or garage-full of goods for a year or more. In many situations involving friends and family, money isn't charged for storage, although payment certainly can be appropriate when bulky or valuable objects are stored for a considerable period of time. This is especially true when the goods are stored in a place (for example, a garage or spare room) that might otherwise be rented or used.

Form 63 covers the basics of storing personal property, including the names of the parties (we call them "property owner" and "property custodian"); a description of the property being stored and its condition and value; storage location, term, and payment; who's responsible for theft of or damage to property during the rental period; and how the custodian will deal with abandoned property never reclaimed by the owner. This storage contract includes a dispute resolution clause that provides for negotiation, mediation, and/or arbitration as a means for the parties to resolve any disputes that may arise over the agreement. (See the Introduction for more on dispute resolution procedures.)

It is especially important that you carefully identify property and its value and condition. One common dispute involves the property owner who claims that a valuable item is missing, while the custodian says it was never present in the first place. The best way to prevent this is to make a thorough list of the items to be stored. In this age of digital cameras and camera-equipped phones, it's a good idea to take pictures and attach them to the contract. In Clause 1, you should identify each item as thoroughly as possible, including (as appropriate) the make, model, year, color, and condition. Also, when you specify the value of the property (Clause 8), be sure to specify whether you mean the replacement value or the fair market value of the property, such as a TV set. (You'll be asked to make a choice.) Replacement value is how much it would cost for you to buy another of this item, such as the cost of a new TV set. Fair market value is how much you would get for an item, such as a TV set, if you sold it—for example, online or at a garage sale. Whichever you choose, specify the value of each item you store, to reduce the chance of a misunderstanding if any items are damaged or missing. Use Clause 9 to spell out any defects or damage in the property being stored (such as a stain on a sofa).

Clause 13 commits the property custodian to use reasonable care while storing the property, but the custodian will not be responsible for damage due to inherent flaws or the property's inherent defective condition. The optional part of the clause specifies that the property will be insured by the owner, and that the custodian will also cover the property subject to the limits and limitations of the owner's own homeowner's or other insurance policy. Homeowners' policies will generally cover damage or loss to another's property up to a certain amount, and typically will not cover automobiles.

Use Clause 14 to describe any special terms of the storage—for example, if you want the custodian to start the car at least once a week while it's in storage.

Signing Instructions

Both parties must sign this Storage Contract for it to be valid. Print out two copies of the form (or enough for each person who will be signing the form to have a separate copy). Each person should sign and date all copies of the form and keep a signed document with all original signatures.

Home Repairs and Maintenance

Form 64: Home Maintenance Agreement 93

Form 65: Home Repairs Agreement 94

Form 66: Contractor Mid-Job Worksheet 94

This chapter contains three agreements that cover home maintenance and repairs, as well as other work you plan to have done at your residence, such as painting or yard work. To get the job done right, your most important task is to find a contractor who has done excellent work for a number of other people in your community. (Our forms use the term "contractor" for someone who does home repairs or maintenance.) But even with a highly recommended person, serious misunderstandings between a homeowner and contractor can easily arise if the key job specifications, payment details, and work schedule haven't been carefully worked out and written down before the work begins. That's the purpose of these forms. These written agreements will help you get the work done right, on time, and within your budget.

CAUTION

The first two forms in this chapter are not suitable for complicated jobs where the contractor will have to replace or install significant materials. You'll need a more detailed contract than the ones provided here if you're planning on remodeling a kitchen, adding a room, putting on a new roof, painting the complete exterior or interior, or doing any other similarly large project. A large firm doing major home repairs and remodeling will usually present you with its own contract. The forms in this chapter can help you analyze an agreement proposed by a contractor and make sure the basics are covered.

State Licensing and Registration Requirements for Home Repair Work

Almost all states have licensing requirements for certain categories of highly skilled home improvement and construction work. For example, most states license people who do residential electrical and plumbing work or who build new structures. By contrast, there is less uniformity among the states as to whether licensing is required for contractors who do general repair and remodeling work, such as framing, drywall installation, paneling, deck construction, siding, and painting.

License and registration requirements are often tied to the following factors:

- **Size of the project**—a license may be required for work on any job over a specified amount, such as $5,000.

- **Type of job**—some states require a license for plumbing or electrical work but not for painting, for example.

- **Location of contractor**—most states regulate contracting work of any type that is done by out-of-state contractors.

Most states that require a license for general repair and remodeling tasks require some experience and skills training, as well as some evidence of financial responsibility or effective customer recourse policy. For details, call your state's Consumer Protection Office or visit its site on the Web to find out whether your state regulates the type of contractor you are hiring, and if so, the name and phone number of the agency that does the regulating, such as the State Contractors' Licensing Board. Then contact the agency directly for information. Many state agencies publish and distribute free consumer information on home repair work and may even have license information online. To find your state agency, check out the Federal Citizen Information Center's Consumer Action website at www.consumeraction.gov.

CAUTION

Beware of unlicensed contractors. Even where licenses are required, you can always find someone unlicensed who will do the work, usually promising a cheap price. Be wary about accepting these offers when the work requires a license—unlicensed contractors are not bonded, meaning that their work isn't insured. And, of course, an unlicensed contractor is almost sure to work without getting a building permit, which may cause problems later.

Some states require people who do home repair and remodeling work to register with the state. Registration usually does not require demonstrated experience or training. It is primarily designed to keep track of people offering contractor services so that homeowners can locate them if something goes wrong during or after the job.

Local Permits and Approvals for Home Repair Work

In addition to state licensing and registration rules, homeowners often must obtain a permit from a city or county agency for jobs that involve structural alterations, additions, substantial remodeling, or new electrical wiring or plumbing installations. Permits are usually not required for casual carpentry, minor plumbing and electrical repairs, or replacing a window or door.

In addition to a local permit, if the house is part of a condominium complex or planned unit development, a homeowner's association or "architectural review committee" will likely insist on formal approval of the work, especially if the work affects the home's exterior appearance. Homeowner association approval is usually necessary for new windows, exterior painting, roofing, and room additions.

Either the homeowner or the contractor must be responsible for getting information about the necessary permits. If the job requires a permit or approval but no one obtains it, the homeowner may have to redo some or all of the work if a later inspection reveals deficiencies. Also, the value of the home may be adversely affected when it comes to resale if the buyer learns of the nonpermit work.

Independent Contractor Versus Employee

Our contracts (Clause 4) assume that the person who will come to your house is an independent contractor, not your employee. As long as the contractor is doing one job or occasional work, this is legal. If a person will work for you regularly (an everyday gardener, for example), the law probably requires that you treat the individual as an employee, for whom you are legally required to pay income taxes, Social Security, and other benefits.

RESOURCE

For more information on the difference between an independent contractor and an employee, see IRS Form SS-8, available on the IRS website at www.irs.gov, or by phone at 800-424-FORM.

Dispute Resolution Clause

The two forms in this chapter do not include a dispute resolution clause mandating mediation and arbitration to resolve disputes before going to court. If you would like to include a dispute resolution clause in either of these forms, see the Introduction to this book, where this is explained.

Form 64: Home Maintenance Agreement

Form 64 is intended for unskilled labor on a one-time job that isn't expected to last for more than a day or two and doesn't need a significant amount of materials. Typical jobs that fall into this category are hauling refuse, cleaning a garage or house, washing windows, and gardening and other yard work. Such jobs are usually performed by one person who supplies the required tools.

This form is easy to complete. Simply spell out the details of the work and the amount, form, and schedule of payment.

Signing Instructions

You (the homeowner) and the contractor must sign this Home Maintenance Agreement for it to be valid. Print out two copies of the form and have each party sign and date both copies of the form. Give the contractor one of the signed documents and keep the other for your own records.

Form 65: Home Repairs Agreement

Form 65 covers home repairs done by skilled labor for a job that isn't expected to take more than a few days, such as installing new locks or windows, nonstructural carpentry repairs, touch-up painting, masonry work, or roofing repairs. Use it to spell out the who (names of the homeowner and contractor), what and how (specific details of the job, such as painting the kitchen or installing new bathroom floor), how much (dollar amount and details of payment), and when (beginning and ending dates) of the work.

TIP

Don't pay too much up front—just enough to let the contractor purchase the materials needed to get started. It is usually best to agree to make periodic payments that are tied to measurable, easy-to-define goals. Clause 2 is the place to spell out the details of your payment arrangement. For example, you may decide to pay one lump sum at the end of the work, or pay in increments (such as half at the beginning of work and half at the end), or pay an hourly rate for work done.

Simple home repairs probably won't require a contractor's license or permit, but if they do, Clauses 4 and 5 of the Home Repairs Agreement allow you to spell out the details regarding licenses and permits. If you don't need them, follow the instructions in the introduction for deleting unnecessary contract clauses. Clause 6 specifies that the contractor must carry insurance and accept responsibility for injuries that occur during the course of the work.

Signing Instructions

You (the homeowner) and the contractor must sign this Home Repairs Agreement for it to be valid. Print out two copies of the form and have each party sign and date both copies of the form. Give the contractor one of the signed documents and keep the other for your own records.

Form 66: Contractor Mid-Job Worksheet

If you've hired a contractor to perform home or business repair or maintenance, you probably have a good idea of what work will be done and what it's going to cost. For extensive jobs, you may have a full-blown contract, which you've accepted by signing it; or, you may have a written bid that you've orally agreed to. Or, you may have only an oral bid and acceptance— basically, you and the contractor had a conversation and came to an understanding of the work and the cost. All of these methods for recording the scope of the work and the cost are legal and enforceable—although, of course, a written understanding is always preferable.

Having a clear understanding of the extent and cost of the work does not mean, however, that events will always turn out as planned. In fact, anyone who has done even modest remodeling will tell you that you will always have surprises as work progresses. For all but the simplest of jobs, you're likely to have lots of questions, which will pop up as you arrive home at night to survey the day's work or, more likely, as you lie in bed at night. You'll be wondering, "Will it look like this when it's done?" "Is this the final color?" "Can I change the placement of that fixture?" "Should we do this while we're at it?" and so on. Most importantly, if the scope of the work changes or the time needed to do it increases, you'll want to know how, if at all, these changes will affect the cost of the job.

It's important that you and your contractor have continuing, clear communication about the progress of your repair or remodeling job. You also should not let important questions go unanswered during the brief exchange you typically have with your contractor each morning. The best way to make sure that all of your questions are addressed is to write them down as they occur to you and go over the list with your contractor on a daily basis. Even the busiest contractor will pause as you approach with clipboard in hand, and will take a few minutes to go over your questions.

Our Contractor Mid-Job Worksheet, which you'll date as of the day of your discussion, provides a place for you to list your issues and gives you room to record the answer and, possibly, the plan. You'll be able to note whether the intended resolution will vary the bid and, if so, by how much. (To be extra careful, after deciding whether the bid will be affected, you can ask your contractor to initial or sign the form.) You'll also be able to record whether the work or variation was actually done and whether it's satisfactory.

This worksheet is valuable primarily as a way to preserve and present your questions, but it has other uses, as well. If there is uncertainty later about what you agreed to—and whether it would cost additional money—you'll have a record of the discussion and the plan. If worse come to worst and you and the contractor get into a legal squabble, your notes will be valuable evidence as well.

Use our Contractor Mid-Job Worksheet on a daily basis if your project is multifaceted and moving quickly; or use it weekly if progress is slow. Be sure to keep all worksheets in a safe place (in a folder or binder, along with the original contract), and keep all documents for at least ten years (the typical time period in which you can sue for most construction defects).

Signing Instructions

For each issue you discuss with your contractor, fill in a row on the Contractor Mid-Job Worksheet to keep track of decisions the two of you reach. Once you reach agreement on a given issue, have your contractor initial the last column, and place your initials next to the contractor's. ●

Handling Personal Finances

Form 67: Daily Expenses...98

Form 68: Monthly Income...99

Form 69: Monthly Budget...99

Form 70: Statement of Assets and Liabilities...100

Form 71: Assignment of Rights..100

Form 72: Notice to Terminate Joint Account...101

Form 73: Notice to Stop Payment of Check..102

Form 74: Request for Credit Report...103

Form 75: Dispute Incorrect Credit Report Entry...104

Form 76: Dispute Credit Card Charge..105

Form 77: Demand Collection Agency Cease Contact.....................................106

You may not think too much about monthly budgets, credit reports, or stopping payment on a check unless you are having financial problems. But by being proactive—reviewing your finances in advance and knowing your legal rights—you can often avoid legal and money problems. The forms in this chapter are designed for you to get a handle on your personal finances—budgeting, dealing with debts and debt collectors, and reviewing your credit report—whether you're trying to avoid problems or are in the midst of a crisis.

RESOURCE

Detailed information and forms on dealing with debts, planning a budget, rebuilding your credit, and other similar topics can be found in *Solve Your Money Troubles: Get Debt Collectors Off Your Back & Regain Financial Freedom* and *Credit Repair*, both by Robin Leonard and John Lamb (Nolo).

Form 67: Daily Expenses

Creating a budget—comparing your average monthly expenses to your total monthly income—is the most effective way to start putting your financial house in order. Although it's not hard to do, budgeting is a three-step process. Step one is to get a clear picture of how you spend your money. You can do that using Form 67 (Daily Expenses), on which you record everything you spend over the course of a week. Step two is to total up your monthly income using Form 68. The final step is comparing the two and figuring out where you might need to make some changes. For that you can use Form 69.

Here's how to use Daily Expenses (Form 67):

1. Make ten copies of the Daily Expenses form (if you're using the tear-out form) or print a new copy each week. You will use nine copies of the form to record your expenses for about two months. By using your expense figures for two months, you'll avoid creating a budget based on a week or a month of unusually high or low expenses. If you and another adult (such as a spouse or partner) share finances, make nine copies for each of you. You will use the tenth copy to record other expenses.

2. Begin recording your expenses on the first of a month; record that date in the blank at the top of one copy of the form.

3. Record every expense you pay by cash or cash equivalent—check, ATM or debit card, or automatic bank withdrawal—on that week's form. Include deposits into savings accounts, certificates of deposit, or money market accounts, and purchases of investments. Do not record credit card charges. When you make a payment on a credit card bill, however, list the amount of your payment and the items it covers.

4. At the end of the week, total your weekly expenses. Put away the completed Daily Expenses form, take out another copy, and fill it out according to Step 3. Repeat until you have two full months of expenses recorded.

5. At the end of the two months, take out the tenth sheet. Anywhere on it, list seasonal, annual, semi-annual, or quarterly expenses that you incur each year but which did not come due during your two-month recording period. Common examples are property taxes, car registration, charitable gifts, magazine subscriptions, tax preparation fees, and auto and house insurance payments. Divide the annual cost of these items by 12 to figure out the monthly amount.

6. Total up all expenses for the two months you tracked, including two months' worth of the expenses described in Step 5. Divide the total by two to calculate your average monthly expenses.

Signing Instructions

There are no signing instructions for this form. Simply fill it out and use it to evaluate your spending patterns and prepare a budget.

Form 68: Monthly Income

Use Form 68 together with Form 67 to help you create a budget. On Form 68, total up your monthly income. Be sure to include income information for both people if you and another adult share finances.

Part A is for jobs for which you receive a salary or wages. Part B is for self-employment income, including sales commissions. Part C is for investment income, and Part D is for other sources of income, such as bonus pay, alimony or child support, pension or retirement income, and public assistance.

When you are done listing all sources of income, add them all up for your total monthly income. If your income varies each month, repeat this process for two or three months to determine your average monthly income.

> **TIP**
>
> **Don't include income that is automatically reinvested.** As you list your income, you may be inclined to include your interest and dividends that are automatically reinvested, such as retirement plan income and stock dividends, to get a true sense of your earnings. But the purpose of creating a budget is to keep track of your actual expenses and the income you have available to pay those expenses. By listing income you don't actually receive, you will be left with the impression that you have more income to cover your expenses each month than you actually have available.

Signing Instructions

There are no signing instructions for the Monthly Income form. Simply fill it out and use it to prepare a monthly budget.

Form 69: Monthly Budget

After you've kept track of your expenses (Form 67) and income (Form 68) for a couple of months, you're ready to create a budget using Form 69. Follow these steps:

1. Using your actual expenses, project your monthly expenses for the categories relevant to you on Form 69 (Monthly Budget). Be sure to include the monthly equivalent of any quarterly, semi-annual, or annual expenses that you noted on your tenth sheet of Form 67 (Daily Expenses).

2. Enter your projected monthly expenses into the projected (Proj.) column on Form 69. Remember, this is just an estimate based on two months of recordkeeping. Enter the total at the end of the form, near the bottom of the column.

3. Enter your projected monthly income (bottom line of Form 68) below your total projected expenses on Form 69.

4. Figure out the difference. If your expenses exceed your income, you may have to cut your projected expenses or increase your income to make ends meet.

5. During each month, write down your actual expenses in each category. Do this as accurately as possible—remember, creating a budget is really designed to help you adopt a sound spending plan, not to fill in the "correct" numbers. Check your actual monthly expenditures periodically to help you keep an eye on how you're doing. Are you keeping close to your projected figures?

If you are not, you will need to change the projected amount for those categories.

TIP

When a large payment comes due. While you have included one-twelfth of your quarterly, semi-annual, and annual expenses in each month's projection, those expenses and other unanticipated ones don't arise every month. Ideally, your budget provides for a cushion each month—that is, your income exceeds your expenses—so you'll be able to handle the large payments when they come due by using that month's cushion or the savings you've built up from the excess each month. If you don't have the cash on hand to pay the large payment, you will have to cut back in other expense categories.

Signing Instructions

There are no signing instructions for this Monthly Budget form. Simply fill it out and use it to balance your income and expenses.

Form 70: Statement of Assets and Liabilities

Subtracting what you owe (liabilities) from what you own (assets) reveals your net worth. A net worth statement can help you and a lender analyze your eligibility for a loan.

To find your net worth, use Form 70, Statement of Assets and Liabilities. Fill in as much information as you can. Don't worry about listing every asset or debt; the information on this form changes daily as your assets change value and the balances on your debts rise or fall. You can estimate the date of purchase, or write N/A in this column if you don't know.

What values should you use for your assets? As best you can, you will want to include an asset's current market value—the amount you could get if you sold the item on the open

market. This means you are not looking at what you could get in a forced sale—such as a house repossession or foreclosure, or if you had to sell all your personal belongings at a garage sale. Instead, you're looking at what your home could bring in under normal selling conditions, how much you could get for your car by selling it through the paper or to a dealer, and how much your household goods are worth, considering they generally depreciate about 20% a year.

CROSS-REFERENCE

For a related form, specifically geared toward determining eligibility for a home loan, see Form 52, Family Financial Statement, in Chapter 6.

Signing Instructions

There are no signing instructions for this Statement of Assets and Liabilities. Simply fill this form out and update it from time to time. Use it to determine your net worth, information that will be useful should you apply for a loan.

Form 71: Assignment of Rights

You can use this form to transfer property or money that you are entitled to receive (for example, under a contract or promissory note) to another person. This is called "assigning" your right to receive the property or money. In legal terms, you are the "assignor": the person transferring a right to property or money to another person, who is the "assignee." For example, if Bette signed a promissory note owing you money and you owe Roger money, you might assign your right to Bette's money to Roger. You are the assignor and Roger is the assignee. Or, you might assign your right to receive income from a book contract to your teenage son so that the money would be taxed in his bracket, not yours. (See a tax adviser before you do this, though.)

This Assignment of Rights form provides for one or two assignors and one or two assignees. There may be situations in which two people have the right to receive money or property and jointly transfer that right, or in which two people are granted the right to receive money or property. This typically, but not exclusively, arises when a husband and wife jointly have the right to money or property or are jointly granted such a right. (Chapter 5 includes a discussion of marital property.)

Often the assignment covers a set period, especially when you assign the right to receive payments. Form 71 (Clauses 3 and 4) allows you to specify the beginning and ending dates of the assignment; if you don't have an exact end date in mind, you can simply say that the assignment will end when a specific event occurs or you revoke the assignment.

Here are some questions to ask when considering an assignment:

- **If you are assigning rights based on a previously existing contract, does the contract allow the assignment?** Be sure to read the contract carefully and make sure you can assign your rights under it. For example, leases and installment purchase contracts for motor vehicles typically prohibit assignment without the lessor's or lender's advance written consent. Mortgages and deeds of trust also typically cannot be assigned.

- **Are there tax implications of the assignment?** If you assign money to another person and receive something of equal value in return, there should be no tax implications. If, however, you assign your right to receive money to another person as a gift and the IRS learns of the assignment, the IRS will treat the assignment as a taxable transaction. For many assignments, this won't be a problem because you can make a tax-free gift of up to $13,000 per individual per year (2009 figure). But if you are assigning more than that, you should get tax advice.

- **Does the assignment substantially change the obligations of the person with whom you signed a contract?** If the contractual obligations will become more onerous, you may not be allowed to make the assignment. For example, if you have signed a contract with Happy Housekeepers to clean your house once a week for $75, you may not assign this obligation to a neighbor whose house would require a lot more time and effort to clean.

Signing Instructions

You must sign the Assignment of Rights form for it to be valid. Print out two copies of the form (or enough for each person who will be signing the form to have a separate copy). Each person (assignor and assignee) should sign and date all copies of the form and keep a signed document with all original signatures.

Form 72: Notice to Terminate Joint Account

If you are separating from or divorcing a spouse or partner, you will want to close any joint credit cards or accounts immediately. This involves notifying all creditors of your request to close joint accounts so that no new charges can be made. You should send this notice to every creditor, including credit card issuers, banks, department stores, and other retailers, with whom you and your spouse or partner hold a joint credit account. Send it to the customer service address on the back of a billing statement, not to the address where you send payments. You must complete a separate Notice to Terminate Joint Account for each credit card account you want to close. Be sure you enter the full names of the joint account holders exactly as they appear on the account, and include the correct account number.

The only way to make sure that an account is truly closed is to insist, as this notice does, that the creditor do a "hard close," so that no new charges can be made. (You can close your account even if you haven't paid off the balance. In that case, the account will remain active only for the purpose of paying off the balance.) This notice states that if a "hard close" is not done, you will not be responsible for any charges made on the account. While such a letter may not fully protect you, it is better than doing nothing and puts the burden on the creditor to show why the account wasn't closed as you requested.

If time is of the essence, call the creditor and request a hard close. Follow up by sending a signed copy of Form 72, along with a cover letter referring to your earlier phone call. You might also be able to close accounts on the card issuer's website.

Signing Instructions

Print out a copy of the Notice to Terminate Joint Account form and sign it in the space provided. Make two copies of the signed form and mail the original and one of the copies to the creditor you wish to notify of the joint account termination. Include a stamped, self-addressed envelope. The creditor will sign the copy and return it to you in the self-addressed envelope as a receipt.

Send the form by certified mail, return receipt requested, and keep a copy of the form and receipt for your records. You may later need it as proof that you properly notified the creditor of your intent to close the joint account.

TIP

Don't overlook home equity lines of credit. You and your ex may have applied for a home equity line of credit a while ago and forgotten about it. Equity credit lines that supply a checkbook can be used just like a joint checking account. Because the risk of leaving an equity line of credit open is so great (you could lose your home if your ex is irresponsible with the funds), we recommend closing it in person. Pay a visit to your banker to request that the account be closed or frozen. Even if you have the checkbook, request that the account be closed so that your ex can't request more checks. Get a written record that the bank has closed the account.

Form 73: Notice to Stop Payment of Check

It's not unusual to write a check, hand it over or mail it to the recipient, and then change your mind and want to stop payment. For example, you might not notice that delivered goods were defective until after the delivery person was paid and left. Many other situations give rise to the need to put a stop payment on a check.

The first thing to do is call the bank, savings and loan, credit union, or other financial institution where your account is located to make an oral request to stop payment. Ask how much the charge is, if any, for this service. Then immediately send or, better yet, drop off a written confirmation of your stop payment notice, Form 73. Include payment for any required charge with your notice.

In many situations, the stop payment notice lasts only six months or a year. If you fear the person to whom you wrote the check will try to cash it much later, you may need to renew your stop payment notice. Banks, savings and loans, credit unions, and other financial institutions have the option of rejecting checks they deem too old, often six months or older, but they usually don't exercise this right. In fact, most people who work in a bank or other financial institution never look at the date of the check. They simply post it to the account. If the money is there to cover it, the check is paid.

Signing Instructions

Print out three copies of the Notice to Stop Payment of Check form. Sign the copies and mail or give two of them to the appropriate bank or financial institution along with a stamped, self-addressed envelope. As requested in this form, the financial institution should then sign and return one of the copies, acknowledging receipt of your letter. Keep a copy for your records.

Form 74: Request for Credit Report

If you want to repair your credit, establish credit, or apply for a loan, your first step is to get a copy of your credit report. This is a file maintained by a credit bureau that sells information to banks, lenders, landlords, and others who routinely evaluate customers' creditworthiness. Credit reports contain personal information about you, including your current and past use of credit cards; loans (home, car, student, and the like); any defaults on bills such as utility payments or doctor's bills; public records, such as lawsuits; and inquiries by creditors.

The federal Fair Credit Reporting Act (FCRA) now requires each major national credit bureau—Equifax, Experian, and TransUnion—to provide you one free copy of your credit report each year.

You can request your free report by one of these means:

- Telephone—1-877-322-8228
- Internet—www.annualcreditreport.com
- Mail—Annual Credit Report Request Service, P.O. Box 10528, Atlanta, GA 30348-5283

You must provide your name, address, Social Security number, and date of birth when you order. You also may be required to provide information that only you would know, such as the amount of your monthly mortgage payment.

You can get an additional copy of your credit report by contacting one of the three major national credit bureaus:

- Equifax, 800-685-1111; www.equifax.com
- Experian, 888-397-3742; www.experian.com
- TransUnion, 800-888-4213; www.transunion.com

If you need additional copies of your credit report, the cost is usually less than $10 (and free in some cases, listed below), but check first for the exact amount.

You are entitled to a free additional copy of your credit report if:

- You've been denied credit or insurance because of information in your credit file. (In that case, you are entitled to a free copy of your report from the credit bureau that reported the information. A creditor that denies you credit or insurance will tell you the name and address of the credit bureau reporting the information that led to the denial.) You must request your free copy within 60 days of being denied; you should provide a copy of the denial letter.

- You are unemployed and planning to apply for a job within 60 days following your request for your credit report. It's a good idea to include documents verifying your unemployment (such as a recent unemployment check or layoff notice). You must also provide a statement swearing that the information is true. You are entitled to one free report in a 12-month period.

- You receive public assistance. Enclose a statement swearing that this is true and provide a copy of your most recent public assistance check as verification. You are entitled to one free report in any 12-month period.

- You reasonably believe your credit file contains errors due to someone's fraud, such as using your credit card, name, or Social Security number. Here, too, you will need to enclose a statement swearing that this is true. You are entitled to one free report in any 12-month period.

- You are a victim of identity theft or fraud, or think that you may be. The FCRA gives consumers the right to request free credit reports in connection with fraud alerts.

  - If you suspect in good faith that you are, or may be, a victim of identity theft or another fraud, you can instruct the major bureaus to add a "fraud alert" to your file. You can request a free copy of your report from each bureau once it places the fraud alert in your file.

  - If you are a victim of identity theft, you can send the major bureaus an identity theft report and instruct them to add an extended fraud alert to your file. You can request two free copies of your credit report from each bureau during the next 12 months once it places the extended fraud alert in your file.

Signing Instructions

Sign your Request for Credit Report and mail it certified mail, return receipt requested, to the credit bureau. Keep a copy of the letter for your files. Include payment and any supporting documentation required, as noted above.

RESOURCE

To avoid credit report problems by making sure you're not a victim of identity theft, see *Stopping Identity Theft: 10 Easy Steps to Security,* by Scott Mitic (Nolo).

Form 75: Dispute Incorrect Credit Report Entry

Under the federal Fair Credit Reporting Act, you have the right to dispute all incorrect or incomplete information in your credit file, such as an incorrect name, employer, account, or tax history, a lawsuit older than seven years or one you weren't involved in, or a bankruptcy older than ten years. If you have carefully reviewed your credit report and identified inaccurate or incomplete information you want changed or removed, complete the "request for reinvestigation" form that was enclosed with your credit report. If the credit bureau did not enclose such a form, use Form 75 to spell out the information you want corrected or deleted from your credit report. Enclose copies of any documents you have that support your claim. Once the credit bureau receives your request, it must investigate the items you dispute and contact you, usually within 30 days. For more information, see *Credit Repair,* by Robin Leonard and John Lamb (Nolo).

You can also dispute inaccurate or incomplete items of information online by going to the credit bureau's website (contact information appears in the instructions for Form 74). Look for the button or link for submitting disputes online. (If you have documents that support your position, it's better to use Form 75 and enclose copies of the documents.)

Signing Instructions

Sign your Dispute Incorrect Credit Report Entry form and mail it certified mail, return receipt requested, to the credit bureau that prepared the report you are disputing. Include copies of any documents supporting your claim. Keep a copy of the letter for your files.

Form 76: Dispute Credit Card Charge

If you use a credit or charge card but don't receive the product you purchased, or you received a defective item, you can legally refuse to pay if you meet certain criteria:

- **Dispute concerning a purchase made with a credit card issued by the seller, such as department store or gas station.** You can legally refuse to pay if you first attempt in good faith to resolve the dispute with the merchant who refuses to replace, repair, or otherwise correct the problem.

- **Dispute concerning a purchase made with a credit card, such as Visa or MasterCard, not issued by the seller.** You can legally refuse to pay if you first attempt in good faith to resolve the dispute with the merchant who refuses to replace, repair, or otherwise correct the problem. But, you can withhold payment only if the purchase was for more than $50 and was made within the state in which you live or was within 100 miles of your home.

You may withhold only the balance on the disputed item or service that is unpaid when you first notify the seller or card issuer of the problem. (To cover yourself as fully as possible, make sure that the card issuer receives your dispute within 60 days after the date of the first credit card statement showing the disputed purchase.)

If you are entitled to withhold payment, complete and mail Form 76 to the credit card company at the address for disputed charges (not the billing address) and explain why you aren't paying. Explain how you tried to resolve the problem with the merchant. Attach a copy of the credit card bill showing the disputed item, along with any additional documentation of your attempt to resolve the dispute, such as a letter you sent to a merchant regarding a defective item.

The card issuer cannot tell a credit reporting agency that the amount you withheld is delinquent until the dispute has been settled, provided that you do not withhold more than you are entitled. Nor can the issuer "freeze" or place a hold on any funds that you may have on deposit with it. However, the issuer can tell a credit reporting agency that your failure to pay is "disputed," so it's important not to abuse this right.

For more information on credit card problems, check the Federal Trade Commission website at www.ftc.gov.

CAUTION
Do not use this form if the problem is unauthorized use of your credit card—for example, charges made by someone who stole your card. In this situation, promptly report your loss to the police and the credit card issuer to limit your liability for unauthorized charges. Then call the three major credit bureaus to report fraud (contact information appears in the instructions for Form 74).

Signing Instructions

Sign your Dispute Credit Card Charge letter and mail it to the credit card issuer, along with copies of any documents supporting your claim. Keep a copy of the letter and your original supporting documentation for your files.

Form 77: Demand Collection Agency Cease Contact

If you owe money and your debt has been passed along to a collection agency, you will no doubt be contacted by a collector working for the agency. Many people don't understand that they have the legal right under federal law (the Fair Debt Collection Practices Act, 15 U.S.C. § 1692 and following) to tell a bill collector who works for a collection agency to leave them alone. (This does not apply to in-house collectors—for example, at a bank, department store, or hospital—unless your state has enacted a similar restriction on in-house collectors.) To pursue this right, you must put your demand in writing (that's the purpose of Form 77) and send it to the collection agency. By law, all collectors from the agency must then cease all phone calls, letters, and other communications with you, unless they are contacting you to notify you that:

- collection efforts against you have ended, or
- the collection agency or the creditor will invoke a specific remedy against you, such as suing you.

Alternatively, you can inform the collector that you are represented by an attorney and instruct that all communications be directed to the attorney (you must provide the attorney's name and address).

TIP

It's usually best not to ignore the debt or try to hide from the collector. Usually, the longer you put off resolving the issue, the worse the situation and consequences will become. Whether you negotiate directly with the collector or obtain a lawyer's assistance, many counselors feel the best strategy almost always is to engage the collector, at least initially.

Signing Instructions

Sign your Demand Collection Agency Cease Contact letter and mail it to the collection agency, along with copies of any documents supporting your demand. It's best to send this letter by certified mail and request a return receipt. Keep a copy of the letter and your original documents for your files.

Dealing With Junk Mail and Telemarketing Calls

Form 78: Notice to Remove Name From List 109

Form 79: Notice to Add or Retain Name but Not Sell or Trade It 111

Form 80: Telemarketing Phone Call Log..111

Form 81: Notice to Put Name on Company's "Do Not Call" List 112

Form 82: Demand for Damages for Excessive Calls..113

The telephone is—depending on one's mood—either a boon or a scourge of modern life. One of its undeniably bad aspects is its wide use by telemarketers. Fortunately, there are two federal laws—the Telephone Consumer Protection Act (47 U.S.C. § 227) and the Telemarketing and Consumer Fraud and Abuse Prevention Act (15 U.S.C. § 6101)—that put some limits on how telemarketers must act. Most states also have laws to curb abusive telemarketing. Some provisions are part of an effort to curb telemarketing fraud; others are aimed at reducing annoyance to consumers. For example, before you pay (usually by credit card) for something purchased from a telemarketer, the seller must accurately state the total cost, quantity of goods or services, and all other important conditions and restrictions. A seller must also explain its refund policy or state that it doesn't allow a refund, exchange, or cancellation.

Even more common than telemarketing fraud are legitimate but incredibly annoying phone calls that we most often get at dinnertime. It may be some consolation that federal law at least prohibits telemarketers from making these calls before 8 a.m. and after 9 p.m. (local time) unless they have your permission to call. Telemarketers also must put you on a "do not call list" if you so request (see "Do Not Call Registries," below). And that's where the forms in this chapter come in—we show you how to tell a company to stop calling you and what to do if it doesn't.

Sometimes, your mailbox can become just as irritating as your telephone. For most of us, catalogues, credit card offers, and all kinds of other junk mail take up more space than our first-class mail. Moreover, this never-read junk mail is an incredible waste of environmental resources. Again, fortunately, some federal laws (for example, amendments to the Fair Credit Reporting Act that restrict credit bureaus' use of your name for marketing purposes) can help you get off various mailing lists. In this chapter, we provide you with the easy-to-use forms to accomplish this.

RESOURCE

The Privacy Rights Clearinghouse is a nonprofit consumer organization with extensive information and advice on consumer rights regarding junk mail, telemarketing, and related privacy issues. For more information, see their website at www.privacyrights.org or call 619-298-3396.

"Do Not Call" Registries

The federal government created a National Do Not Call Registry to make it easier for you to stop getting telemarketing sales calls you don't want. You can register online at www.donotcall.gov or call toll-free, 888-382-1222, from the number you wish to register. Registration is free. Your number stays on the list for five years, and then you'll have to reregister it. You can ask to have your number taken off the register at any time. Telemarketers must update their "do not call" lists with names from the National Do Not Call Registry at least once every 31 days. Telemarketers can be fined up to $11,000 for each violation.

Placing your number on the National Do Not Call Registry will stop most, but not all, unwelcome calls. For example, you may still be called by nonprofits, or by companies you've recently contacted or with which you've done business.

Before the federal Do Not Call Registry opened, more than half the states started their own registries of telephone subscribers who do not want to receive telemarketing calls. These state laws continue to be valid if they impose more restrictions on intrastate telemarketing (calls made and completed within the state) than the federal law. In order to do business in these states, telemarketers must buy the "do not call" list and abide by the wishes of the persons named on the list. Violators are subject to fines. Some state registries are free; others charge a small fee to put your name on the list.

All registries exempt some categories of callers (as does the National Do Not Call Registry). For example, many states allow charities, companies seeking payment of debts, and those calling on behalf of political candidates to continue to call you. If an organization is exempt from whichever registry you participate in, you can still follow the procedures outlined below to get on that organization's "do not call" list. (See the instructions for Form 81.)

Some, but not all, of the states are transferring their "do not call" registries to the National Do Not Call Registry. If you want to know whether your state has a separate registry, contact your state attorney general or consumer protection agency.

If your number is listed on a "do not call" registry and you get a call from a telemarketer, report the call to the appropriate agency, either state or national. Most registries provide complaint forms online. You can also check with your local consumer protection office or state Attorney General (see "How to Complain to Government Agencies," below, for information on contacting these agencies).

Form 78: Notice to Remove Name From List

It's quite possible that you want to receive some catalogs, promotional mailings, or telemarketing phone calls, but not others. To get yourself onto only the lists you want to be on requires a two-step approach. First, send

---

How to Complain to Government Agencies

In addition to taking all of the steps suggested in this chapter, it is also a good idea to complain to government enforcement agencies about abusive phone calls and letters. You can simply send a copy of the written notice, such as Form 82, Demand for Damages for Excessive Calls, to one or more of the following agencies:

- **State Attorneys General.** You can find contact information for your state Attorney General's office from the National Association of Attorneys General at www.naag.org. This is also a good resource to find out more about your state telemarketing laws.

- **State Consumer Protection Office.** To find the consumer protection office in your state, visit the Federal Consumer Information website at www.consumeraction.gov/caw_state_resources.shtml.

- **Federal Trade Commission.** Consumer Response Center, 600 Pennsylvania Avenue, NW, Washington, DC 20580; toll-free 877-382-4357; www.ftc.gov. The FTC strongly encourages consumers to file complaints from its website, using FTC forms.

- **Federal Communications Commission.** Consumer Inquiries and Complaints Division, 445 12th Street, SW, Washington, DC 20554; 888-225-5322 (voice); 888-835-5322 (TTY); www.fcc.gov.

Form 78 to all companies that collect names in order to sell them to direct marketers and telemarketers, telling them to remove your name. Provide them with all spellings of your name, and the names of any other household members on the mailing label. If you're receiving junk mail for previous occupants at your address, provide their names, too. Then, send Form 79 to only those businesses whose materials or phone calls you want to receive.

Dozens of companies gather names and addresses to sell to direct marketers and telemarketers. While some lists are larger than others, you will get yourself off of most lists if you send Form 74, Notice to Remove Name from List, to the major credit bureaus:

- Experian Marketing Solutions, 475 Anton Blvd, Costa Mesa, CA 92626; www.experian.com
- Equifax, Options, P.O. Box 740241, Atlanta, GA 30374; www.equifax.com
- TransUnion, Name Removal Option, P.O. Box 97328, Jackson, MS 39288; www.transunion.com

One phone call to 888-5OPTOUT will get you off the lists of all three of these credit bureaus.

The three credit bureaus listed above give you the choice of opting out for five years or permanently. If you opt out, you will no longer appear on lists offered by the credit bureaus, but you will continue to receive mailings based on lists from other sources.

Other places to send Form 78 include:

- Mail Preference Service, Direct Marketing Association, P.O. Box 282, Carmel, NY 10512; 212-768-7277, or www.dma consumers.org. To register, you must complete a form online or download the form and mail it in; there's a $1 fee either way. This service is a good step towards getting rid of junk mail, but it's not a cure-all. Members of the Direct Marketing Association must comply with the "do not write" list. Even so, you may continue to receive unsolicited mail from DMA members with whom you already do business. While the list also is available to businesses that are not DMA members, they have no obligation to comply with it. The Direct Marketing Association will keep your name in its files for five years. After that time, you should send another letter.
- R.L. Polk & Company, Attn: Name Deletion File, 26955 Northwestern Highway, Southfield, MI 48034; 800-873-7655.
- Donnelly Marketing, Inc., Data Base Operations, 416 South Bell, Ames, IA 50010; 888-633-4402.
- National Demographics and Lifestyles, Customer Service Department, 1621 18th Street, #300, Denver, CO 80202. Most warranty cards—also called product registration cards—are sent to this company, not to the manufacturer. The cards are used to gather names for mailing lists and to inform customers about product recalls. Often, the cards have nothing to do with whether you get the benefit of the warranty. Usually, you're covered even if you don't send in the warranty card. Check with the manufacturer to find out whether this is the case. Send Form 78 to this company to get your name removed from their list.

Another way to reduce your junk mail is to contact the customer service departments of the companies that send you catalogs you don't want or other unwanted mail and ask to be taken off their mailing list. After you call, send Form 78.

Finally, privacy-conscious consumers can complete and return the "opt out" portion of the "privacy notices" that financial institutions and businesses send them when they open accounts. These consumers opt out of every use of their personal information possible under the institution's or business' privacy policy. Doing this reduces the distribution of the consumer's personal information somewhat, and also cuts down the number of offers and solicitations that the consumer receives.

Usually, the privacy notice will include a detachable "opt out" or "privacy preference" form. If not, look in the privacy notice for an "800" number and call it to register your preferences. In the absence of a form or an 800 number, you can create your own opt-out letter. For a sample, go to the Privacy Rights Clearinghouse's website, www.privacyrights.org. Click on the Financial Privacy link, then on Fact Sheets and scroll down to Fact Sheet 24(a) on financial privacy and the sample opt-out letter.

Signing Instructions

Sign and date your Notice to Remove Name From List, and mail it to some or all of the companies listed above that sell lists of names to direct marketers and telemarketers. Keep a copy of the notice for your files.

RESOURCE

An excellent resource for getting off of direct marketing and telemarketing lists is *Stop Junk Mail Forever (Telemarketing and Spamming, Too)*, by Marc Eisenson, Nancy Castleman, and Marcy Ross (Good Advice Press, www.goodadvicepress.com/sjmf.htm).

Form 79: Notice to Add or Retain Name but Not Sell or Trade It

After sending Form 78 to get your name off the lists of all businesses that sell lists of names to direct marketers and telemarketers, use Form 79 to get onto (or keep yourself on) the lists maintained by businesses whose mailings and/or phone calls you do want to receive. This notice states that you do not want your name sold, traded, or shared with any other company or business. Also, you can specify whether or not you want to accept telemarketing phone calls from the company.

Signing Instructions

Sign and date your Notice to Add or Retain Name and mail it to the companies whose mailings and/or phone calls you do want to receive. Keep a copy of the notice for your files.

Form 80: Telemarketing Phone Call Log

A federal law, the Telephone Consumer Protection Act, requires every telemarketer to keep a list of consumers who say that they do not want to be called again. If you tell a telemarketer not to call you, but you get another call within 12 months, you can sue the company on whose behalf the call is made for up to $500. (The telemarketer can take up to 30 days to put your number on its "do not call" list.) If the court finds that the telemarketer willfully or knowingly violated the law, the court can award you up to $1,500. Most states' small claims courts allow claims of at least $2,000, so you can sue on your own, without hiring a lawyer.

Some states also have telemarketing laws. Often, those laws are even stricter than federal law. Contact your state Consumer Protection Office to find out more about your state's telemarketing laws (see "How to Complain to Government Agencies," above, for information on contacting these agencies).

Use Form 80 to keep a log of telemarketing phone calls. You will need to note the date, the time of the call, the company on whose behalf the call is being made, the telemarketer's name (probably a fake, but write it down anyway), the product being sold, and the fact that you stated "put me on a 'do not call' list." Telemarketers may not block their phone numbers from being identified, so if you have caller ID you can write down the caller's name and phone number whenever possible and include it on the form. This information will help you recognize repeat callers, and will provide a form of identification if the caller refuses to give a name. You will need this evidence to prove that you received more than one call from the same telemarketing company.

If you follow up with a letter, such as Form 81, asking to be put on the "do not call" list, note this on the call log, too.

Suing a company whose telemarketer violates the Telephone Consumer Protection Act presents at least two practical problems. First, you must be able to locate the company (see the instructions for Form 81 for suggestions). Second, the court in your state must be able to assert jurisdiction over the company. This is difficult (and practically speaking, often impossible) if it's located in another state.

Signing Instructions

There are no signing instructions for the Telemarketing Phone Call Log. Simply fill it out every time you get a call from a telemarketer.

Form 81: Notice to Put Name on Company's "Do Not Call" List

Proving that a telemarketer willfully violated the law by calling you more than once may be difficult. One way you can generate evidence of a company's willful act is to *always* end your phone call by stating "Put me on your 'do not call' list," and follow up with a letter stating the same. Include all of your telephone numbers in the letter. You can use Form 81 for this purpose.

You can also use Form 81 to stop calls that are not prohibited by the "do not call" list—for example, calls from companies that you do business with.

You will need to find out the mailing address of the company on whose behalf the call is made in order to send your letter. Here are a few suggestions:

- Ask the telemarketer who calls you for the company's address. Telemarketers are required by law to give you the telephone number or the address of the company. Despite the law, many telemarketers will claim they don't know the information or can't tell you. If that happens, contact your State Consumer Protection Office (see "How to Complain to Government Agencies," above).

- If it's a local company, or you know the city in which the company is located, see if you can find the address online or in your phone book; if you find a phone number, but not the address, call and ask for the mailing address.

- Consult *Hoover's Handbook of American Business: Profiles of Major U.S. Companies.* Your local library should have a copy, or you can visit the website at www.hoovers.com. The site contains a lot of self-promotional ads and other companies' banners, but you can get the information you need if you keep trying.

- Try using a search engine such as Google to locate the company's address.

Form 81 also may be used to eliminate telemarketing calls from one or more specific companies rather than eliminating all calls by registering with the National Do Not Call Registry.

Signing Instructions

Sign and date your Notice to Put Name on Company's "Do Not Call" List and mail it to the company whose telemarketer has called you. Keep a copy of the notice for your own records. You may need this if you end up suing the company for excessive calls (as described under Form 82).

Form 82: Demand for Damages for Excessive Calls

You can use Form 82 after you receive a second (or third or fourth) telemarketing call on behalf of the same company. (Remember, it can take up to 30 days for your number to get on the "do not call" list.) It details the history of telemarketing phone calls you have received on behalf of the company and your requests to be put on the "do not call" list. Form 82 spells out your right to monetary compensation for a violation of the federal Telephone Consumer Protection Act as explained in the discussion of the Telemarketing Phone Call Log (Form 80), above. It specifies that you will seek all appropriate remedies in court if you do not get the requested compensation within 30 days. You will need to find out the mailing address of the company in order to send your letter. See the discussion under Form 81, Notice to Put Name on Company's "Do Not Call" List for some suggestions on obtaining the address.

In addition to locating the company on whose behalf the calls were made, the court in your state must be able to assert jurisdiction over it. This is difficult (and practically speaking, often impossible) if the company is located in another state.

Signing Instructions

Sign your Demand for Damages for Excessive Calls letter and mail it to the company on whose behalf the telemarketing calls were made. Keep a copy for your files. ●

Hiring Child Care, Elder Care, or Household Help

Form 83: Child Care Agreement 118

Form 84: Child Care Instructions 120

Form 85: Elder Care Agreement 121

Form 86: Housekeeping Services Agreement 121

Many people hire others to work regularly in their homes—for example, to take care of children during the workday, care for elderly parents, or clean the house. These relationships are often set up informally, with no written agreement. But informal arrangements can be fraught with problems. If you don't have a written agreement clearly defining responsibilities and benefits, you and those helping you are all too likely to have different expectations about the job. This can lead to serious disputes—even to one or both parties bitterly backing out of the arrangement. Far better to draft a clear written understanding of what the job entails.

The agreements in this chapter are for hiring child and elder care providers and other household workers who are employees, not independent contractors. When you hire an employee, you set the hours, responsibilities, and pay rate of the worker. Legally, most babysitters and household workers who work for you on a regular basis are considered employees for whom you are required to pay taxes, Social Security, and other benefits described below. In contrast, independent contractors typically own their own businesses and work for you only occasionally.

This chapter also includes a Child Care Instructions form you can use for either a full-time child care provider or an occasional babysitter.

RESOURCE

For information on hiring independent contractors, see *Working With Independent Contractors*, by Stephen Fishman (Nolo).

CAUTION

Do not use this form if you hire a child or elder care worker or housecleaner through a placement agency. If you use an agency that sets and collects the worker's fee from you, pays the worker, and controls the terms of the work, the agency will have its own contract for you to complete. People you hire through an agency are not your employees—they are the employees of their agencies.

Legal Obligations for Employees

Assuming your child care worker, elder care worker, or housecleaner is your employee, you have legal obligations to that person, obligations that include a certain amount of paperwork and recordkeeping. You do not have to put this information in your child or elder care or housekeeping agreement, but you need to be aware of your responsibilities.

Social Security and Income Taxes. If you pay a child care or elder care worker $1,600 or more in a calendar year, you must make Social Security (FICA) payments on those wages and withhold the employee's share of FICA. You do not have to deduct income taxes from wages paid to an employee for working in your home unless the employee requests it and you agree to do so. You make these payments by attaching Schedule H, Household Employment Taxes, to your annual Form 1040.

Unemployment Compensation. If you pay a household employee $1,000 or more in a three-month period, you must pay quarterly taxes under the Federal Unemployment Tax Act (FUTA), using IRS Form 940 or 940-EZ. As with FICA, you pay this amount by attaching Schedule H, Household Employment Taxes, to your annual Form 1040.

Workers' Compensation. Your state may require you to provide workers' compensation insurance against job-related injuries or illnesses suffered by your employees. Check with your state department of labor or employment.

Minimum Wage and Overtime. The federal minimum hourly wage is $6.55, increasing to $7.25 on July 24, 2009. Your child care or elder care worker may be entitled to minimum wage, depending upon their particular hours and earnings. If your state minimum wage is higher, you will need to pay the state wage. In addition, under federal law, most domestic workers (other than live-in workers) qualify for overtime pay. Workers must be paid overtime at a rate one-and-a-half times the regular rate for all hours worked beyond a 40-hour workweek. You can check the U.S. Department of Labor website, www.dol.gov, for current information about federal and state minimum wage laws.

New Hire Reporting Form. Within a short time after you hire someone—20 days or fewer, depending on your state's rules—you must file a New Hire Reporting Form with a designated state agency. The information on the form becomes part of the National Directory of New Hires, used primarily to locate parents to collect child support. To find out about your state's new hire reporting requirements—and the location of the state agency where you must send this information—go to www.acf.dhhs.gov.

Federal ID Number. If you hire a household employee, you must obtain a federal employer identification number (EIN), required by the IRS of all employers for tax filing and reporting purposes. The form you need is IRS Form SS-4, Application for Employer Identification Number.

IRS Resources

The IRS has a number of publications and forms that might help you. Call the IRS at 800-424-FORM or visit its website at www.irs.gov to download these forms and publications. Start with Publication 926, *Household Employers' Tax Guide*, which describes the major tax responsibilities of employers. You may also want to look at:

- Form SS-8, which contains IRS definitions of independent contractor and employee, and
- Form SS-4, Application for Employer Identification Number.

Reality Check

Many families don't comply with the law that requires them to pay taxes or Social Security for household workers, some of whom are undocumented aliens. This chapter is not intended to preach about the law, but to alert you to the laws that affect your relationships with child and elder care and housekeeping workers. No question, if you fail to pay Social Security and to meet your other legal obligations as an employer, there may be several negative consequences.

- You may be assessed substantial financial penalties. For example, if your full-time elder care provider files for Social Security five years from now and can prove prior earnings, but no Social Security has been paid, the IRS could back-bill you at high interest rates.

- If you don't meet a state requirement to provide workers' compensation insurance and your child care worker is injured while on the job and can't work for a few months, you may be in hot water if the worker files for workers' compensation. You will probably be held liable for the worker's medical costs and a portion of any lost wages, as well as be fined for not having the insurance in the first place.

- You will not be able to take a child care tax credit on your federal income taxes. The credit is based on your work-related expenses and income.

Form 83: Child Care Agreement

A child care provider who takes care of your children in your house, either part time or full time, may live out (often called a caregiver or babysitter) or live in (an au pair or nanny). The responsibilities of the position may vary widely, from performing a whole range of housekeeping services to only taking care of the children.

Use Form 83 to spell out your agreement about the child care worker's responsibilities, hours, benefits, amount and schedule of payment, and other important aspects of the job. The best approach is to be as detailed as possible.

Start by filling in your name, address, phone numbers, and other contact information for yourself (and a second parent if another parent will be signing the Child Care Agreement) and your child care provider. List your children's names and birth dates.

Here's some advice on filling in various sections of the Child Care Agreement:

Location and Schedule of Care (Clause 4). Provide the address where child care will be provided (typically your home) and the days and hours of care, such as 8 a.m. to 6 p.m. weekdays. Live-in nannies or au pairs often work some weeknights and weekends.

Beginning Date (Clause 5) and Training or Probation Period (Clause 6). Specify the date employment will begin and the length of any training or probation period, such as the first 15 or 30 days of child care. This is the time to make sure that the relationship will work for everyone involved. A training period helps your child care provider get to know your home and neighborhood and the exact way you want things done. If there will be no training or probation period, you can skip this clause.

Responsibilities (Clause 7). The responsibilities of the child care position may vary depending on many factors, including the number and age of your children; whether the child care worker lives in or out; the hours worked; your family situation and needs; and the skills and background of the child care provider. In some households, particularly with infants and toddlers, the babysitter or au pair only takes care of the children and does not do housework, except for doing the children's laundry. In other families, especially with older children, the employee may function more as a housekeeper, cook, and chauffeur. You should specify the child care worker's responsibilities in as much detail as possible, including cooking, bathing, and personal care for your children, social and recreational activities (such as arranging the children's play dates), transportation (driving kids to and from school or practices), shopping and errands for the family, housecleaning, ironing, and laundry.

EXAMPLE:

Here's an example of responsibilities for a live-in au pair taking care of an infant (Kate) and preschooler (Tom):

The child care provider's primary responsibility is to provide loving care of Kate and Tom. This includes playing with and reading to them, taking them to the park as weather permits, making sure they have naps as needed, and preparing their meals and snacks. The care provider will bathe Kate and Tom every other day, more frequently if necessary. Other responsibilities include driving Tom to "Baby Gym" twice a week, doing the children's laundry, and keeping their rooms tidy.

Wage or Salary (Clause 8). You should specify exactly how the child care provider will be paid, such as an hourly rate or weekly salary. How much you pay depends on many factors, including the number and ages of your children; the type of care provided and responsibilities; the number of hours, time of day, and regularity of the schedule; the experience and training of the employee; benefits such as room and board; and the going rate in your community. Check local sources to find out what similar workers are being paid—neighborhood listservs are a great source for this type of information. Before you fill in this section, be sure you understand your legal obligations when hiring an employee, such as minimum wage rules, as described above.

Payment Schedule (Clause 9). You can decide to pay your child care provider weekly (say, on Friday), twice per month (such as on the 15th and on the last day of the month), or once per month.

Benefits (Clause 10). In addition to payment, you may offer the child care provider any benefits you wish, such as paid vacations and holidays, health insurance, or sick leave.

Termination Policy (Clause 11). If things don't work out, the Child Care Agreement provides a termination policy that allows either the parents or the child care provider the right to terminate the agreement at any time, for any reason, and without notice.

Additional Provisions (Clause 12). Describe any additional terms of this agreement, such as a schedule for salary reviews, a no smoking policy, or a requirement that the child care provider take a first aid course.

Modifications (Clause 13). This agreement provides that any changes to it must be made in writing and signed by all parties to the agreement. This protects both the parents and the child care provider against misunderstandings over major issues that were agreed to verbally.

Signing Instructions

To make the Child Care Agreement valid, the parent(s) and the child care provider must sign it. (If you and your children's other parent are living in the same home and raising your kids together, it's best if both of you sign this document.) Print out two copies of the form. You, your children's other parent (if signing the form), and the caregiver must sign and date the form where indicated. Give one of the signed originals to the child care provider and keep the other for your records.

Shared In-Home Care

Some families pool their resources and share an in-home child care provider. These arrangements are ideal for neighbors or coworkers with children who are close in age. Just as a written agreement between a family and a child care worker can clarify expectations and prevent conflicts, a written understanding between the two families who are sharing a child care provider can accomplish the same objectives. If you share in-home care with another family, be sure you agree on the key issues before drafting your contract with the child care worker, including location of the care, splitting expenses, termination procedures, and supervision. The other parents should make their own child care arraangements with the care provider.

RESOURCE

For more about sharing care for children, elders, and disabled family members, as well as dozens of other ideas, see *The Sharing Solution: How to Save Money, Simplify Your Life, and Build Community*, by Janelle Orsi and Emily Doskow (Nolo).

Form 84: Child Care Instructions

Use this form to provide important information for babysitters and child care providers, such as phone numbers of doctors, instructions about meals and naps, and other details of your child's care, including any allergies or health conditions your child has.

The "temporary contact" section of the Child Care Instructions form (Clause 3) is the place to provide information about where you can be reached while you are away from the kids—for example, if you are going out for dinner and to the movies on a Saturday night. Clause 3 will change most frequently. If you do not want to update your Child Care Instructions every time you go out, you can skip this section and give the information to your babysitter on a separate piece of paper.

Form 84 has space for you to fill in the names, addresses, and phone numbers of people that your babysitter or child care provider can contact if they can't reach you in an emergency. We suggest that you list at least two or three friends, relatives, or neighbors who live nearby and are well known to your children and family. The form will print out with a reminder to call 911 in case of emergency. If you wish to list another emergency number for the police, fire department, or poison control, you may do so.

Finally, the Child Care Instructions form has space to provide additional important information a babysitter or child care provider needs to know about your family or home, such as the location of first aid supplies, the phone number of a local taxi service, or the fact that you have a rule against smoking in the house.

CROSS-REFERENCE

Use a separate form to authorize medical care. While these Child Care Instructions provide important medical information about your child, such as any medications or allergies, this form does not authorize your babysitter or child care provider to arrange medical care for your child. For that, you will need to use the Authorization for Minor's Medical Treatment (Form 2).

Signing Instructions

There is no need to sign the Child Care Instructions. Simply fill in the information and print out the form after reading it carefully to make sure all information is complete and correct. Give the babysitter or child care provider a copy and keep one posted in a prominent place, such as on your refrigerator. Be sure to review and update your Child Care Instructions from time to time.

Form 85: Elder Care Agreement

Many older people remain at home or live with relatives rather than enter a residential facility for extended recovery or long-term care. Often this requires hiring someone (an elder care provider) to help with their personal and medical care, cooking, housekeeping, and other services. An elder care provider (sometimes called a home health aide) can either live out or live in, and work full or part time. The responsibilities of this position may vary, from performing a wide range of housekeeping services to attending to the personal and health care needs of the older adult (or adults, in case the elder care worker is taking care of two people, such as both of your parents). Responsibilities may range from dispensing medicine to helping with bathing to driving to doctor's appointments, activities, or social functions.

Use Form 85 to spell out your written agreement about the elder care worker's responsibilities, hours, benefits, amount and schedule of payment, and other important aspects of the job. The best approach is to be as detailed as possible. Follow the directions for the Child Care Agreement (Form 83) when completing this form.

Signing Instructions

To make the Elder Care Agreement valid, the employer(s) and the elder care provider must sign it. Start by printing out two copies of the form. You (the employer) and the caregiver must sign and date the form where indicated. Give one of the signed originals to the elder care provider and keep the other for your records.

RESOURCE

For more about sharing care for children, elders, and disabled family members, as well as dozens of other ideas, see *The Sharing Solution: How to Save Money, Simplify Your Life, and Build Community*, by Janelle Orsi and Emily Doskow (Nolo).

Form 86: Housekeeping Services Agreement

If you hire the same person every week to clean your house, a written contract can be a valuable way to define the worker's responsibilities and benefits. If your housecleaner will be your employee, use this form to spell out the housecleaner's hours, benefits, amount and schedule of payment, termination policy, and other aspects of the job. Your agreement should cover regular weekly cleaning tasks (Clause 5)—for example, cleaning the bathroom and mopping the kitchen floor—as well as occasional projects, such as washing blinds. Be sure to spell out other responsibilities as well (Clause 6), such as cooking, laundry, ironing, shopping, gardening, and yard work. The best approach is to be as detailed as possible. Follow the directions for the Child Care Agreement (Form 83, above) when completing this form.

Signing Instructions

To make the Housekeeping Services Agreement valid, the employer(s) and the housekeeper must sign it. Finalizing your housekeeping services agreement is easy. Start by printing out two copies of the form. You (the employer) and the housekeeper must sign and date the form where indicated. Give one of the signed originals to the housekeeper and keep the other for your records.

Living Together

Form 87: Agreement to Keep Property Separate 124

Form 88: Agreement for a Joint Purchase 125

Form 89: Agreement to Share Property 126

Form 90: Declaration of Legal Name Change...127

contract is no more than an agreement to do (or not to do) something. It contains promises made by one person in exchange for another's actions. Marriage is a contractual relationship, even though the "terms" of the contract are rarely stated explicitly, or even necessarily known by the marrying couple. Saying "I do" commits a couple to a well-established set of state laws and rules governing, among other things, the couple's property rights should one spouse die or the couple split up. (Prenuptial agreements are a way people who plan to marry can modify the contract imposed on married people by state law.)

On the other hand, unmarried couples—gay and straight—do not automatically agree to any state-imposed contractual agreement when they begin living together. Nor does simply living together for a certain period of time entitle you to a property settlement (or inheritance) should you split up (or one of you die) as it would if you were married.

Fortunately, when it comes to financial and property concerns, unmarried couples have the right to create whatever kind of living together contract they want. Sometimes these agreements are made in anticipation of ending a relationship. But more often, the purpose is to record the couple's needs and expectations as to money and property—either at the start of the relationship or when the couple makes a major purchase.

This chapter includes some basic property-ownership agreement forms for unmarried couples. It also includes a basic name change form.

RESOURCE

Nolo's *Living Together: A Legal Guide for Unmarried Couples*, by Ralph Warner, Toni Ihara, and Frederick Hertz, and *A Legal Guide for Lesbian &*

Gay Couples, by Denis Clifford, Frederick Hertz, and Emily Doskow, cover the main legal issues affecting unmarried couples in areas of property and money, estate planning, children, house ownership, medical decisions, and separation. And if you're a same-sex couple considering marriage or registration, see *Making It Legal: A Guide to Same-Sex Marriage, Domestic Partnership & Civil Unions*, by Frederick Hertz and Emily Doskow (Nolo).

Form 87: Agreement to Keep Property Separate

Especially in the first year or two after getting together, unmarried couples usually keep all or most of their money and property separate—with the occasional exception of a joint account to pay household bills or an agreement to purchase one or more items jointly.

You may think at first that a decision to keep your property ownership separate is so simple there is no need for a written agreement. Think again. Because most states recognize oral contracts between unmarried couples, the lack of a written agreement can be an invitation for one partner to later claim the existence of an oral property-sharing agreement. This is just what commonly occurs in the so-called "palimony cases" that regularly hit the headlines.

To avoid the possibility of future misunderstandings about property ownership, use the Agreement to Keep Property Separate to confirm that each of you plans to keep your property and income separate unless you have a specific written agreement that says otherwise—for example, to purchase a sofa bed together. Form 87 keeps all of your property separate, including property you brought into the relationship as well as property you purchased or received by gift or inheritance while living together.

Here are a few things to keep in mind when you're using this form:

- Clause 2 states that you will attach a separate list of major items you own to the agreement and includes Attachments A and B for this purpose. You will want to be very specific in describing the items you list.

- Clause 4 specifies that if you register under a domestic partnership program that makes you responsible for each other's basic living expenses, you agree to only the minimal level of reciprocal financial responsibility. Without this type of disclaimer, registering as domestic partners may imply that you intend to share ownership of property—and if you are in a same-sex couple and you register as domestic partners or enter a civil union in one of the states that allows it, the law may impose property sharing on you. Of course, if you do not register as domestic partners, you can simply delete this sentence of Clause 4.

- Clause 5 provides that you will share expenses for household items and services equally. If you have a different arrangement, or want to spell out how you will split expenses on non-household items, such as insurance or car repairs, you can edit Clause 5 accordingly.

- Clause 6 refers to a joint ownership agreement that you may prepare from time to time relating to a specific item—for example, if you purchase a television or computer together. (You can use Form 88 for this purpose.)

- Clause 9 provides for mediation if a dispute arises out of this agreement. "Resolving Disputes," in the Introduction, discusses mediation and dispute resolution procedures.

Signing Instructions

You and your partner must sign this Agreement to Keep Property Separate for it to be valid. Print out two copies of the form, so you'll each have your own copy. Each person should sign and date both copies of the agreement and keep a signed document for their own records. Keep your agreement in a safe place along with other important documents, such as insurance and financial papers, lease, copies of wills, and the like.

FORM
This form contains a space for the acknowledgment of a notary public. To have a form notarized, you must go to the notary before signing it. (See the Introduction for general advice on having a form notarized.) Notarization will add a measure of legal credibility, but it is not legally required.

Form 88: Agreement for a Joint Purchase

Many couples make purchases item by item, witih the understanding that whoever makes the purchase owns the property. George buys the kitchen table and chairs, and Edna buys the lamp and stereo. If they split up, each keeps the property that person bought. In this situation, George and Edna would use the Agreement to Keep Property Separate (Form 87). Couples can also pool money for their purchases. Edna and George can jointly own everything bought during the relationship, and divide it all 50-50 if they separate. In this case, the Agreement to Share Property (Form 89) would be appropriate.

While these types of consistent approaches to property ownership may simplify things, they are not required by either law or logic. Edna and George could choose a combination of the two methods. Some items may be separately owned, some pooled 50-50, and some shared in proportion to how much money each contributed toward the purchase price or how much labor each put into upkeep.

Many unmarried couples opt for a basic keeping-things-separate approach, at least when they first get together. Despite this, however, an unmarried couple will often want to own one or more major items together, as would be the case if they pool income to buy a new bed and an expensive sound system. Clause 6 in the Agreement to Keep Property Separate (Form 87) allows you to do this.

Whatever type of property is purchased, it is important that your joint ownership agreement be written down. This is especially true if you have previously signed an agreement (such as Form 87) to keep the bulk of your property separate. Form 88 allows you to record your joint ownership agreement for a specific purchase quickly and easily. Simply fill in the details of your joint purchase, including the item or property bought, the percentage of ownership (such as 50-50 or 60-40) each of you has, and how you will deal with the property should you split up. For example, you may specify that one person automatically has the right (of first refusal) to buy out the other's share, or you may agree to do a simple coin toss or come up with your own approach depending upon the particular property.

Signing Instructions

You and your partner must sign this Agreement for a Joint Purchase for it to be valid. Print out two copies of the form, so you'll each have your own copy. Each person should sign and date both copies of the agreement and keep a signed document for their own records. Keep your agreement in a safe place along with other important documents, such as insurance and financial papers, lease, copies of wills, and the like.

CAUTION

Don't use the Agreement for a Joint Purchase if you're buying a car or house together. Check with your state's motor vehicles department for rules regarding the language that should be used to establish joint ownership of a motor vehicle. Also, houses and other real property will have their own specialized rules for ownership and taking title.

Form 89: Agreement to Share Property

Especially if you have been together several years or more and have begun to purchase property jointly (a new car or bed, for example), you may want to do what a fair number of unmarried couples do—abandon your agreement to keep property separate, and instead treat property either of you purchases as jointly owned. If this is your understanding, write it down. Use Form 89 to establish that all property acquired after a certain date—except that given to or inherited by one partner, or that which is clearly specified in writing as separate property, is to be jointly owned by both, and equally divided should you separate.

Note that Clause 3 states that you will attach a list of the property each of you owned prior to the date of your agreement, as well as a list of jointly owned property and includes Attachments A, B, and C for this purpose. You may be as detailed as you want in preparing these separate property lists, but at least include major items (valued at $100 or more).

Clause 9 provides for mediation if a dispute arises out of this agreement. The Introduction discusses mediation and dispute resolution procedures.

Signing Instructions

You and your partner must sign this Agreement to Share Property for it to be valid. Print out two copies of the form, so you'll each have your own copy. Each person should sign and date both copies of the agreement and keep a signed document for their own records. Keep your agreement in a safe place along with other important documents, such as insurance and financial papers, lease, copies of wills, and the like.

FORM

This form contains a space for the acknowledgment of a notary public. To have a form notarized, you must go to the notary before signing it. (See the Introduction for general advice on having a form notarized.) Notarization will add a measure of legal credibility, but it is not legally required.

CAUTION

Giving or receiving property for the purpose of evading creditors is illegal. A contract agreeing to keep all property separate will protect you from your partner's creditors and avoid any suggestion of impropriety.

Form 90: Declaration of Legal Name Change

Committed unmarried partners occasionally prefer to use the same last name, or a hyphenated version of both last names. But doing this means that one or both partners must change their existing name.

The best way to change your name is by court order. This is usually fairly simple—you fill out and file at the courthouse a short petition, publish legal notice of your intention to change your name in a local legal newspaper, and attend a routine court hearing. This is the foolproof way to change your name. Although it used to be more common to change one's name simply by using the new name for a period of time, it is more and more difficult to find agencies that will honor this way of changing your name, called a "usage method name change." After you change your legal name, you will need to notify the relevant agencies. That's the purpose of Form 90, the Declaration of Legal Name Change, which officially states that you have changed to a new name. Use it to change your personal records, identity cards, and documents. Getting official agencies such as the Department of Motor Vehicles and Social Security Administration to accept your name change is particularly important to getting your new name accepted. Once you follow those agencies' procedures and actually get official documents in your new name, it will be easy to switch over other accounts and documents.

CAUTION

Illegal reasons to change your name. You cannot change your name to defraud creditors, for any illegal purpose, to benefit economically by the use of another person's name, or to invade someone's privacy (don't name yourself Madonna or George Bush). Otherwise, you can change your name for any reason and assume any name you wish.

RESOURCE

If you live in California, you can get all the forms and instructions you need to do your own legal name change in *How to Change Your Name in California*, by Lisa Sedano and Emily Doskow (Nolo).

Signing Instructions

You must sign this Declaration of Legal Name Change form for it to be valid. Print out enough copies for every agency and organization you wish to notify of your name change. Keep a signed copy for your own records.

Settling Legal Disputes

Form 91: Demand Letter...130

Form 92: Online Auction Buyer Demand Letter 131

Form 93: Request for Refund or Repair of Goods Under Warranty 132

Form 94: Accident Claim Worksheet...134

Forms 95–100: Releases...134

Form 95: General Release 136

Form 96: General Mutual Release...137

Form 97: Release for Damage to Real Estate...137

Form 98: Release for Property Damage in Auto Accident 137

Form 99: Release for Personal Injury 137

Form 100: Mutual Release of Contract Claims...138

Becoming involved in any legal dispute can be harrowing. Many people lose time, money, and sleep trying to right their wrongs, even informally. Then, take it to the next step—the prospect of facing an unpredictable court trial can scare even the bravest person. That's why it's so easy to appreciate the curse that says, "May you have a lawsuit in which you know you are right."

Fortunately, most legal disputes are resolved long before anyone sees the inside of a courtroom—one person demands a settlement, the other person counters, and the negotiations continue from there. If settlement still proves elusive, it's common to turn for assistance to a mediator who will attempt to help the parties come to an agreement. ("Resolving Disputes," in the Introduction, discusses mediation and other means of resolving disputes.)

This chapter presents useful tools you can use to try and resolve your dispute. And if you do settle, it also provides several releases that you or the other party should sign so neither of you risks being hauled into court after you write or receive the check you believe settles the matter.

RESOURCE

Additional information and sample forms for settling disputes can be found in *Everybody's Guide to Small Claims Court*, by Ralph Warner, and *Mediate, Don't Litigate*, by Peter Lovenheim and Lisa Guerin (available only as an eBook at www.nolo.com). Sample forms for settling a claim with an insurance company can be found in *How to Win Your Personal Injury Claim*, by Joseph Matthews. For a detailed discussion of representing yourself in court, see *Represent Yourself in Court*, by Paul Bergman and Sarah Berman-Barrett. All titles are published by Nolo.

Form 91: Demand Letter

Assuming your dispute has escalated to the point where you and the other party can no longer civilly discuss a compromise, your next step in trying to resolve it is to send a demand letter clearly stating what you want. That's the purpose of Form 91. Studies show that in as many as one-third of all disputes, your demand letter will serve as a catalyst to arriving at a settlement. It is fair to ask why demand letters work so frequently to resolve disputes that couldn't simply be talked out. The answer seems to be that a written document often serves as a wake-up call that convinces the other party you really are serious about going to court if you can't settle the matter. Also, your demand letter gives you a chance to organize the facts of your case. This means if you wind up in mediation, arbitration, or court (such as small claims court), you will have already done much of your preparation.

When writing your demand letter, here are some suggestions:

• Be polite. Avoid personally attacking your adversary.

• Concisely review the main facts of the dispute—including who, what, where, and when. (See "How to Word a Demand," below.) Even though your adversary knows this information, a judge, mediator, or other third party may eventually see your letter.

• Ask for exactly what you want—the return of property, a specific amount of money, or whatever.

• Conclude by stating that if the problem isn't resolved within a set period of time (seven to ten days is often good), you will take further action, such as filing a court case.

The demand letter included here indicates that you are willing to try mediation. Mediation, a nonadversarial process involving a neutral person (a mediator) is usually a great way for people to resolve differences. If you are not willing to try mediation (that is, you plan to sue if your demands aren't met), delete the mediation language in the demand letter.

How to Word a Demand

When writing a demand letter, describe in your own words exactly what happened. Specify dates, names of people with whom you dealt, and the damages you have suffered. Here's an example:

On September 21, 20xx, I took my car to your garage for service. Shortly after I picked it up the next day, the engine caught fire because of your failure to connect the fuel line to the fuel injector properly. Fortunately, I was able to douse the fire without injury. As a direct result of the engine fire, I paid ABC Garage $1,281 for necessary repair work. I enclose a copy of the invoice. Also, I was without the use of my car for three days and had to rent a car to get to work. I enclose a copy of an invoice showing the rental cost of $145. In total, I was out $1,426.

Signing Instructions

Sign the Demand Letter and send it certified mail (return receipt requested) to the person with whom you're having a dispute. Keep a copy of the letter. You may need it later if you end up filing a lawsuit.

Form 92: Online Auction Buyer Demand Letter

Online auctions, such as those held on eBay, have become increasingly popular. Unfortunately, not everyone who buys goods via an online auction has a satisfactory experience. If you have a dispute with an online auction seller, use this demand letter to alert the seller of your complaint and to establish your claim. (For more on demand letter strategies, see Form 91 above.)

This demand letter gives you the option of proposing to the buyer that the two of you use an online dispute resolution service to resolve your claim. Make sure to look at the websites (suggested sites are listed on Form 92) for these dispute resolution companies first to understand how they work before proposing that option to the buyer.

Online Auctions: Think Before You Bid

Are you a novice buyer, unfamiliar with how auction sites work? If so, review the auction site's rules and find out what the company does if a problem occurs. Also, compare the price of the item elsewhere—not every item for sale at an online auction is a bargain.

Most important, learn as much as you can about the seller. Use common sense. Possible danger signs are if the seller:

- has a history of negative feedback
- is using a post office box
- wants payment in cash
- is outside the U.S.
- wants your Social Security or driver's license number, or
- uses a free email account—that is, a service such as Yahoo! or Hotmail that doesn't require a credit card to obtain an account.

For more advice on how to protect yourself, check out the Internet Fraud Watch's online auction page at www.fraud.org/tips/internet/onlineauctions.htm.

Signing Instructions

If you have the seller's physical address, sign the Online Auction Buyer Demand Letter and send it via certified mail, return receipt requested. If not, send it by email. Keep a copy of the letter. You may need it later if you wind up filing a lawsuit.

Form 93: Request for Refund or Repair of Goods Under Warranty

Use this form to request compensation when an item you purchased, such as a VCR or bicycle, is defective. Most new products you buy (and even some used ones) come with a warranty that offers protection if the product fails during the warranty period. Here are the basic rules regarding warranties:

- If a product comes with a written warranty from either the seller or the manufacturer, you have the right to rely on it.

- If a seller makes a statement describing a product's feature—for example, "This sleeping bag will keep you warm at 25 degrees below zero"—and you make your purchase because of the statement, then the statement is an express warranty that you have a right to rely on.

- For most purchases, you automatically have an implied warranty of merchantability, meaning that the item will work for its intended use—for example, a lawnmower will cut grass. If the item doesn't work, you should be able to return it for a refund or replacement.

If a warranty is breached—for example, a TV set with a one-year warranty breaks after two weeks' time—ask the seller for redress. Simply call or visit the store, explain the problem,

and ask for a refund or replacement of the defective TV set. If the seller refuses, use this form to notify the seller and manufacturer of your demand for them to make good under the warranty. Give them a reasonable chance—such as 30 days—to make necessary repairs, replace the defective product, or refund the purchase price. Most reputable sellers and manufacturers will. Form 93 states that you may take further action, such as filing a court action, if your request is unmet.

> **TIP**
>
> **If you are using this form to request warranty coverage, make sure the product warranty covers your situation.** Read the warranty to see how long it lasts; whom you contact for warranty service (seller or manufacturer); your options if the product fails (refund, replacement, or repair); what parts and problems are covered (some warranties cover replacement of parts but not labor, or cover only problems due to faulty material or workmanship); and any conditions (such as registration) or limitations that may apply.

Here's how to prepare a Request for Refund or Repair of Goods form:

Start by filling in the name(s) and address(es) of the seller or manufacturer (depending upon the particular warranty and your complaint). If you have a written manufacturer's warranty, check it for the appropriate address to send requests for warranty coverage; this may be the seller/dealer or the manufacturer. If you are not sure, ask the seller from whom you purchased the item. This may be a retail store, catalog distributor, or website. In many cases, you will need to mail or deliver the product along with your request for warranty coverage to either the seller/dealer or the manufacturer.

If you do not have a written manufacturer's warranty and the dispute is with the seller, send this form to the seller. It shouldn't be too hard for you to determine the name and address of the seller, assuming you made an in-person or catalog purchase. For online purchases, you may have to search the seller's website to locate an address. If you can't find this on the site, look for a phone number to call for the address. If all else fails, ask your local reference librarian for suggestions on how to get the seller's address.

Fill in the item name or description. If possible, include the model number—for example, Tasty Toaster Model 9333.

Next, fill in the purchase price, date, and place of purchase.

Describe the problem (reason you are demanding redress) and why you are dissatisfied with your purchase. Provide as much detail as possible, including what your written warranty (if any) says; what you were told by whom when you made the purchase; how you have used the product; what has gone wrong; and what efforts you have made to obtain a new item or refund. For example, if you called the seller, provide the date and details of the phone conversation. If you have already sent the seller an informal note about the problem, mention that and attach a copy of the note to this form. If you are enclosing anything, such as a copy of the purchase receipt as proof of purchase or a copy of the written warranty, be sure to say so in this section of the form. See "How to Complain About a Defective Product."

Indicate whether or not the item is enclosed. Whether you are seeking redress by mail or in person, you may need to return the item, such as a broken toaster or punctured tires. This will not always be feasible—for example, in the case of a shattered mirror.

How to Complain About a Defective Product

Here are a couple of examples of how to explain your dissatisfaction with a product you've purchased and why you're seeking redress:

Complaint about manufacturer's warranty. *On May 21, 20xx, I purchased a Tasty Toaster (Model 9333) from the Toaster Store, 195 Main Street, Columbus, Ohio. This toaster came with a one-year warranty (copy enclosed). Last week, the toaster coils overheated and the toaster simply does not work. I have owned the toaster only four months, used it only occasionally, and have not subjected it to any extraordinary usage.*

Complaint about store's warranty. *On April 16, 20xx, I purchased an UpHill Bicycle (model number 12345ht) from CycLeader, 3300 Sharper Avenue, Denver, Colorado. In the presence of my friend, Randy Jacobs, I explained to the store clerk, "Mark," that I planned to use the bicycle for off-road mountain cycling throughout Colorado. The clerk assured me that the tires on this particular UpHill bicycle could "handle any surface." Just last week, less than a month after I purchased the bike, both tires punctured while I was cycling on a much-used mountain bike trail near Greeley. When I asked for a partial refund so as to purchase new tires, the store manager claimed that no one named Mark currently works at CycLeader and claimed that this model UpHill bicycle would never have been sold for off-road use.*

Specify what type of compensation you want. Read your warranty (if any) to find out what kind of redress may be available and to make sure that the warranty covers your situation. Some manufacturer warranties promise only to repair or replace a defective item; others will give you the additional choice of seeking a full or partial refund of your purchase price. If you don't care, or don't have a written warranty, ask for either a refund or a replacement item.

Indicate when you want to receive the requested compensation. We suggest 30 days, after which you will take further action such as filing a lawsuit.

Signing Instructions

Sign the Request for Refund or Repair of Goods form and include any relevant material, such as a copy of the written warranty (often part of the owner's manual that came with the item from the manufacturer), the advertisement that you relied on when making your purchase, your receipt, previous correspondence with the seller, or the item itself. If you are addressing this form to the manufacturer, send a copy to the seller, too. You may also want to send a copy of this letter to a state or local consumer agency or the Better Business Bureau. See "How to Complain to Government Agencies," at the end of Form 101 in Chapter 15.

Keep a copy of your form and attached materials for your records. You may need this if you end up filing a small claims court case.

Form 94: Accident Claim Worksheet

Many types of legal disputes involve claims against a person, business, or insurance company arising out of an accident where you were injured or your property was damaged or both. This includes both car accidents and "slip and falls." Use Form 94, the Accident Claim Worksheet, to keep track of the names, addresses, and phone numbers of parties and witnesses involved, along with communications with them, dates of relevant events and conversations, details from insurance companies, and other information you will need to process an accident claim. It is for your personal reference and is not intended to become part of your claim.

CAUTION

Get witness statements in writing as soon as possible. Don't count on an eyewitness's memory for too long, especially given the fact that the witness is likely to be contacted by the other party. Ask the witness to make and sign a note about what happened as soon after the accident as possible.

Signing Instructions

There are no signing instructions for the Accident Claim Worksheet. Simply fill it in for use in preparing a claim after an accident.

CROSS-REFERENCE

Use Form 102, Notice of Insurance Claim, to notify the appropriate insurance company of the accident.

Forms 95–100: Releases

A common means of settling minor disputes (such as an argument about an unpaid loan, a minor fender bender, or a golf ball crashing through a window) is for one party to pay the other a sum of money in exchange for giving up any legal claim related to the incident. Another way to settle a claim is for the person in the wrong to do something of benefit for the other. For example, if your neighbor's dog destroys your garden, you might agree to take no further action if your neighbor agrees to replace your most valuable plants and build a fence.

In either situation, you'll want to write out your agreement in the form of a contract, commonly called a release. A release usually consists of no more than one party saying, "I'll pay a certain amount or do a certain thing," and the other party saying that, "In exchange, I'll forever give up my legal claim against you."

What Makes a Release Legally Enforceable?

To be legally enforceable, a release must satisfy two contract law requirements:

- **The release must be voluntary.** Each side must enter into the agreement voluntarily. If a party was coerced into signing an agreement because of the other's threats or intimidation, a court may consider it involuntary and therefore unenforceable. Courts are quite leery about tossing out a release for this reason, however. For example, in a dispute involving the repair of a bicycle, one party telling the other "I'll sue for $100,000 tomorrow if you don't agree to this release" is not the kind of threat that will make a release unenforceable. The threat or coercion must be both significant and within the realm of possibility.

- **The agreement must be arrived at fairly.** Judges are usually unwilling to enforce any agreement that is the product of deceit or the result of one side taking undue advantage of the other. For example, if a person is persuaded to sign a release two hours after an accident that left her groggy, or doesn't understand the meaning of the document or the rights being waived because of limited English, a court will likely not uphold it.

Releases are powerful documents. If you sign one forever giving up a legal claim in exchange for $500, and learn six months later that the extent of what you lost is much greater than you realized when you signed the release, you are out of luck unless a court declares the release unenforceable for one of the above reasons.

Questions to Ask Before Signing a Release

In most situations where both sides understand the dispute and the consequences of various settlement options, you can confidently sign a release, knowing that the dispute will be finally put to rest. But it is always wise for you and the other party to answer the following questions before signing on the dotted line:

- Do you both understand the issues that underlie the dispute?
- Do you both understand what the release accomplishes?

If the answer to these questions is yes, it's wise to ask another three additional questions, but this time just of yourself:

- Do I understand the alternative to a settlement—the legal result I am likely to obtain (and the time and dollars I am likely to spend to get it) if I go to court rather than accepting the release and settling the matter?
- Have I discussed my decision to sign the release with someone who has good business sense and is not emotionally involved with the issue or parties?
- If a lot of money is involved, have I consulted an attorney with practical experience in this field?

If big bucks are at stake and the answer to either of the last three questions is "no," or even a waffling "maybe," do the necessary homework before agreeing to release the other party.

This chapter contains several release forms, including a General Release, Form 95 (to settle a dispute when only one party is alleged to have been injured or suffered damages), and a General Mutual Release, Form 96 (to settle a dispute when both parties claim the other is at fault and that each has suffered injury or damage). We also include specific releases for damage to real estate (Form 97), property damage in an automobile accident (Form 98), personal injury (Form 99), and contract claims (Form 100). Review them all to see which one is most appropriate to your situation.

Note on Legal Terminology

The person with the claim who releases the other is called the "releasor." The "releasee" is the person responsible for the injury or the claim who agrees to pay money or promises to do something of value (or not to do anything) in exchange for the release. This is called "paying consideration." To be binding, all contracts, including releases, require an exchange of consideration. The exchange of consideration (such as payment of a specific sum of money) should ideally occur before the release is signed. If this is not possible or feasible, the release should specify when the payment or consideration will be provided.

Making the Release Binding on Others

If one of the parties dies, you want the release to be binding on that person's heirs. Our release forms include language about "successors, assigns, and heirs." In addition, in all community property states (and in some non-community property states), one spouse is generally liable for the debts of the other spouse, and is entitled to recover monies owed to the other—even if the first spouse had nothing to do with the event leading up to the liability. For this reason, our release forms are binding on spouses and require the spouse's

signature that signifies consent to the deal. The discussion of promissory notes in Chapter 5 explains the basics of the community property system.

Signing Instructions for Release Forms

You must sign the Release for it to be valid. Print out two copies of the form. All parties to the release, including spouses (if any) should sign and date both copies of the document in the appropriate spaces. Print the name(s) of the spouse(s) in the blank line provided; if one or both of the parties is not married, write "N/A" on the blank line. Each party should keep one copy of the release, signed by all parties.

Form 95: General Release

A General Release is appropriate for settling personal disputes over a contract, debt, or minor personal injury when only one party is alleged to have been injured or suffered damage. (This form is not appropriate, however, if both parties claim the other is at fault and that each has suffered damage or injury as a result. This requires a mutual release, in which case you would use Form 96.)

TIP

You can't release what you don't own. If you've assigned your rights to someone else, that person becomes the releasor, not you. Paragraph 4 of the General Release form represents your promise that you own the right that is the subject of the release.

Form 96: General Mutual Release

Form 96 is appropriate for settling disputes—for example, over a debt or minor personal injury—where both parties say the other is at fault and each claims damage or injury as a result. Here the main point is often to trade legal releases—in which case the value or consideration is each person's mutual relinquishment of the legal rights involved in the dispute (Clause 3 of this form). It is not unusual, however, for the person who has suffered the more serious loss (or who was less at fault) to receive additional consideration (Clause 4 of this form). This may be a cash payment or other benefit—for example, free use of a spa facility owned by one of the parties.

If the dispute concerns an oral or written contract, use Form 100, Mutual Release of Contract Claims.

Form 97: Release for Damage to Real Estate

Form 97 is appropriate for settling disputes between landowners that arise when one owner's property is damaged by another's action or inaction. Common examples include one person's tree overhanging another's yard or pool, or an uphill neighbor digging a ditch that diverts rain runoff onto a downhill neighbor's property. And, of course, walls, fences, view-blocking trees, and noise can all lead to serious disagreements between neighbors.

RESOURCE

Before you settle a neighbor dispute, it will help if you understand the legal issues—for example, if a tree grows on the border, which neighbor owns it? For answers to this and similar questions, see *Neighbor Law: Fences, Trees, Boundaries & Noise*, by Cora Jordan and Emily Doskow (Nolo).

Form 98: Release for Property Damage in Auto Accident

Use Form 98 to settle claims over minor property damage from an auto accident. Do not use it if personal injuries are involved. In that case, use Form 99, Release for Personal Injury.

Form 99: Release for Personal Injury

Use Form 99 when one party has suffered a relatively minor personal injury because of another's actions.

CAUTION

Don't sign a release involving personal injuries unless the parties are sure that the scope of the injury is fully known. For example, be sure that an injury has completely healed and your doctor has examined you, clearly established the scope of your injury, and unequivocally stated that you have fully recovered and that there will be no further problem. It is almost never wise to sign very soon after an injury—you never know what problems may develop later.

Here are a few examples of language describing an injury for use in Clause 2:

- Cat scratches sustained on both arms after Releasor was attacked by Releasee's cat, Roscoe.
- Cuts Releasor sustained from a shattered window when a baseball hit by Releasee's son broke a window in Releasor's house.

RESOURCE

For detailed advice on filing a personal injury claim, see *How to Win Your Personal Injury Claim*, by Joseph Matthews (Nolo).

Form 100: Mutual Release of Contract Claims

This final release can be used to settle a disagreement that arises from the breach of a written or oral contract. Unlike the General Release (Form 95) or the General Mutual Release (Form 96), this release is useful only for dealing with contract disputes.

What If One of the Parties to a Release Doesn't Follow Through?

If either of the people signing the release doesn't pay the money or do the promised deed, the other has a choice. The wronged party can take the appropriate legal steps concerning the original dispute as though no release had been signed. Or, either person could go to court and ask a judge to enforce the release (after all, it's a contract). A judge will consider whether the release was voluntary and whether the agreement was arrived at fairly.

You can use small claims court to enforce the release if the amount is within the jurisdictional limits of the court. This is a good option, especially if the only thing involved is money.

Miscellaneous Forms for Personal Use

Form 101: Complaint Letter 140

Form 102: Notice of Insurance Claim 141

Form 103: Notice to Cancel Certain Contracts 142

Form 104: Cancel Membership or Subscription Notice 143

Form 105: Request to Begin Special Education Process 144

Form 106: Identity Theft Worksheet 145

The forms in this chapter are designed to help with various consumer issues, including writing a complaint letter to a government agency, asking your school to evaluate your child's eligibility for special education services, and dealing with identity theft.

Form 101: Complaint Letter

Every state and the federal government prohibit unfair or deceptive trade acts or practices. This means that a seller can't deceive, abuse, mislead, defraud, or otherwise cheat you. If you think you've been cheated by someone selling a service or product, and you have been unable to resolve the problem directly, you should let the appropriate federal, state, and local government offices know. Although law enforcement in the area of consumer fraud is not uniformly great, many hardworking investigators do their jobs well. The more agencies you notify, the more likely it is that someone will take notice of your complaint and act on it—especially if more than one consumer has registered a complaint about the same company.

Your first step is to draft a complaint letter, using this form. Be as detailed as possible regarding your complaint, including the name and title of the person you dealt with, the dates and details of the service or product problem, and any follow-up communication. Keep your language neutral and state the facts of the situation. See "How to Word a Complaint," below, for sample language. To back up your complaint, attach copies (never the originals) of all purchase receipts, contracts, warranties, advertisements, and other written documents relating to your complaint.

Finally, your letter will be more persuasive if you suggest a solution, such as a refund, or at least request a reply from the person investigating your complaint.

How to Word a Complaint

Here's an example of language to include in a complaint letter:

I wish to complain about a business called Celebrity Cards located in your state. About three months ago, I received a package of cards from this company, unsolicited. I received a second package two months ago. Last month I received a bill from the company for $50 plus shipping and handling. I never ordered these cards and I wrote to the company to say so. (A copy of my letter is attached.) I also stated that I considered the unsolicited items sent to my home to be a gift. Just this week, I received a second bill and a threat to send this debt to a collection agency and report it to a credit bureau.

Compile a list of agencies and their addresses where you will send your complaint letter. Start by checking www.usa.gov for information about federal, state, and local agencies. This will help you identify the appropriate federal agency to receive your complaint, depending on the nature of your problem. For example, a complaint about a mail order company or an online auction would go to the Federal Trade Commission (www.ftc.gov), which handles fraudulent, deceptive, and unfair business practices. See "How to Complain to Government Agencies," below, for a list of resources.

Be sure to send a copy of your letter to the company you are complaining about.

How to Complain to Government Agencies

Depending on the problem, you can send a copy of your complaint letter to one or more of the following agencies. You can also contact your local district attorney's consumer fraud division regarding local consumer protection services available, or the National Fraud Information Center at www.fraud.org or by phone at 800-876-7060.

- **State Attorneys General.** You can find contact information for your state Attorney General's office from the National Association of Attorneys General at www.naag.org.

- **State Consumer Protection Office.** Your state consumer protection office can also provide advice, including the name of the appropriate licensing board that handles consumer complaints (for example, if your complaint concerns a licensed professional such as a contractor or lawyer).

- **Federal Trade Commission.** Division of Enforcement, 600 Pennsylvania Avenue, NW, Washington, DC 20580; 877-382-4357; www.ftc.gov

- **Federal Communications Commission.** 445 12th Street, SW, Washington, DC 20554; 888-225-5322 (voice); 888-835-5322 (TTY); www.fcc.gov

Signing Instructions

There are no specific signing instructions for this Complaint Letter. Simply sign the form and send it to the appropriate government agencies with a copy to the company you're complaining about. Be sure to include copies of any relevant material such as previous correspondence with the seller. Keep a copy of your complaint letter and attached materials for your records. You may need this if you end up filing a small claims court case or taking other legal action.

CROSS-REFERENCE
If your complaint involves a defective product under warranty, use Form 93, Request for Refund or Repair of Goods Under Warranty.

Form 102: Notice of Insurance Claim

If you're planning to make a claim against an insurance company—because you were in a car accident, suffered a slip and fall or animal bite, or something similar—you can use Form 102 to notify the appropriate company or companies. Depending on the circumstances, send your letter to the insurance company of the individual or business you believe was at fault. If you were in a car accident, send your insurance claim notice to the insurance company of the owner and the driver of the vehicle involved in the accident. If you were in a slip-and-fall, such as at a store, send your notice to the insurance company of the owner of the building where the accident occurred and of the owner of the store where you had the slip and fall. You will need to get the name and address of the insurance company from the appropriate party—for example, the person driving the car involved in the accident.

If you are covered by your own auto, homeowner's, business, or other policy, be sure to notify your own insurer. You can begin by contacting your agent or broker by phone, but it's a good idea to mail or fax in a written claim as well, keeping a copy for yourself.

Your insurance claim notice (Form 102) should be a simple letter giving only basic information and asking for a written response.

It should not discuss fault, responsibility, or the details of your injuries. Make sure your notice includes the following:

- Your name, address, and phone number.
- The date, approximate time of day, and general location of the accident or incident.
- The type of accident (such as motor vehicle or animal bite) and an indication of whether you were injured or suffered property damage in the accident.
- If a vehicle was involved: details on the driver's car (such as make, model, and license plate number) and driver's license number.

If you completed the Accident Claim Worksheet (Form 94), you should already have this information at hand.

Form 102 includes a request that the insurance company confirm by return letter whom it represents, liability coverage of the insured, and whether the company is aware of anyone else who might be responsible for the accident. If the insurance company does not feel you provided sufficient information, it may send you its own form to complete.

Signing Instructions

There are no specific signing instructions for the Notice of Insurance Claim form. Simply sign the form and send it to the other party's company with a copy to your own insurance company. Keep a copy of your insurance claim notice for your records. You may need this if you end up filing a small claims court case or taking other legal action.

RESOURCE

For more about personal injury claims, see *How to Win Your Personal Injury Claim*, by Joseph Matthews (Nolo).

Form 103: Notice to Cancel Certain Contracts

Under the Federal Trade Commission (FTC) "cooling-off rule," consumers have the right to cancel certain types of consumer contracts within three days of signing. This right-to-cancel law applies to door-to-door sales contracts for more than $25 and contracts for more than $25 made anywhere other than the seller's normal place of business—for instance, at a sales presentation at a friend's house, hotel or restaurant, outdoor exhibit, computer show, or trade show. (Real estate, insurance, public car auctions, and craft fairs are exempted from coverage.)

The cooling-off rule applies only to goods or services primarily intended for personal, family, or household purposes. It does not apply to sales made as part of a request for a seller to do home repairs or maintenance (but purchases made beyond the maintenance or repair request are covered).

To take advantage of this right to cancel, you have until midnight of the third business day following the day you signed the contract to cancel the contract either in person or by mail. If you were not given notice of this right and a cancellation form when you signed the contract, simply use Form 103.

After canceling, the seller must refund your money within ten days. Then, the seller must either pick up the items purchased or reimburse you within 20 days for your expense of mailing the goods back to the seller (many states give the seller 40 days). If the seller doesn't come for the goods or make an arrangement for you to mail them back, you can keep them.

RESOURCE

For more information on the federal cooling-off rule, see www.ftc.gov or call 877-FTC-HELP.

Signing Instructions

To cancel a contract under the FTC cooling-off rule, sign and date one copy of the Notice to Cancel Certain Contracts. Mail it to the seller or the address given for cancellation (if different from the place of purchase). Keep a copy of the notice for your own file. Be sure your envelope is postmarked before midnight of the third business day after the contract date. (Saturday is considered a business day, while Sundays and federal holidays are not.) It is a good idea to send this form by certified mail so you can get a return receipt. You may need this later as proof that you properly canceled the contract.

Form 104: Cancel Membership or Subscription Notice

Use Form 104 to provide written confirmation that you wish to cancel membership in a club or organization, or that you wish to cancel your subscription to a magazine, newspaper, or other periodical.

Look in the front of the publication for the address of the department that handles subscriptions. Check mailings from membership groups for similar information. If there is not a separate membership or subscription department, send your Cancel Membership or Subscription Notice to the main address.

Fill in the requested information, specifically your name, address, and identifying information as listed on mailing labels on the magazine or on printed materials you receive from the membership organization. If there is a business name or second name listed on the subscription or membership materials, fill in both names.

State the date you want to cancel the particular subscription or membership, such as "effective May 1, 20xx." If you want, you may specify the reason you are canceling a magazine subscription or other periodical, or no longer want to receive mailings from a membership organization. You may also request a refund for the remainder of the subscription or membership period if you think it is appropriate.

EXAMPLE 1:

I want to cancel my subscription to *Beef Roundup* because I have recently become a vegetarian.

EXAMPLE: 2

I want to cancel my subscription to *Beef Roundup* because I am offended by your recent series on the lifestyles of vegetarians. Please refund the value of my remaining issues.

Signing Instructions

Sign the Cancel Membership or Subscription Notice in the space provided. Make a copy of the form and mail the original to the publisher or organization whose periodical or membership you wish to cancel. If applicable, attach a copy of the mailing label or payment invoice to your notice. Keep a copy of the form for your records.

Form 105: Request to Begin Special Education Process

This form can be used by parents who believe their child is in need of special help from their school district. A federal law—the Individuals with Disabilities Education Act (IDEA)—gives parents and guardians the right to request evaluations (assessments) of their children for physical or psychological disabilities that may affect their ability to learn. Upon your request, the school must present you with an assessment plan, listing all testing to be done on your child. Assessments usually include objective tests of your child's abilities in all areas of suspected disability (for example, reading, memory, motor skills, or vision). In addition to formal tests, assessments often include subjective information relating to your child's educational status, such as comments by teachers, the school psychologist, or a classroom aide.

The IDEA requires the school to provide special services (an Individualized Education Program, or IEP) to a child found to have disabilities. "Special education" is the broad term used to describe the educational system for children who have disabilities, such as mental retardation; autism; specific learning disabilities; hearing, speech, language, orthopedic or visual impairment; or serious emotional disturbance.

Your child's eligibility for special education will depend on the results of the assessment. This letter starts the formal process by requesting an initial assessment of your child's eligibility for special education, an assessment plan, and general information on the IEP process.

This letter also asks the school district to provide a copy of your child's school file, including all tests, report cards, disciplinary records, and teacher notes about your child, so you can learn everything they already know about your child at school. This information is crucial as you assess your child's difficulties and the need for special education services. You have a legal right to inspect and review any educational record relating to your child. If your child has not yet been found eligible for services under the IDEA, you have the right to a copy of the school's file under the Family Educational Rights and Privacy Act (FERPA) (20 U.S.C. § 1232[g]). State laws also may give you a right to your child's file. Rules vary in different states, but you should be entitled to obtain the file without unnecessary delay. You may be charged for the copies as long as the fee "does not effectively prevent you from exercising your right to inspect and review the records" (34 C.F.R. § 300.617).

Once you send this letter, the school district is required by federal law to inform you of the regulations, guidelines, and procedures that apply to special education services and to begin the process of evaluation (assessment).

Send this Request to Begin Special Education Process to the special administrator at your child's school. Ask your child's teacher or the school principal for this person's name and address. Be sure to include a brief summary of your child's difficulties at school, such as developmental delays in language or reading problems, that you have noticed or have been told about by teachers, doctors, friends, or anyone who has spent time with your child.

RESOURCE

For a comprehensive and thorough guide to special education laws and services, see *The Complete IEP Guide,* by Lawrence Siegel (Nolo). If you know or suspect that your child has a learning disability, check out *Nolo's IEP Guide: Learning Disabilities,* also by Lawrence Siegel (Nolo).

Signing Instructions

There are no specific signing instructions for the Request to Begin Special Education Process. Simply sign the form and keep a copy for your records.

Form 106: Identity Theft Worksheet

Identity theft has become an epidemic, affecting millions of Americans. Despite the mounting number of victims of identity theft, many people don't know what to do if it happens to them. If you believe that you are a victim of identity theft or fear that you may soon become one—for example, if you lost your wallet or gave personal information to a stranger—take these simple steps immediately. The order in which you take these steps will depend on your situation. For instance, if someone stole your wallet, you would likely want to start by contacting the relevant authorities and canceling all the accounts that are tied to the stolen cards.

Describing Your Child's Special Needs

It is very common for parents to recognize that their child has problems with school and simply not know what to do about them. It may be that your child's difficulties can be isolated and addressed very specifically, or the problems may be more wide-ranging. Following are some examples of difficulties your child may be experiencing in school that you should mention in your letter to the special education administrator. Be as specific as possible, but do not worry about listing everything. Don't get bogged down in things such as special classes or eligibility. Just write down what you have observed about your child's behavior, focusing on specific patterns. Keep in mind that this is just the beginning of the process. Trained professionals and assessments will help determine whether your intuition is correct.

- academic problems in reading, spelling, or math
- delays in developmental areas, such as language or fine motor skills
- difficulties processing or retaining information, such as understanding simple instructions or problems with short- or long-term memory
- social or emotional problems
- trouble sleeping, eating, or getting along with family
- sustained difficulties in paying attention or staying focused
- inappropriate or hyperactive behavior, or
- delays in physical milestones, or other physiological difficulties, such as hearing loss, sight problems, difficulties with mobility, or handwriting problems.

Form 106 will help you keep track of what you've done, whom you've spoken to, and what else you'll need to do to protect your personal information.

Regardless of your situation, be sure to follow every step.

1. **Start a log.** Keep notes of your conversations and correspondence with authorities and financial institutions, including dates, names, and phone numbers. Also keep track of all time spent and expenses you incur; you can deduct theft-related expenses on your income tax return if you itemize deductions, and you may be able to seek compensation if you ever sue the thief.

2. **Check your homeowners' insurance policy.** Many now include coverage for certain administrative costs of dealing with identity theft, including attorney fees. Give your carrier a call to find out how they can help and what you'll need to keep track of. Unfortunately, the insurance typically won't cover any amounts that were actually stolen.

3. **Contact the credit bureaus to place a fraud alert.** Call one of the three major credit bureaus (Equifax, Experian, or TransUnion), and ask to have a free credit report sent to you, and to have your account flagged with a fraud alert. Activating a fraud alert removes you from all preapproved credit and insurance offers for two years, and requests creditors to contact you before opening any new accounts or making any changes to your existing accounts. When activating a fraud alert, whichever one of three main credit bureaus you contact is required to notify the other two (but follow up to make sure this happens). If you make additional calls to the credit bureaus on other subjects, be sure to contact all three, as they are not required to communicate

with each other after your initial fraud-alert call. Here are the numbers to call:

Equifax: 800-525-6285

Experian: 888-397-3742

TransUnion: 800-680-7289

4. **Review your credit reports.** After you receive your credit reports from the three credit bureaus, review them thoroughly. Make sure that all your personal information, including name, address, and Social Security number, is correct and that there are no fraudulent accounts or inquiries. Immediately report any suspicious information or activity to the credit bureau that issued the credit report. And in two to three months, order another report to ensure that no new fraudulent activity has occurred. Depending on where you live, a nominal fee may apply when you order a follow-up credit report.

5. **Close any accounts that have been accessed fraudulently:** Contact all creditors, including banks, credit card companies, and other service providers, with whom there has been fraudulent activity. Close all accounts the thief opened or used fraudulently. Request that creditors notate closed accounts as "account closed at consumer's request," because a mark of "card lost or stolen" can reflect poorly on your credit report.

> **TIP**
> **If your ATM or debit card was stolen, do not use your old PIN for your new card.** Choose a password that is obscure but that you will remember. Do not use common numbers such as your birth date.

If a thief stole checks or opened bank accounts in your name, contact one of the major check verification companies to report the fraudulent activity and to stop payment on stolen checks. For a complete listing of check verification companies, visit www.fightidentitytheft.com. When disputing new unauthorized accounts, use the Identity Theft Affidavit available at the Federal Trade Commission website, www.ftc.gov.

6. **Call the police.** File a report of the crime with your local police department. Provide as much evidence as you can, and ask the officer to list all fraudulently accessed accounts on the police report. Be sure to ask for a copy of the police report, because creditors will probably ask to see it. Remember to log the phone numbers and names of all the law enforcement agents with whom you speak; creditors may want this information. It's also recommended that you file a police report in the community where the crime occurred.

7. **Report the fraud to the Federal Trade Commission (FTC).** When you file a claim with the FTC, your information will be entered into an electronic database used to prevent future identity thefts. The FTC also uses identity theft claims to assist law enforcement agencies in finding and arresting identity thieves.

RESOURCE

To file a claim with the FTC, visit www.ftccomplaintassistant.gov or call the FTC's Identity Theft Hotline at 877-438-4338.

Further Steps

Depending on the severity of your identity theft case, there are several other actions you may wish to pursue.

- **Contact the local postal inspector.** If you believe that someone has changed your address through the post office or has committed mail fraud, call the U.S. Postal Service at 800-275-8777 or visit www.usps.gov/websites/depart/inspect to obtain the phone number for your local postal inspector. If you discover that mail in your name is being sent to an address other than your own, ask the local postmaster to forward all mail in your name to your own address.

- **Contact the Social Security Administration (SSA).** If you believe that your Social Security number has been used to fraudulently obtain welfare or Social Security benefits, visit www.socialsecurity.gov/oig/guidelin.htm or call the SSA Fraud Hotline at 800-269-0271.

- **Deal with debt collectors.** While you are handling your identity theft case, debt collectors may ask you to pay outstanding bills from fraudulently activated credit accounts. Inform the debt collector by phone and in writing that you are a victim of identity theft and that you are not responsible for the unpaid bill. In your letter, be sure to include copies of documents, such as a police report, that demonstrate that you are the victim of identity theft. With some exceptions, the company is legally prohibited from contacting you once they receive your letter. Request all pertinent information (e.g., name, phone number, address, account number) relating to both the debt collector and the referring credit issuer, and ask whether they want you to fill out the FTC's fraud affidavit form (available at www.ftc.gov/bcp/conline/pubs/credit/affidavit.pdf). Finally, ask the debt collector to confirm in writing that you are not responsible for the outstanding debt and that the account has been closed.

- **Contact the U.S. State Department.** If your passport was stolen or if you believe someone may be fraudulently ordering a passport in your name, contact the U.S. State Department at 202-955-0430 or visit www.travel.state.gov/passport_services.html.

- **Contact the Department of Motor Vehicles (DMV).** If your driver's license was stolen or if someone is using the number to facilitate fraud, contact your state's DMV (for state-specific DMV contact information, visit www.aamva.org). Most states will put a fraud alert on your license if you ask for one. You should also request a new license number and fill out the DMV's complaint form.

RESOURCE

Where to go for more information. For comprehensive identity theft information, including sample credit dispute letters and forms to help you log conversations, visit www.ftc.gov/bcp/conline/pubs/credit/idtheft.htm

To avoid identity theft in the future, see *Stopping Identity Theft: 10 Easy Steps to Security*, by Scott Mitic (Nolo).

For state and federal identity theft laws and other victim resources, visit www.idtheftcenter.org.

For links to additional identity theft websites, visit www.privacyrights.org.

Signing Instructions

There are no specific signing instructions for the Identity Theft Worksheet. Simply use the form to keep track of what you've done to follow up on an identity theft.

How to Use the CD-ROM

Installing the Files Onto Your Computer...150
    Windows XP and Vista...150
    Macintosh 150

Using the Word Processing Files to Create Documents......................................151
    Opening a File...151
    Editing Your Document..151
    Printing Out the Document 152
    Saving Your Document...152

List of Files on the CD-ROM 153

The CD-ROM included with this book can be used with Windows computers. It installs files that use software programs that need to be on your computer already. It is not a standalone software program.

In accordance with U.S. copyright laws, the CD-ROM and its files are for your personal use only.

Please read this appendix and the "Readme. htm" file included on the CD-ROM for instructions on using the CD-ROM. For a list of files and their file names, see the end of this appendix.

Note to Macintosh users: This CD-ROM and its files should also work on Macintosh computers. Please note, however, that Nolo cannot provide technical support for non-Windows users.

Note to eBook users: You can access the CD-ROM files mentioned here from the bookmarked section of the eBook, located on the left hand side.

How to View the README File

To view the "Readme.htm" file, insert the CD-ROM into your computer's CD-ROM drive and follow these instructions:

Windows XP and Vista

1. On your PC's desktop, double-click the **My Computer** icon.

2. Double-click the icon for the CD-ROM drive into which the CD-ROM was inserted.

3. Double-click the file "Readme.htm."

Macintosh

1. On your Mac desktop, double-click the icon for the CD-ROM that you inserted.

2. Double-click the file "Readme.htm."

Installing the Files Onto Your Computer

To work with the files on the CD-ROM, you first need to install them onto your hard disk. Here's how:

Windows XP and Vista

Follow the CD-ROM's instructions that appear on the screen.

If nothing happens when you insert the CD-ROM, then:

1. Double-click the **My Computer** icon.

2. Double-click the icon for the CD-ROM drive into which the CD-ROM was inserted.

3. Double-click the file "Setup.exe."

Macintosh

If the **101 Law Forms CD** window is not open, double-click the **101 Law Forms CD** icon. Then:

1. Select the **101 Law Forms** folder icon.

2. Drag and drop the folder icon onto your computer.

Where Are the Files Installed?

Windows

By default, all the files are installed to the **101 Law Forms** folder in the **Program Files** folder of your computer. A folder called **101 Law Forms** is added to the **Programs** folder of the **Start** menu.

Macintosh

All the files are located in the **101 Law Forms** folder.

Using the Word Processing Files to Create Documents

The CD-ROM includes word processing files that you can open, complete, print, and save with your word processing program. All word processing files come in rich text format and have the extension ".rtf." For example, the file for the Pet Care Agreement discussed in Chapter One is on the file "Form06.rtf." RTF files can be read by most recent word processing programs including MS *Word*, Windows *WordPad*, and recent versions of *WordPerfect*.

The following are general instructions. Because each word processor uses different commands to open, format, save, and print documents, refer to your word processor's help file for specific instructions.

Do not call Nolo's technical support if you have questions on how to use your word processor or your computer.

Opening a File

You can open word processing files with any of the three following ways:

1. Windows users can open a file by selecting its "shortcut."

   i. Click the Windows **Start** button.

   ii. Open the **Programs** folder.

   iii. Open the **101 Law Forms** folder.

   iv. Open the chapter's subfolder.

   v. Click the shortcut to the file you want to work with.

2. Both Windows and Macintosh users can open a file by double-clicking it.

   i. Use **My Computer** or **Windows Explorer** (Windows XP or Vista) or the **Finder** (Macintosh) to go to the **101 Law Forms** folder.

   ii. Double-click the file you want to open.

3. Windows and Macintosh users can open a file from within their word processor.

   i. Open your word processor.

   ii. Go to the **File** menu and choose the **Open** command. This opens a dialog box.

   iii. Select the location and name of the file. (Navigate to the version of the **101 Law Forms** folder that you've installed on your computer.)

Editing Your Document

Here are tips for working on your document.

- Refer to the book's instructions and sample agreements for help.

- Underlines indicate where to enter infor-mation, frequently including bracketed instructions. Delete the underlines and instructions before finishing your document.

- Signature lines should appear on a page with at least some text from the document itself.

Editing Forms That Have Optional or Alternative Text

Some files have check boxes that appear before text. Check boxes indicate:

- Optional text that you can choose to include or exclude.
- Alternative text that you select to include, excluding the other alternatives.

If you are using the tear-out files in Appendix B, mark the appropriate box to make your choice.

If you are using the CD-ROM, we recommend doing the following:

Optional text

Delete optional text you do not want to include and keep that which you do. In either case, delete the check box and the italicized instructions. If you choose to delete an optional numbered clause, renumber the subsequent clauses after deleting it.

Alternative text

Delete the alternatives that you do not want to include first. Then delete the remaining check boxes, as well as the italicized instructions telling you that you need to select one of the alternatives provided.

Printing Out the Document

Use your word processor's or text editor's **Print** command to print out your document.

Saving Your Document

Use the **Save As** command to save and rename your document. You will be unable to use the **Save** command because the files are "read-only." If you save the file without renaming it, the underlines that indicate where you need to enter your information will be lost, and you will be unable to create a new document with this file without recopying the original file from the CD-ROM.

List of Files on the CD-ROM

The following files are in rich text format (RTF).

File Name	Form Title
Form01.rtf	Form 1: Temporary Guardianship Authorization for Care of Minor
Form02.rtf	Form 2: Authorization for Minor's Medical Treatment
Form03.rtf	Form 3: Authorization for Foreign Travel With Minor
Form04.rtf	Form 4: Housesitting Instructions
Form05.rtf	Form 5: Children's Carpool Agreement
Form06.rtf	Form 6: Pet Care Agreement
Form07.rtf	Form 7: Authorization to Drive a Motor Vehicle
Form08.rtf	Form 8: Power of Attorney for Finances (Limited Power)
Form09.rtf	Form 9: Power of Attorney for Real Estate
Form10.rtf	Form 10: Notice of Revocation of Power of Attorney
Form11.rtf	Form 11: Property Worksheet
Form12.rtf	Form 12: Beneficiary Worksheet
Form13.rtf	Form 13: Will for Adult With No Children
Form14.rtf	Form 14: Will for Adult With Child(ren)
Form15.rtf	Form 15: Will Codicil
Form16.rtf	Form 16: Request for Death Certificate
Form17.rtf	Form 17: Notice to Creditor of Death
Form18.rtf	Form 18: Executor's Checklist
Form19.rtf	Form 19: General Notice of Death
Form20.rtf	Form 20: Obituary Information Fact Sheet
Form21.rtf	Form 21: Notice to Deceased's Homeowners' Insurance Company
Form22.rtf	Form 22: Notice to Deceased's Vehicle Insurance Company
Form23.rtf	Form 23: Apartment-Finding Service Checklist
Form24.rtf	Form 24: Rental Application
Form25.rtf	Form 25: Fixed-Term Residential Lease
Form26.rtf	Form 26: Month-to-Month Residential Rental Agreement
Form27.rtf	Form 27: Landlord-Tenant Agreement to Terminate Lease
Form28.rtf	Form 28: Consent to Assignment of Lease
Form29.rtf	Form 29: Landlord-Tenant Checklist
Form30.rtf	Form 30: Notice of Needed Repairs
Form31.rtf	Form 31: Tenant's Notice of Intent to Move Out
Form32.rtf	Form 32: Demand for Return of Security Deposit
Form33.rtf	Form 33: Loan Comparison Worksheet
Form34.rtf	Form 34: Authorization to Check Credit and Employment References
Form35.rtf	Form 35: Monthly Payment Record

File Name	Form Title
Form36.rtf	Form 36: Promissory Note—Installment Payments With Interest
Form37.rtf	Form 37: Promissory Note—Installment Payments With Interest and Balloon Payment
Form38.rtf	Form 38: Promissory Note—Installment Payments Without Interest
Form39.rtf	Form 39: Promissory Note—Lump Sum Payment With Interest
Form40.rtf	Form 40: Promissory Note—Lump Sum Payment Without Interest
Form41.rtf	Form 41: Cosigner Provision
Form42.rtf	Form 42: Security Agreement Provision for Promissory Note
Form43.rtf	Form 43: Security Agreement
Form44.rtf	Form 44: U.C.C. Financing Statement
Form45.rtf	Form 45: Release of U.C.C. Financing Statement
Form46.rtf	Form 46: Agreement to Modify Promissory Note
Form47.rtf	Form 47: Overdue Payment Demand
Form48.rtf	Form 48: Demand to Make Good on Bad Check
Form49.rtf	Form 49: Ideal House Profile
Form50.rtf	Form 50: House Priorities Worksheet
Form51.rtf	Form 51: House Comparison Worksheet
Form52.rtf	Form 52: Family Financial Statement
Form53.rtf	Form 53: Monthly Carrying Costs Worksheet
Form54.rtf	Form 54: Mortgage Rates and Terms Worksheet
Form55.rtf	Form 55: Moving Checklist
Form56.rtf	Form 56: Motor Vehicle Bill of Sale
Form57.rtf	Form 57: Boat Bill of Sale
Form58.rtf	Form 58: Computer System Bill of Sale
Form59.rtf	Form 59: General Bill of Sale
Form60.rtf	Form 60: Bill of Sale for Dog
Form61.rtf	Form 61: Personal Property Rental Agreement
Form62.rtf	Form 62: Notice of Termination of Personal Property Rental Agreement
Form63.rtf	Form 63: Storage Contract
Form64.rtf	Form 64: Home Maintenance Agreement
Form65.rtf	Form 65: Home Repairs Agreement
Form66.rtf	Form 66: Contractor Mid-Job Worksheet
Form67.rtf	Form 67: Daily Expenses
Form68.rtf	Form 68: Monthly Income
Form69.rtf	Form 69: Monthly Budget
Form70.rtf	Form 70: Statement of Assets and Liabilities
Form71.rtf	Form 71: Assignment of Rights
Form72.rtf	Form 72: Notice to Terminate Joint Account
Form73.rtf	Form 73: Notice to Stop Payment of Check

File Name	Form Title
Form74.rtf	Form 74: Request for Credit Report
Form75.rtf	Form 75: Dispute Incorrect Credit Report Entry
Form76.rtf	Form 76: Dispute Credit Card Charge
Form77.rtf	Form 77: Demand Collection Agency Cease Contact
Form78.rtf	Form 78: Notice to Remove Name From List
Form79.rtf	Form 79: Notice to Add or Retain Name but Not Sell or Trade It
Form80.rtf	Form 80: Telemarketing Phone Call Log
Form81.rtf	Form 81: Notice to Put Name on Company's "Do Not Call" List
Form82.rtf	Form 82: Demand for Damages for Excessive Calls
Form83.rtf	Form 83: Child Care Agreement
Form84.rtf	Form 84: Child Care Instructions
Form85.rtf	Form 85: Elder Care Agreement
Form86.rtf	Form 86: Housekeeping Services Agreement
Form87.rtf	Form 87: Agreement to Keep Property Separate
Form88.rtf	Form 88: Agreement for a Joint Purchase
Form89.rtf	Form 89: Agreement to Share Property
Form90.rtf	Form 90: Declaration of Legal Name Change
Form91.rtf	Form 91: Demand Letter
Form92.rtf	Form 92: Online Auction Buyer Demand Letter
Form93.rtf	Form 93: Request for Refund or Repair of Goods Under Warranty
Form94.rtf	Form 94: Accident Claim Worksheet
Form95.rtf	Form 95: General Release
Form96.rtf	Form 96: General Mutual Release
Form97.rtf	Form 97: Release for Damage to Real Estate
Form98.rtf	Form 98: Release for Property Damage in Auto Accident
Form99.rtf	Form 99: Release for Personal Injury
Form100.rtf	Form 100: Mutual Release of Contract Claims
Form101.rtf	Form 101: Complaint Letter
Form102.rtf	Form 102: Notice of Insurance Claim
Form103.rtf	Form 103: Notice to Cancel Certain Contracts
Form104.rtf	Form 104: Cancel Membership or Subscription Notice
Form105.rtf	Form 105: Request to Begin Special Education Process
Form106.rtf	Form 106: Identity Theft Worksheet

Tear-Out Forms

Form #/Name   **Chapter**

Form 1: Temporary Guardianship Authorization for Care of Minor 1

Form 2: Authorization for Minor's Medical Treatment 1

Form 3: Authorization for Foreign Travel With Minor 1

Form 4: Housesitting Instructions 1

Form 5: Children's Carpool Agreement 1

Form 6: Pet Care Agreement 1

Form 7: Authorization to Drive a Motor Vehicle 1

Form 8: Power of Attorney for Finances (Limited Power) 1

Form 9: Power of Attorney for Real Estate 1

Form 10: Notice of Revocation of Power of Attorney 1

Form 11: Property Worksheet 2

Form 12: Beneficiary Worksheet 2

Form 13: Will for Adult With No Children 2

Form 14: Will for Adult With Child(ren) 2

Form 15: Will Codicil 2

Form 16: Request for Death Certificate 3

Form 17: Notice to Creditor of Death 3

Form 18: Executor's Checklist 3

Form 19: General Notice of Death 3

Form 20: Obituary Information Fact Sheet 3

Form 21: Notice to Deceased's Homeowners' Insurance Company 3

Form 22: Notice to Deceased's Vehicle Insurance Company 3

Form #/Name	Chapter

Form 23: Apartment-Finding Service Checklist...4

Form 24: Rental Application...4

Form 25: Fixed-Term Residential Lease..4

Form 26: Month-to-Month Residential Rental Agreement 4

Form 27: Landlord-Tenant Agreement to Terminate Lease.............................4

Form 28: Consent to Assignment of Lease 4

Form 29: Landlord-Tenant Checklist..4

Form 30: Notice of Needed Repairs..4

Form 31: Tenant's Notice of Intent to Move Out...4

Form 32: Demand for Return of Security Deposit...4

Form 33: Loan Comparison Worksheet...5

Form 34: Authorization to Check Credit and Employment References.........5

Form 35: Monthly Payment Record 5

Form 36: Promissory Note—Installment Payments With Interest.................5

Form 37: Promissory Note—Installment Payments With Interest and
Balloon Payment...5

Form 38: Promissory Note—Installment Payments Without Interest...........5

Form 39: Promissory Note—Lump Sum Payment With Interest....................5

Form 40: Promissory Note—Lump Sum Payment Without Interest...............5

Form 41: Cosigner Provision 5

Form 42: Security Agreement Provision for Promissory Note........................5

Form 43: Security Agreement..5

Form 44: U.C.C. Financing Statement..5

Form 45: Release of U.C.C. Financing Statement...5

Form 46: Agreement to Modify Promissory Note...5

Form 47: Overdue Payment Demand...5

Form 48: Demand to Make Good on Bad Check..5

Form 49: Ideal House Profile..6

Form #/Name	Chapter

Form 50: House Priorities Worksheet	6
Form 51: House Comparison Worksheet	6
Form 52: Family Financial Statement	6
Form 53: Monthly Carrying Costs Worksheet	6
Form 54: Mortgage Rates and Terms Worksheet	6
Form 55: Moving Checklist	6
Form 56: Motor Vehicle Bill of Sale	7
Form 57: Boat Bill of Sale	7
Form 58: Computer System Bill of Sale	7
Form 59: General Bill of Sale	7
Form 60: Bill of Sale for Dog	7
Form 61: Personal Property Rental Agreement	8
Form 62: Notice of Termination of Personal Property Rental Agreement	8
Form 63: Storage Contract	8
Form 64: Home Maintenance Agreement	9
Form 65: Home Repairs Agreement	9
Form 66: Contractor Mid-Job Worksheet	9
Form 67: Daily Expenses	10
Form 68: Monthly Income	10
Form 69: Monthly Budget	10
Form 70: Statement of Assets and Liabilities	10
Form 71: Assignment of Rights	10
Form 72: Notice to Terminate Joint Account	10
Form 73: Notice to Stop Payment of Check	10
Form 74: Request for Credit Report	10
Form 75: Dispute Incorrect Credit Report Entry	10
Form 76: Dispute Credit Card Charge	10
Form 77: Demand Collection Agency Cease Contact	10

Form #/Name	Chapter

Form 78:   Notice to Remove Name From List 11

Form 79:   Notice to Add or Retain Name but Not Sell or Trade It 11

Form 80:   Telemarketing Phone Call Log.. 11

Form 81:   Notice to Put Name on Company's "Do Not Call" List 11

Form 82:   Demand for Damages for Excessive Calls.. 11

Form 83:   Child Care Agreement... 12

Form 84:   Child Care Instructions 12

Form 85:   Elder Care Agreement... 12

Form 86:   Housekeeping Services Agreement.. 12

Form 87:   Agreement to Keep Property Separate 13

Form 88:   Agreement for a Joint Purchase 13

Form 89:   Agreement to Share Property 13

Form 90:   Declaration of Legal Name Change.. 13

Form 91:   Demand Letter... 14

Form 92:   Online Auction Buyer Demand Letter 14

Form 93:   Request for Refund or Repair of Goods Under Warranty.......................... 14

Form 94:   Accident Claim Worksheet.. 14

Form 95:   General Release 14

Form 96:   General Mutual Release... 14

Form 97:   Release for Damage to Real Estate.. 14

Form 98:   Release for Property Damage in Auto Accident 14

Form 99:   Release for Personal Injury 14

Form 100: Mutual Release of Contract Claims.. 14

Form 101: Complaint Letter 15

Form 102: Notice of Insurance Claim 15

Form 103: Notice to Cancel Certain Contracts... 15

Form 104: Cancel Membership or Subscription Notice.. 15

Form 105: Request to Begin Special Education Process 15

Form 106: Identity Theft Worksheet... 15

Temporary Guardianship Authorization for Care of Minor

Child

Name: _____

Permanent address: _____

Phone: _____ Birthdate: _____

Child's School or Day Care

(Leave this section blank if your child is not in school or any type of child care program.)

School or child care program: _____ Grade (if in school): _____

Teacher: _____

School address: _____

Phone: _____

Other child care program (such as after-school program): _____

Address: _____

Phone: _____

Reponsible adult: _____

Child's Doctor, Dentist, and Insurance

Doctor (or HMO): _____

Address: _____

Phone: _____

Name of medical insurer/health plan: _____

Policy number: _____ Phone: _____

Dentist: _____

Address: _____

Phone: _____

Name of dental insurer/dental plan: _____

Policy number: _____ Phone: _____

Parents (or Legal Guardians)

Parent 1

Name: _____

Address: _____

_____

Home phone: _____ Work phone: _____

Cell phone or pager: _____ Email: _____

Parent 2

Name: _____

Address: _____

_____

Home phone: _____ Work phone: _____

Cell phone or pager: _____ Email: _____

Temporary Guardian

Name: _____

Address: _____

_____

Home phone: _____ Work phone: _____

Cell phone or pager: _____ Email: _____

Relationship to minor: _____

Emergency Contact

In case of emergency, if the guardian cannot be reached, please contact: _____

_____

Home phone: _____ Work phone: _____

Cell phone or pager: _____ Email: _____

Authorization and Consent of Parent(s) or Legal Guardian(s)

If there is more than one parent, the use of the singular incorporates the plural.

1. I affirm that I have legal custody of the minor child named above, who is my child.

2. I give my full authorization and consent for my child to live with and travel with the temporary guardian, and for the temporary guardian to establish a place of residence for my child.

3. I give the temporary guardian permission to act in my place and make decisions pertaining to my child's educational, recreational, and religious activities.

4. I give the temporary guardian permission to authorize medical and dental care for my child, including but not limited to medical examinations, X-rays, tests, anesthesia, surgical operations, hospital care, or other treatments that, in the temporary guardian's sole opinion, are needed or useful for my child. Such medical treatment shall be provided only upon the advice of and supervision by a physician, surgeon, dentist, or other medical practitioner licensed to practice in the United States.

5. This authorization shall cover the period from _____ to _____.

6. While the temporary guardian cares for my child, the costs of my child's upkeep, living expenses, and medical and dental expenses shall be paid as follows: _____

    _____

    _____

    _____.

I declare under penalty of perjury under the laws of the state of _____
that the foregoing is true and correct.

_____   _____
Parent 1's signature   Date

_____   _____
Parent 2's signature   Date

Consent of Temporary Guardian

I solemnly affirm that I will assume full responsibility for the minor who will live with me during the period designated above. I agree to make necessary decisions and to provide consent for the minor as set forth in the above Authorization and Consent of Parent(s). I also agree to the terms of the costs of the minor's upkeep, living expenses, and medical and dental expenses as set forth in the above Authorization and Consent of Parent(s).

I declare under penalty of perjury under the laws of the state of _____
that the foregoing is true and correct.

_____   _____
Temporary guardian's signature   Date

Certificate of Acknowledgment of Notary Public

State of _____

County of _____ } ss

On _____, _____, before me, _____,
a notary public in and for said state, personally appeared _____,
who proved to me on the basis of satisfactory evidence to be the person whose name is subscribed to the within instrument and acknowledged to me that he or she executed the same in his or her authorized capacity and that by his or her signature on the instrument, the person, or the entity upon behalf of which the person acted, executed the instrument.

I certify under PENALTY OF PERJURY under the laws of the State of _____
that the foregoing paragraph is true and correct.

WITNESS my hand and official seal.

_____

Notary Public for the State of _____

My commission expires _____

[NOTARY SEAL]

Authorization for Minor's Medical Treatment

Child

Name: _____

Birthdate: _____ Age: _____ Grade in school: _____

Doctor (or HMO): _____

Address: _____

Phone: _____

Name of medical insurer/health plan: _____

Policy number: _____ Phone: _____

Allergies (medications): _____

Allergies (other): _____

Conditions for which child is currently receiving treatment: _____

_____

Other important medical information: _____

_____

Dentist: _____

Address: _____

Phone: _____

Name of dental insurer/dental plan: _____

Policy number: _____ Phone: _____

Parents (or Legal Guardians)

Parent 1

Name: _____

Address: _____

_____

Home phone: _____ Work phone: _____

Cell phone or pager:_____ Email: _____

Additional contact information: _____

Parent 2

Name: _____

Address: _____

_____

Home phone: _____ Work phone: _____

Cell phone or pager: _____ Email: _____

Additional contact information: _____

Other Adult to Notify in Case Parent(s) Cannot Be Reached

Name: _____

Address: _____

_____

Home phone: _____ Work phone: _____

Cell phone or pager: _____ Email: _____

Authorization and Consent of Parent(s) or Legal Guardian(s)

I affirm that I have legal custody of the minor child indicated above. I give my authorization and consent for

_____ *[name of supervising adult]*, who is a(n) _____

_____

[title and name of organization, if appropriate] to authorize necessary medical or dental care for my child. Such medical treatment shall be provided upon the advice of and supervised by any physician, surgeon, dentist, or other medical practitioner licensed to practice in the United States.

_____   _____
Parent 1's signature   Date

_____   _____
Parent 2's signature   Date

Certificate of Acknowledgment of Notary Public

State of _____

County of _____ } ss

On _____, _____, before me, _____,

a notary public in and for said state, personally appeared _____,

who proved to me on the basis of satisfactory evidence to be the person whose name is subscribed to the within instrument and acknowledged to me that he or she executed the same in his or her authorized capacity and that by his or her signature on the instrument, the person, or the entity upon behalf of which the person acted, executed the instrument.

I certify under PENALTY OF PERJURY under the laws of the State of _____
that the foregoing paragraph is true and correct.

WITNESS my hand and official seal.

_____

Notary Public for the State of _____

My commission expires _____

[NOTARY SEAL]

Authorization for Foreign Travel With Minor

To Whom It May Concern:

This letter concerns my child, _____

[name of child], a United States citizen and a minor born on _____, _____,

[child's date of birth], who carries a United States passport with the number _____.

I affirm that I have legal custody of my child, and that there are no pending divorce or child custody proceedings that involve my child. I give my full authorization and consent for my child to travel outside of the United States with _____

[name of adult with whom child will travel], who is the _____ *[state adult's relationship with child]* of my child. The purpose of the travel is _____

_____

[specify vacation, touring, to visit relatives, to accompany adult on business trip, or other reason].

I have approved the following travel plans:

Dates of travel	Destinations/Accommodations
_____	_____
_____	_____
_____	_____
_____	_____
_____	_____
_____	_____

Furthermore, I hereby authorize _____

[name of adult with whom child will travel] to modify the travel plans specified above as he/she deems necessary.

I declare under penalty of perjury under the laws of the state of _____ *that the foregoing is true and correct.*

Parent 1's signature: _____ Date: _____

Printed name: _____

Address: _____

_____

Home phone: _____ Work phone: _____

Cell phone or pager: _____ Email: _____

Parent 2's signature: _____ Date: _____

Printed name: _____

Address: _____

_____

Home phone: _____ Work phone: _____

Cell phone or pager: _____ Email: _____

Certificate of Acknowledgment of Notary Public

State of _____

County of _____ } ss

On _____, _____, before me, _____,
a notary public in and for said state, personally appeared _____,
proved to me on the basis of satisfactory evidence to be the person whose name is subscribed to the within
instrument and acknowledged to me that he or she executed the same in his or her authorized capacity and
that by his or her signature on the instrument, the person, or the entity upon behalf of which the person
acted, executed the instrument.

I certify under PENALTY OF PERJURY under the laws of the State of _____
that the foregoing paragraph is true and correct.

WITNESS my hand and official seal.

_____

Notary Public for the State of _____

My commission expires _____

[NOTARY SEAL]

Authorization for Foreign Travel With Minor

Housesitting Instructions

Home Owner(s)

Name(s): _____

Home address: _____

Home phone: _____

Temporary address(es) and phone numbers while housesitter is staying at home (or attach schedule):

_____

Plants and Garden. What to water when.

_____

Newspapers and Mail. What to do about mail and newspapers; what to save, what to throw out.

_____

Garbage and Recycling. Details of garbage pickup and recycling—what, where, when.

_____

Appliances. Where to find manuals/booklets on different major and minor appliances, plus odds and ends of information as to location and operation of DVD player, vacuum cleaner, stove, etc.

_____

Lights. Any special details on lights, timers, automatic night light, and external motion-sensitive lights.

_____

Windows, Doors, Security Systems, and Keys. Details on how locks and security system work, and who has extra keys.

_____

Smoke Detectors and Fire Extinguishers. Details on location and functioning of smoke detectors and fire extinguishers.

_____

Utilities. Details on location and use of thermostat, gas and water shut-off valves, fuse box, and spare fuses.

_____

Tools and Supplies. Location of house supplies, such as tools, light bulbs, batteries, iron, cleaning supplies, and first aid kit.

_____

Vehicles. Details on cars, whether they need to be started once a week, etc.

_____

Neighbors and Friends. Names and phone numbers (home and work) of neighbors and friends who can help with any questions.

_____

Repair People and Service Contacts. Names and phone numbers of repairperson, plumber, insurance agent, etc.

_____

Miscellaneous. Anything else you want the housesitter to know.

_____

_____   _____
Signature   Date

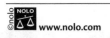

Children's Carpool Agreement

1. The purpose of this carpool is to transport children to _____ [*name of activity*], located at _____ [*address*].

2. The carpool will begin on _____ [*date*] and end on_____ [*date*].

3. Inbound trip: The carpool will pick up _____ [*the first child to be picked up*] at _____ [*time*] and pick up the rest of the children in this order: _____ _____ [*list the pickup order*].

4. Return trip: The carpool will meet the children at _____ [*time*] and deliver the children to the addresses listed below in this order: _____ _____ [*list the drop-off order*].

5. Special agreements (waiting time, alternate drop-off sites, etc.): _____ _____ .

6. The members of the carpool and the riders are:

Child 1

Child's name: _____

Inbound pickup address: _____

Outbound drop-off address: _____

Parent(s)' or guardian(s)' name(s): _____

Parents'/guardians' home address: _____

Parents'/guardians' work address: _____

Parents'/guardians' contact information:

Home phone: _____ Work phone: _____

Cell phone: _____ Email: _____

Names, phone numbers, and relationship to you/child of two people, other than those listed above, to call in an emergency: _____

Name and phone number of child's physician: _____

Driver's name: _____

Driver's license number: _____

Driver's address, if different from above: _____

Driver's phone, if different from above: _____

Model, make, and license number of vehicle(s) driver expects to use: _____ _____

Name of insurance company: _____

Child 2

Child's name: _____

Inbound pickup address: _____

Outbound drop-off address: _____

Parent(s)' or guardian(s)' name(s): _____

Parents'/guardians' home address: _____

Parents'/guardians' work address: _____

Parents'/guardians' contact information:

Home phone: _____ Work phone: _____

Cell phone: _____ Email: _____

Names, phone numbers, and relationship to you/child of two people, other than those listed above, to call in an emergency: _____

_____

Name and phone number of child's physician: _____

Driver's name: _____

Driver's license number: _____

Driver's address, if different from above: _____

Driver's phone, if different from above: _____

Model, make, and license number of vehicle(s) driver expects to use: _____

_____

Name of insurance company: _____

Child 3

Child's name: _____

Inbound pickup address: _____

Outbound drop-off address: _____

Parent(s)' or guardian(s)' name(s): _____

Parents'/guardians' home address: _____

Parents'/guardians' work address: _____

Parents'/guardians' contact information:

Home phone: _____ Work phone: _____

Cell phone: _____ Email: _____

Names, phone numbers, and relationship to you/child of two people, other than those listed above, to call in an emergency: _____

_____

Name and phone number of child's physician: _____

Driver's name: _____

Driver's license number: _____

Driver's address, if different from above: _____

Driver's phone, if different from above: _____

Model, make, and license number of vehicle(s) driver expects to use: _____

_____

Name of insurance company: _____

8. By signing this Agreement, I agree to abide by its terms to the best of my ability. I understand that any member of the carpool can cease participation without notice but agree to give as much notice as is possible under the circumstances. I understand that if a member is not fulfilling his or her responsibilities, that member may be asked to leave. I understand that this document is not a legally binding agreement and is entered into in a spirit of cooperation and a shared desire to make the carpool work well for the benefit of the children and their parents or guardians.

_____   _____

Parent or Guardian Signature   Date

_____   _____

Parent or Guardian Signature   Date

_____   _____

Parent or Guardian Signature   Date

Pet Care Agreement

Pet Owner

Name: _____

Home address: _____

_____

Home phone: _____ Work phone: _____

Cell phone or pager: _____ Email: _____

Temporary address while pet is in Caregiver's care: _____

Phone: _____ Cell phone or pager: _____ Email: _____

[if more than one temporary address, attach itinerary]

Caregiver

Name: _____

Home address: _____

_____

Home phone: _____ Work phone: _____

Cell phone or pager: _____ Email: _____

Pet(s)

Caregiver will take care of: _____

_____

_____

[list name, species, breed, age, and, if necessary, any distinguishing characteristics]

Dates of Care

Caregiver will care for the animal(s) from_____ *[beginning date]*

until _____ *[ending date]*.

Reimbursement and Compensation

Owner will reimburse Caregiver for reasonable out-of-pocket expenses, including veterinary bills incurred while caring for the animal(s). Owner will also compensate Caregiver as follows:

☐ no compensation

☐ payment of $ _____

☐ other: _____

Care Instructions

Caregiver will exercise reasonable care to protect the animal(s) from sickness, injury, and theft, and will follow these instructions:

Food

Type of food: _____

Amount: _____ Frequency: _____

Special instructions:_____

_____

Medication

1. Name: _____ Dosage: _____

   Special instructions: _____

2. Name: _____ Dosage: _____

   Special instructions: _____

Exercise

Frequency and type: _____

Special instructions: _____

Grooming

Frequency and type: _____

Special instructions: _____

Veterinary Care

Name: _____

Address: _____

Phone: _____ Veterinary insurance company and policy no. _____

Special instructions: _____

Emergency Contact

If Caregiver becomes unable to care for the pet(s), Caregiver will contact _____

_____ [name] at _____ [phone number] to try to make

substitute arrangements for care of the pet(s) and will promptly notify Owner. If arrangements cannot be

made, Caregiver will turn the pet(s) over to _____ [name] at

_____ [phone number] and promptly notify Owner.

Disputes

If any dispute arises under this agreement, the parties agree to select a mutually agreeable third party to help them mediate it, and to share equally any costs of mediation.

Additional Terms

_____

_____

_____

Entire Agreement

This agreement contains the entire agreement between Owner and Caregiver. Any modifications must be in writing.

Signatures

_____

Pet owner's name

_____   _____

Signature   Date

_____

Caregiver's name

_____   _____

Signature   Date

www.nolo.com

Pet Care Agreement

Authorization to Drive a Motor Vehicle

Vehicle Owner ("Owner")

Name: _____

Address: _____

_____

Home phone: _____ Work phone: _____

Cell phone or pager: _____ Email: _____

Vehicle

Make, model, and year of vehicle: _____

Vehicle license plate number: _____

State of registration: _____ Vehicle identification number (VIN): _____

Insurance company: _____

Insurance policy number: _____

Person Authorized to Drive ("Borrower")

Name: _____

Address: _____

_____

Home phone: _____ Work phone: _____

Cell phone or pager: _____ Email: _____

Driver's license number: _____

Motor vehicle insurance company (if any): _____

Insurance policy number (if any): _____

Authorization and Consent of Vehicle Owner

I am the lawful owner of the vehicle indicated above. I give my authorization and consent for Borrower to use this vehicle as follows:

Dates of use: _____

Area in which vehicle may be used: _____

Any restrictions or conditions on use: _____

I declare under penalty of perjury under the laws of the state of _____ *that the foregoing is true and correct.*

_____   _____

Owner's signature   Date

Power of Attorney for Finances (Limited Power)

I, _____ *[your name],*

of _____ *[your city and state],*

appoint _____

[name of your attorney-in-fact] to act in my place for the purposes of:

_____

_____

_____

_____

This power of attorney takes effect on _____,
and shall continue until terminated in writing, or until _____,
whichever comes first. In the event of my incapacity or death, this power of attorney shall terminate immediately.

I grant my attorney-in-fact full authority to act in any manner both proper and necessary to the exercise of the foregoing powers, and I ratify every act that my attorney-in-fact may lawfully perform in exercising those powers.

I agree that any third party who receives a copy of this document may act under it. Revocation of the power of attorney is not effective as to a third party until the third party has actual knowledge of the revocation. I agree to indemnify the third party for any claims that arise against the third party because of reliance on this power of attorney.

Signed: This _____ day of _____,

State of: _____ County of: _____

Signature: _____, Principal

Social Security number: _____

Witnesses

On the date written above, the principal declared to me that this instrument is his or her financial power of attorney, and that he or she willingly executed it as a free and voluntary act. The principal signed this instrument in my presence.

Witness 1

_____
Signature

_____
Name

_____
Address

Witness 2

_____
Signature

_____
Name

_____
Address

Certificate of Acknowledgment of Notary Public

State of _____

County of _____ } ss

On _____, _____, before me, _____,
a notary public in and for said state, personally appeared _____,
who proved to me on the basis of satisfactory evidence to be the person whose name is subscribed to the
within instrument and acknowledged to me that he or she executed the same in his or her authorized
capacity and that by his or her signature on the instrument, the person, or the entity upon behalf of which the
person acted, executed the instrument.

I certify under PENALTY OF PERJURY under the laws of the State of _____
that the foregoing paragraph is true and correct.

WITNESS my hand and official seal.

_____

Notary Public for the State of _____

My commission expires _____

[NOTARY SEAL]

Acknowledgment of Attorney-in-Fact

By accepting or acting under the appointment, the attorney-in-fact assumes the fiduciary and other legal
responsibilities and liabilities of an agent.

Name of Attorney-in-Fact: _____

Signature of Attorney-in-Fact: _____

Power of Attorney for Real Estate

RECORDING REQUESTED BY
AND WHEN RECORDED MAIL TO

_____

_____

_____

Power of Attorney for Real Estate

I, _____ ,

name of principal

of _____ , _____ _____ ,

city   county

_____ , appoint _____

state   name of attorney-in-fact

_____ , of _____ ,

city

_____ , _____ ,

county   state

to act in my place with respect to the real property described as follows:

_____

_____

_____

_____

_____

_____

_____

_____

_____

_____

_____

_____

_____

_____

_____

_____

_____

_____

_____

My attorney-in-fact may act for me in any manner to deal with all or any part of any interest in the real property described in this document, under such terms, conditions, and covenants as my attorney-in-fact deems proper. My attorney-in-fact's powers include but are not limited to the power to:

1. Accept as a gift or as security for a loan, reject, demand, buy, lease, receive, or otherwise acquire ownership or possession of any estate or interest in real property.

2. Sell, exchange, convey with or without covenants, quitclaim, release, surrender, mortgage, encumber, partition or consent to the partitioning of, grant options concerning, lease, sublet, or otherwise dispose of any interest in the real property described in this document.

3. Maintain, repair, improve, insure, rent, lease, and pay or contest taxes or assessments on any estate or interest in the real property described in this document.

4. Prosecute, defend, intervene in, submit to arbitration, settle, and propose or accept a compromise with respect to any claim in favor of or against me based on or involving the real property described in this document.

However, my attorney in fact shall not have the power to:

_____

_____

_____

_____

_____

_____

_____

_____

_____

_____

_____

_____

_____

_____

_____

_____

I further grant to my attorney-in-fact full authority to act in any manner both proper and necessary to the exercise of the foregoing powers, including _____

_____

and I ratify every act that my attorney-in-fact may lawfully perform in exercising those powers.

This power of attorney takes effect on _____, and shall continue until terminated in writing, or until _____, whichever comes first. In the event of my incapacity or death, this power of attorney shall terminate immediately.

I agree that any third party who receives a copy of this document may act under it. Revocation of the power of attorney is not effective as to a third party until the third party has actual knowledge of the revocation. I agree to indemnify the third party for any claims that arise against the third party because of reliance on this power of attorney.

Signed this _____ day of _____, _____.

State of _____, County of _____.

_____   _____
Signature   Social Security number

Witnesses

On the date written above, the principal declared to me that this instrument is his or her power of attorney for real estate, and that he or she willingly executed it as a free and voluntary act. The principal signed this instrument in my presence.

_____   _____
Name   Name

_____   _____
Address   Address

_____   _____
County   County

Certificate of Acknowledgment of Notary Public

State of _____

County of _____ } ss

On _____, _____, before me, _____, a notary public in and for said state, personally appeared _____, who proved to me on the basis of satisfactory evidence to be the person whose name is subscribed to the within instrument and acknowledged to me that he or she executed the same in his or her authorized capacity and that by his or her signature on the instrument, the person, or the entity upon behalf of which the person acted, executed the instrument.

I certify under PENALTY OF PERJURY under the laws of the State of _____ that the foregoing paragraph is true and correct.

WITNESS my hand and official seal.

_____

Notary Public for the State of _____

[NOTARY SEAL]   My commission expires: _____

Signature of Attorney-in-Fact

By accepting or acting under the appointment, the attorney-in-fact assumes the fiduciary and other legal responsibilities of an agent.

_____
Signature of attorney-in-fact

This power of attorney takes effect on _____, and shall continue until terminated in writing, or until _____, whichever comes first.

I agree that any third party who receives a copy of this document may act under it. Revocation of the power of attorney is not effective as to a third party until the third party has actual knowledge of the revocation. I agree to indemnify the third party for any claims that arise against the third party because of reliance on this power of attorney.

Signed this _____ day of _____, _____.

State of _____, County of _____.

_____   _____
Signature   Social Security number

Witnesses

On the date written above, the principal declared to me that this instrument is his or her power of attorney for real estate, and that he or she willingly executed it as a free and voluntary act. The principal signed this instrument in my presence.

_____   _____
Name   Name

_____   _____
Address   Address

_____   _____
County   County

Certificate of Acknowledgment of Notary Public

State of _____

County of _____ } ss

On _____, _____, before me, _____, a notary public in and for said state, personally appeared _____, who proved to me on the basis of satisfactory evidence to be the person whose name is subscribed to the within instrument and acknowledged to me that he or she executed the same in his or her authorized capacity and that by his or her signature on the instrument, the person, or the entity upon behalf of which the person acted, executed the instrument.

I certify under PENALTY OF PERJURY under the laws of the State of _____ that the foregoing paragraph is true and correct.

WITNESS my hand and official seal.

_____

Notary Public for the State of _____

[NOTARY SEAL]   My commission expires: _____

Signature of Attorney-in-Fact

By accepting or acting under the appointment, the attorney-in-fact assumes the fiduciary and other legal responsibilities of an agent.

_____
Signature of attorney-in-fact

This power of attorney takes effect on _____, and shall continue until terminated in writing, or until _____, whichever comes first. In the event of my incapacity or death, this power of attorney shall terminate immediately.

I agree that any third party who receives a copy of this document may act under it. Revocation of the power of attorney is not effective as to a third party until the third party has actual knowledge of the revocation. I agree to indemnify the third party for any claims that arise against the third party because of reliance on this power of attorney.

Signed this _____ day of _____, _____.

State of _____, County of _____.

_____
Signature

_____
Social Security number

Certificate of Acknowledgment of Notary Public

State of _____

County of _____ } ss

On _____, _____, before me, _____, a notary public in and for said state, personally appeared _____, who proved to me on the basis of satisfactory evidence to be the person whose name is subscribed to the within instrument and acknowledged to me that he or she executed the same in his or her authorized capacity and that by his or her signature on the instrument, the person, or the entity upon behalf of which the person acted, executed the instrument.

I certify under PENALTY OF PERJURY under the laws of the State of _____ that the foregoing paragraph is true and correct.

WITNESS my hand and official seal.

_____

Notary Public for the State of _____

[NOTARY SEAL]   My commission expires: _____

Signature of Attorney-in-Fact

By accepting or acting under the appointment, the attorney-in-fact assumes the fiduciary and other legal responsibilities of an agent.

_____
Signature of attorney-in-fact

Notice of Revocation of Power of Attorney

I, _____ [your name],

of _____ [your city and state],

revoke the power of attorney dated _____, empowering

_____ [name of your attorney-in-fact] to act

as my attorney-in-fact. I revoke and withdraw all power and authority granted under that power of attorney.

[if applicable]: That power of attorney was recorded on _____, _____. The reference number is _____.

Signed: This _____ day of _____,

State of: _____ County of: _____

Signature: _____, Principal

Social Security number: _____

Certificate of Acknowledgment of Notary Public

State of _____

County of _____ } ss

On _____, _____, before me, _____,

a notary public in and for said state, personally appeared _____,

who proved to me on the basis of satisfactory evidence to be the person whose name is subscribed to the within instrument and acknowledged to me that he or she executed the same in his or her authorized capacity and that by his or her signature on the instrument, the person, or the entity upon behalf of which the person acted, executed the instrument.

I certify under PENALTY OF PERJURY under the laws of the State of _____ that the foregoing paragraph is true and correct.

WITNESS my hand and official seal.

_____

Notary Public for the State of _____

[NOTARIAL SEAL] My commission expires: _____

Property Worksheet

Property	Name of Any Existing Beneficiary

Real Estate *(list each piece of real estate by address)*

_____   _____

_____   _____

_____   _____

_____   _____

Cash and Other Liquid Assets

Cash

_____   _____

_____   _____

_____   _____

Checking accounts

_____   _____

_____   _____

_____   _____

Savings and money market accounts

_____   _____

_____   _____

_____   _____

Certificates of deposit

_____   _____

_____   _____

_____   _____

Precious metals

_____   _____

_____   _____

_____   _____

Securities (not in retirement accounts)

Mutual funds

_____   _____

_____   _____

_____   _____

Listed and unlisted stocks

_____   _____

_____   _____

_____   _____

_____   _____

Property   **Name of Any Existing Beneficiary**

Securities (continued)
Government, corporate, and municipal bonds

_____   _____

_____   _____

_____   _____

Annuities

_____   _____

_____   _____

_____   _____

Retirement Plan Assets (IRAs, Keoghs, Roth IRAs, 401(k) and 403(b) plans)

_____   _____

_____   _____

_____   _____

Vehicles
Automobiles, trucks, and recreational vehicles

_____   _____

_____   _____

_____   _____

Planes, boats, and other vehicles

_____   _____

_____   _____

Other Personal Property
Household goods

_____   _____

_____   _____

_____   _____

Valuable clothing, jewelry, and furs

_____   _____

_____   _____

_____   _____

Collectibles, including artworks and antiques

_____   _____

_____   _____

_____   _____

Tools and equipment

_____   _____

_____   _____

_____   _____

Property   **Name of Any Existing Beneficiary**

Other Personal Property (continued)
Livestock or other valuable animals

_____   _____

_____   _____

Money owed you (personal loans, etc.)

_____   _____

_____   _____

_____   _____

Death benefits

_____   _____

_____   _____

_____   _____

_____   _____

Life insurance (other than term insurance)

_____   _____

_____   _____

Miscellaneous (any personal property not listed above)

_____   _____

_____   _____

_____   _____

_____   _____

_____   _____

Business Personal Property
Business ownerships (partnerships, sole proprietorships, limited partnerships, limited liability companies, corporations)

_____   _____

_____   _____

_____   _____

_____   _____

Intellectual property (domain names, patents, copyrights, and trademarks—including the right to receive royalties)

_____   _____

_____   _____

_____   _____

Miscellaneous receivables (mortgages, deeds of trust, or promissory notes held by you; any rents due from income property you own; and payments due for professional or personal services or property sold by you for which you have not been fully paid by the purchaser)

_____   _____

_____   _____

_____   _____

Beneficiary Worksheet

Beneficiaries of Specific Gifts in Your Will

Item: _____

Beneficiary(ies): _____

Address(es): _____

Alternate Beneficiary(ies): _____

Address(es): _____

Item: _____

Beneficiary(ies): _____

Address(es): _____

Alternate Beneficiary(ies): _____

Address(es): _____

Item: _____

Beneficiary(ies): _____

Address(es): _____

Alternate Beneficiary(ies): _____

Address(es): _____

Item: _____

Beneficiary(ies): _____

Address(es): _____

Alternate Beneficiary(ies): _____

Address(es): _____

Item: _____

Beneficiary(ies): _____

Address(es): _____

Alternate Beneficiary(ies): _____

Address(es): _____

Item: _____

Beneficiary(ies): _____

Address(es): _____

Alternate Beneficiary(ies): _____

Address(es): _____

Item: _____

Beneficiary(ies): _____

Address(es): _____

Alternate Beneficiary(ies): _____

Address(es): _____

Item: _____

Beneficiary(ies): _____

Address(es): _____

Alternate Beneficiary(ies): _____

Address(es): _____

Item: _____

Beneficiary(ies): _____

Address(es): _____

Alternate Beneficiary(ies): _____

Address(es): _____

Item: _____

Beneficiary(ies): _____

Address(es): _____

Alternate Beneficiary(ies): _____

Address(es): _____

Debts Forgiven

Amount Forgiven:_____ Date of loan: _____

Debtor: _____

Amount Forgiven:_____ Date of loan: _____

Debtor: _____

Amount Forgiven:_____ Date of loan: _____

Debtor: _____

Amount Forgiven:_____ Date of loan: _____

Debtor: _____

Residuary Beneficiary or Beneficiaries

Residuary beneficiary(ies) and percentage each one receives:

_____ _____ %

_____ _____ %

_____ _____ %

_____ _____ %

_____ _____ %

Alternate Residuary Beneficiary or Beneficiaries

Alternate residuary beneficiary(ies) and percentage each one receives:

_____ _____ %

_____ _____ %

_____ _____ %

_____ _____ %

_____ _____ %

⚠ **Do not just fill in and sign this form.** To be legally valid, your will must be printed out (using the CD-ROM that comes with this book) or typed, eliminating all items that don't apply to you. You cannot just fill in the blanks of this form and try to use the completed form as your will.

Will for Adult With No Children

Will of _____

I, _____

a resident of _____ [county], State of _____ ,

declare that this is my will.

1. **Revocation.** I revoke all wills that I have previously made.

2. **Marital Status.** I am ☐ married ☐ single ☐ in a registered domestic partnership or civil union.

3. **Specific Gifts.** I make the following specific gifts:

I leave _____

_____

_____

to _____

or, if he/she/they do/does not survive me, to _____

_____

I leave _____

_____

_____

to _____

or, if he/she/they do/does not survive me, to _____

_____

I leave _____

_____

_____

to _____

or, if he/she/they do/does not survive me, to _____

_____

I leave _____

_____

_____

to _____

or, if he/she/they do/does not survive me, to _____

_____

[repeat as needed]

4. **Residuary Estate.** I leave my residuary estate, that is, the rest of my property not otherwise specifically and validly disposed of by this will, including lapsed or failed gifts, to _____

_____

or, if he/she/they do/does not survive me, to _____

_____.

5. **Beneficiary Provisions.** The following terms and conditions apply to the beneficiary clauses of this will.

   A. **45-Day Survivorship Period.** As used in this will, the phrase "survive me" means to be alive or in existence as an organization on the 45th day after my death. Any beneficiary, except any alternate residuary beneficiary, must survive me to take property under this will.

   B. **Shared Gifts.** If I leave property to be shared by two or more beneficiaries, it shall be shared equally by them unless this will provides otherwise.

   If any beneficiary of a shared specific gift left in a single paragraph of the Specific Gifts clause, above, does not survive me, the gift shall be given to the surviving beneficiaries in equal shares.

   If any beneficiary of a shared residuary gift does not survive me, the residue shall be given to the surviving residuary beneficiaries in equal shares.

   C. **Encumbrances.** All property that I leave by this will shall pass subject to any encumbrances or liens on the property.

6. **Executor.** I name _____

as executor, to serve without bond. If he/she does not qualify, or ceases to serve, I name

_____

as executor, also to serve without bond.

I direct that my executor take all actions legally permissible to probate this will, including filing a petition in the appropriate court for the independent administration of my estate.

I grant to my executor the following powers, to be exercised as the executor deems to be in the best interests of my estate:

   A. To retain property, without liability for loss or depreciation resulting from such retention.

   B. To sell, lease, or exchange property and to receive or administer the proceeds as a part of my estate.

   C. To vote stock; convert bonds, notes, stocks, or other securities belonging to my estate into other securities; and to exercise all other rights and privileges of a person owning similar property.

   D. To deal with and settle claims in favor of or against my estate.

   E. To continue, maintain, operate, or participate in any business which is a part of my estate, and to incorporate, dissolve, or otherwise change the form of organization of the business.

   F. To pay all debts and taxes that may be assessed against my estate, as provided under state law.

   G. To do all other acts, which in the executor's judgment may be necessary or appropriate for the proper and advantageous management, investment, and distribution of my estate.

These powers, authority, and discretion are in addition to the powers, authority, and discretion vested in an executor by operation of law, and may be exercised as often as deemed necessary, without approval by any court in any jurisdiction.

Signature

I subscribe my name to this will this _____ day of _____ , _____ , at

_____ [county], State of _____ .

I declare that it is my will, that I sign it willingly, that I execute it as my free and voluntary act for the purposes expressed, and that I am of the age of majority or otherwise legally empowered to make a will and under no constraint or undue influence.

Signature: _____

Witnesses

On this _____ day of _____ , _____ , the testator,

_____

declared to us, the undersigned, that this instrument was ☐ his ☐ her will and requested us to act as witnesses to it. The testator signed this will in our presence, all of us being present at the same time. We now, at the testator's request, in the testator's presence and in the presence of each other, subscribe our names as witnesses and each declare that we are of sound mind and of proper age to witness a will. We further declare that we understand this to be the testator's will, and that to the best of our knowledge the testator is of the age of majority, or is otherwise legally empowered to make a will, and appears to be of sound mind and under no constraint or undue influence.

We declare under penalty of perjury that the foregoing is true and correct, this _____ day of

_____ , _____ , at _____ [county],

State of _____ .

Witness 1

Signature: _____

Typed or printed name: _____

Residing at: _____

City, state, zip: _____

Witness 2

Signature: _____

Typed or printed name: _____

Residing at: _____

City, state, zip: _____

Do not just fill in and sign this form. *To be legally valid, your will must be printed out (using the CD-ROM that comes with this book) or typed, eliminating all items that don't apply to you. You cannot just fill in the blanks of this form and try to use the completed form as your will.*

Will for Adult With Child(ren)

Will of _____

I, _____

a resident of _____ *[county]*, State of _____,

declare that this is my will.

1. **Revocation.** I revoke all wills that I have previously made.

2. **Marital Status.** I am ☐ married ☐ single ☐ in a registered domestic partnership or civil union.

3. **Children.** I have the following natural and legally adopted children:

Name   Date of Birth

_____   _____

_____   _____

_____   _____

_____   _____

_____   _____

_____   _____

_____   _____

[repeat as needed]

4. **Specific Gifts.** I make the following specific gifts:

I leave _____

_____

_____

to _____

or, if he/she/they do/does not survive me, to _____

_____

I leave _____

_____

_____

to _____

or, if he/she/they do/does not survive me, to _____

_____

I leave _____

_____

to _____

or, if he/she/they do/does not survive me, to _____

_____

I leave _____

_____

_____

to _____

or, if he/she/they do/does not survive me, to _____

_____

[repeat as needed]

5. **Residuary Estate.** I leave my residuary estate, that is, the rest of my property not otherwise specifically and validly disposed of by this will, including lapsed or failed gifts, to _____

_____

or, if he/she/they do/does not survive me, to _____

_____

6. **Beneficiary Provisions.** The following terms and conditions apply to the beneficiary clauses of this will.

   A. **45-Day Survivorship Period.** As used in this will, the phrase "survive me" means to be alive or in existence as an organization on the 45th day after my death. Any beneficiary, except any alternate residuary beneficiary, must survive me to take property under this will.

   B. **Shared Gifts.** If I leave property to be shared by two or more beneficiaries, it shall be shared equally by them unless this will provides otherwise.

   If any beneficiary of a shared specific gift left in a single paragraph of the Specific Gifts clause, above, does not survive me, the gift shall be given to the surviving beneficiaries in equal shares.

   If any beneficiary of a shared residuary gift does not survive me, the residue shall be given to the surviving residuary beneficiaries in equal shares.

   C. **Encumbrances.** All property that I leave by this will shall pass subject to any encumbrances or liens on the property.

7. **Executor.** I name _____

   as executor, to serve without bond. If he/she does not qualify, or ceases to serve, I name

   _____

   as executor, also to serve without bond.

   I direct that my executor take all actions legally permissible to probate this will, including filing a petition in the appropriate court for the independent administration of my estate.

   I grant to my executor the following powers, to be exercised as the executor deems to be in the best interests of my estate:

   A. To retain property, without liability for loss or depreciation resulting from such retention.

   B. To sell, lease, or exchange property and to receive or administer the proceeds as a part of my estate.

   C. To vote stock; convert bonds, notes, stocks, or other securities belonging to my estate into other securities; and to exercise all other rights and privileges of a person owning similar property.

D. To deal with and settle claims in favor of or against my estate.

E. To continue, maintain, operate, or participate in any business which is a part of my estate, and to incorporate, dissolve, or otherwise change the form of organization of the business.

F. To pay all debts and taxes that may be assessed against my estate, as provided under state law.

G. To do all other acts, which in the executor's judgment may be necessary or appropriate for the proper and advantageous management, investment, and distribution of my estate.

These powers, authority, and discretion are in addition to the powers, authority, and discretion vested in an executor by operation of law, and may be exercised as often as deemed necessary, without approval by any court in any jurisdiction.

8. **Personal Guardian.** If at my death any of my children are minors, and a personal guardian is needed, I nominate

_____

to be appointed personal guardian of my minor children. If ☐ he ☐ she cannot serve as personal guardian, I nominate _____

to be appointed personal guardian.

I direct that no bond be required of any personal guardian.

9. **Property Guardian.** If at my death any of my children are minors, and a property guardian is needed, I appoint

_____

as the property guardian of my minor children. If ☐ he ☐ she cannot serve as property guardian, I appoint

_____

as property guardian.

I direct that no bond be required of any property guardian.

10. **Gifts Under the Uniform Transfers to Minors Act.** All property left by this will to _____

_____ [name of minor]

shall be given to _____ [name of custodian]

as custodian for _____ [name of minor]

under the Uniform Transfers to Minors Act of _____ [your state].

If _____ [name of custodian]

cannot serve as custodian, _____

[name of successor custodian] shall serve as custodian. If _____

[your state] allows testators to choose the age at which the custodianship ends, I choose the oldest age allowed by my state's Uniform Transfers to Minors Act.

[repeat as needed for each child]

Signature

I subscribe my name to this will this _____ day of _____, _____, at

_____ [county], State of _____ .

I declare that it is my will, that I sign it willingly, that I execute it as my free and voluntary act for the purposes expressed, and that I am of the age of majority or otherwise legally empowered to make a will and under no constraint or undue influence.

Signature: _____

Witnesses

On this _____ day of _____, _____, the testator,

_____

declared to us, the undersigned, that this instrument was ☐ his ☐ her will and requested us to act as witnesses to it. The testator signed this will in our presence, all of us being present at the same time. We now, at the testator's request, in the testator's presence and in the presence of each other, subscribe our names as witnesses and each declare that we are of sound mind and of proper age to witness a will. We further declare that we understand this to be the testator's will, and that to the best of our knowledge the testator is of the age of majority, or is otherwise legally empowered to make a will, and appears to be of sound mind and under no constraint or undue influence.

We declare under penalty of perjury that the foregoing is true and correct, this _____ day of

_____, _____, at _____ [county],

State of _____.

Witness 1

Signature: _____

Typed or printed name: _____

Residing at: _____

City, state, zip: _____

Witness 2

Signature: _____

Typed or printed name: _____

Residing at: _____

City, state, zip: _____

! ***Do not just fill in and sign this form.*** *To be legally valid, your will codicil must be printed out (using the CD-ROM that comes with this book) or typed, eliminating all items that don't apply to you. You cannot just fill in the blanks of this form and try to use the completed form as your will.*

Will Codicil

First Codicil to the Will of _____

I, _____

a resident of _____ [county], State of _____ ,

declare this to be the first codicil to my will dated _____ , _____ .

FIRST: I revoke the provision of Clause _____ of my will that provided:

[include the exact will language you wish to revoke]

_____

_____

_____

_____

_____

SECOND: I add the following provision to Clause _____ of my will:

[add whatever is desired]

_____

_____

_____

_____

_____

THIRD: In all other respects I confirm and republish my will dated _____ , _____ .

Dated _____ , _____ .

Signature

I subscribe my name to this codicil this _____ day of _____ , _____ .

_____ [county], State of _____ .

   I declare under penalty of perjury that I sign and execute this codicil willingly, that I execute it as my free and voluntary act for the purposes expressed, and that I am of the age of majority or otherwise legally empowered to make a codicil and under no constraint or undue influence.

Signature: _____

Witnesses

On this _____ day of _____, _____,

_____ [codicil maker's name]

declared to us, the undersigned, that this instrument was a codicil to ☐ his ☐ her will and requested us to act as witnesses to it. The testator signed this codicil in our presence, all of us being present at the same time. We now, at the testator's request, in the testator's presence and in the presence of each other, subscribe our names as witnesses and declare we understand this to be the testator's codicil and that to the best of our knowledge the testator is of the age of majority, or is otherwise legally empowered to make a codicil, and appears to be of sound mind and is under no constraint or undue influence.

We declare under penalty of perjury that the foregoing is true and correct, this _____ day of

_____, _____, at _____ [county],

State of _____.

Witness 1

Signature: _____

Typed or printed name: _____

Residing at: _____

City, state, zip: _____

Witness 2

Signature: _____

Typed or printed name: _____

Residing at: _____

City, state, zip: _____

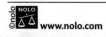

Request for Death Certificate

Date: _____

_____

_____

_____

_____

[insert address of vital statistics office]

Name of deceased: _____

Date of death: _____ Place of death: _____

Place of birth: _____ Social Security number: _____

Please send me _____ certified copies of the death certificate of the above-named person. I have enclosed a check in the amount of $_____ and a stamped, self-addressed envelope. The reason for my request is to administer the affairs of the deceased's estate.

Thank you for your assistance.

Signature: _____

Printed or typed name: _____

Relationship to deceased: _____

Address: _____

_____

Home phone: _____ Work phone: _____

Notice to Creditor of Death

Date: _____

_____

_____

_____

_____

[insert name and address of creditor]

Name of deceased: _____

Deceased's address: _____

Account number: _____ Date of death: _____

To whom it may concern:

I am the representative of the decedent. Please cancel this account at once.

Please also acknowledge that you received this notice by signing the duplicate of this letter and returning it to me in the enclosed stamped, self-addressed envelope.

If there is any outstanding balance on this account, please promptly notify me at the address below.

Thank you for your assistance.

Signature: _____

Printed or typed name: _____

Relationship to deceased: _____

Address: _____

_____

Home phone: _____ Work phone: _____

Receipt acknowledged by:

Signature: _____

Printed or typed name: _____

Title: _____

Date of receipt of notice: _____

Executor's Checklist

☐ **Decide Whether or Not Probate Is Necessary**

Probate isn't necessary for many common assets. No probate is necessary to:

- pass real estate or other assets owned in joint tenancy, tenancy by the entirety, or community property with right of survivorship to the surviving owner

- transfer bank accounts and securities registered in "payable on death" form to beneficiaries

- transfer funds in IRAs and retirement plans to named beneficiaries

- transfer property left to the surviving spouse (in some states)

- transfer assets held in trusts (such as revocable living trusts or bypass trusts) to named beneficiaries.

The deceased's home state may also have streamlined probate procedures for small estates. Whether probate is necessary commonly depends upon the size of the estate, minus all the non-probated assets—that is, anything that can be transferred outside of probate.

If probate is not required, go to "Handling an Estate That Doesn't Go Through Probate," below. If probate is required, go to "Probating an Estate."

☐ **Handling an Estate That Doesn't Go Through Probate**

☐ Locate and secure the deceased person's assets and carefully manage them until you distribute them.

☐ Handle day-to-day details, such as terminating leases and other outstanding contracts, and notifying banks and government agencies of the death—for example, the Social Security Administration, the post office, Medicare, and the Department of Veterans Affairs.

☐ Use money left in the estate to pay continuing expenses—for example, mortgage payments, utility bills, and homeowners' insurance premiums.

☐ Use money left in the estate to pay any debts the deceased person owed. If there isn't enough money to pay them all, consult a lawyer. State law gives certain creditors priority.

☐ Pay income taxes. Income tax returns must be filed for the year in which the person died.

☐ Supervise the distribution of property to the people entitled to inherit it according to the will or state law.

☐ **Probating an Estate**

☐ File the will in the local probate court and ask the court to confirm you as executor. You may want to hire a lawyer to prepare the paperwork or to help you with the process. (See "Decide Whether or Not to Hire a Lawyer," below.)

☐ Send notice of the probate proceeding to the beneficiaries named in the will and, if necessary, to certain close relatives—in most cases, a surviving spouse and children—who would have been entitled to property if there was no valid will.

☐ Locate and secure the deceased person's assets and carefully manage them during the probate process, which commonly takes about a year. Depending on the contents of the will and the financial condition of the estate, this may involve deciding whether to sell real estate or securities owned by the deceased person.

☐ Handle day-to-day details, such as terminating leases and other outstanding contracts, and notifying banks and government agencies of the death—for example, the Social Security Administration, the post office, Medicare, and the Department of Veterans Affairs.

☐ Set up an estate bank account to hold money that comes to the estate—for example, paychecks and stock dividends.

☐ Pay continuing expenses—for example, mortgage payments, utility bills, and homeowners' insurance premiums.

☐ Pay any debts that the estate is legally required to pay. You must also notify creditors of the probate proceeding; the required method of notice will be set out by state law. Creditors then have a certain amount of time—usually about four to six months—to file a claim for payment of any bills or other obligations you haven't voluntarily paid. As executor, you decide whether or not a claim is valid.

☐ Pay income taxes. Income tax returns must be filed for the year in which the person died.

☐ Pay estate taxes if necessary. It's unlikely, but state and federal estate tax returns may be required. Only very large estates owe federal estate tax. (And any amount of property left to a surviving spouse who is a U.S. citizen is estate tax free.) More and more states are collecting estate taxes of their own as well. Some states impose inheritance tax which is paid by the people who inherit the property. Check with your state's taxing authority.

☐ Supervise the distribution of property—such as cash, personal belongings, and real estate—to the people or organizations named in the will or entitled to inherit under state law.

☐ When debts and taxes have been paid and all the property distributed to the beneficiaries, ask the probate court to formally close the estate.

☐ **Decide Whether or Not to Hire a Lawyer**

Hiring a lawyer is often a sensible choice, especially for estates with lots of different types of property, significant tax liabilities, or the potential for disputes among inheritors. But it is not mandatory, and you may decide to handle the paperwork yourself. This makes good sense if you have access to good do-it-yourself materials (from private sources or the probate court itself), particularly if you are a main beneficiary and you don't expect any complications collecting and transferring the assets.

Essentially, handling a probate court proceeding requires shuffling a lot of papers through the court clerk's office; in the vast majority of cases, there are no disputes that require a decision by a judge. You may even be able to do everything by mail. Doing a good job requires persistence and attention to tedious detail.

Here are some ways to get information and help, whether or not you hire a lawyer:

• Some court websites offer very useful booklets, forms, and instructions. Be sure to see what your court offers. Probate court clerks commonly answer basic questions about court procedure but they staunchly avoid saying anything that could be construed as legal advice. Some courts, however, have lawyers on staff who look over probate documents; they may point out errors in your papers and tell you how to fix them.

• In many law offices, lawyers delegate all the probate paperwork to paralegals. In some areas of the country, experienced paralegals have set up shop to help people deal directly with probate paperwork. They do not offer legal advice; they just prepare documents as you instruct them. They can also file papers with the court for you. To find one, look online for "legal document preparers." Make sure that the person you hire has lots of experience in this field and gives you references to check out.

• You may want to consult books written for nonlawyers, such as *The Executor's Guide: Settling a Loved One's Estate or Trust*, by Mary Randolph (Nolo). *How to Probate an Estate in California*, by Julia Nissley (Nolo), leads you through the California probate process step by step. Although the forms included with the book are used only in California, the book contains much information that would be valuable background in any state.

General Notice of Death

Date: _____

_____

_____

_____

_____

[insert name and address of organization]

This letter is to notify you that _____ *[name]*

of _____

_____ *[address]*

died on _____ *[date]*. Please let me know if you would like further information.

Signature: _____

Printed or typed name: _____

Relationship to deceased: _____

Address: _____

_____

Obituary Information Fact Sheet

Name of deceased: _____

Age at death: _____

Location and date of death: _____

Cause of death: _____

Birthplace: _____

Address: _____

Length of time in community: _____

Religious affiliation or membership: _____

High school, college, or graduate degrees: _____

_____

Professional degrees or affiliations: _____

_____

Military service: _____

Profession: _____

Interesting personal facts: _____

_____

Survived by: [*Names of survivors—spouses, siblings, in-laws, children, grandchildren, etc.—and their relationship to deceased*] _____

_____

Predeceased by: [*Names of spouses, siblings, and children who predeceased and when deaths occurred*]

_____

_____

Time and location of funeral arrangements and services: [*often supplied by the funeral home*] _____

_____

_____

For further information, contact:_____

_____

_____

_____

Notice to Deceased's Homeowners' Insurance Company

Date: _____

_____

_____

_____

_____

[insert insurance company name and address]

Name of deceased: _____

Address: _____

Date of death: _____

Homeowners' insurance policy number: _____

This letter is to notify you that your insured, _____

_____ *[deceased's name]*, has died.
I am the executor of the estate and would like to be added as a named insured to this homeowners' insurance policy. Enclosed with this letter you will find a certified death certificate, along with documentation that I am the executor.

Please contact me so that we may discuss this matter. I can be reached using the information below. Please sign and return the copy of this letter in the enclosed stamped and self-addressed envelope.

Thank you for your assistance.

Signature: _____

Printed or typed name: _____

Relationship to deceased: _____

Address: _____ Home phone: _____

Work phone: _____ Email: _____

Receipt acknowledged by:

Signature: _____

Printed or typed name: _____

Title: _____

Date of receipt of notice: _____

Notice to Deceased's Vehicle Insurance Company

Date: _____

_____

_____

_____

_____

[insert insurance company name and address]

Name of deceased: _____

Address: _____

Date of death: _____

Vehicle insurance policy number: _____

Make, model, and year of vehicle: _____

This letter is to notify you that your insured, _____

_____ *[deceased's name]*, has died.

I am the executor of the estate and would like to be added as a named insured to this insurance policy. Enclosed with this letter you will find a certified death certificate for _____

[deceased's name], documentation of my status as executor, and a state-certified copy of my driving record.

Please contact me so that we may discuss this matter. I can be reached using the information below. Please sign and return the second copy of this letter in the enclosed stamped and self-addressed envelope.

Thank you for your assistance.

Signature: _____

Printed or typed name: _____

Relationship to deceased: _____

Address: _____ Home phone: _____

Work phone: _____ Email: _____

Receipt acknowledged by:

Signature: _____

Printed or typed name: _____

Title: _____

Date of receipt of notice: _____

Apartment-Finding Service Checklist

Name of Company: _____

Address: _____

Phone number: _____

Hours: _____

Date: _____

1. Description of listings:

   • geographic areas covered _____

   • type of rentals _____

   • total number of listings _____

   • number of new listings per day _____

   • exclusivity _____

   • type of information available in listing _____

   _____

   _____

2. Ways to access listings, cost, and duration of service:

   ☐ phone _____

   ☐ fax _____

   ☐ email _____

   ☐ pager _____

   ☐ books available in office _____

   ☐ costs _____

   ☐ duration of service _____

3. Free phone available in office for members' use?   ☐ Yes   ☐ No

4. Other services and costs:

   ☐ roommate referrals _____

   ☐ credit screening _____

   ☐ other _____

5. Percentage of members who find a rental unit through service: _____

6. Refund if rental not found through company: _____

7. Length of time in business: _____

8. Other comments: _____

Rental Application

Separate application required from each applicant age 18 or older.

Date and time received by landlord _____

Credit check fee $_____ Received _____

THIS SECTION TO BE COMPLETED BY LANDLORD

Address of Property to Be Rented: _____

    Rental Term: ☐ month-to-month ☐ lease from _____ to _____

    Amounts Due Prior to Occupancy

        First month's rent .... $_____

        Security deposit .... $_____

        Other (specify): .... $_____

                       TOTAL .... $_____

Applicant

Full Name—include all names you use(d): _____

Home Phone: _____ Work Phone: _____ Cell Phone: _____

Email: _____ Fax*:_____

Social Security Number: _____ Driver's License Number/State: _____

Other Identifying Information: _____

Vehicle Make: _____ Model: _____ Color: _____ Year: _____

License Plate Number/State: _____

Additional Occupants

List everyone, including children, who will live with you:

Full Name	**Relationship to Applicant**
_____	_____
_____	_____
_____	_____
_____	_____

Rental History

FIRST-TIME RENTERS: ATTACH A DESCRIPTION OF YOUR HOUSING SITUATION FOR THE PAST FIVE YEARS.

Current Address: _____

Dates Lived at Address: _____ Rent $_____ Security Deposit $_____

Landlord/Manager: _____ Landlord/Manager's Phone: _____

Reason for Leaving: _____

Previous Address: _____

Dates Lived at Address: _____ Rent $_____ Security Deposit $_____

Landlord/Manager: _____ Landlord/Manager's Phone: _____

Reason for Leaving: _____

* By providing this fax number I agree to receive facsimile advertisements from the landlord or management company.

Previous Address: _____

Dates Lived at Address: _____ Rent $_____ Security Deposit $_____

Landlord/Manager: _____ Landlord/Manager's Phone: _____

Reason for Leaving: _____

Previous Address: _____

Dates Lived at Address: _____ Rent $_____ Security Deposit $_____

Landlord/Manager: _____ Landlord/Manager's Phone: _____

Reason for Leaving: _____

Employment History

SELF-EMPLOYED APPLICANTS: ATTACH TAX RETURNS FOR THE PAST TWO YEARS.

Name and Address of Current Employer: _____

_____ Phone: _____

Name of Supervisor: _____ Supervisor's Phone: _____

Dates Employed at This Job: _____ Position or Title: _____

Name and Address of Previous Employer: _____

_____ Phone: _____

Name of Supervisor: _____ Supervisor's Phone: _____

Dates Employed at This Job: _____ Position or Title: _____

ATTACH PAY STUBS FOR THE PAST TWO YEARS, FROM THIS EMPLOYER OR PRIOR EMPLOYERS.

Income

1. Your gross monthly employment income (before deductions): $_____

2. Average monthly amounts of other income (specify sources): $_____

   _____ $_____

   _____ $_____

                                        TOTAL: $_____

Bank/Financial Accounts

	Account Number	Bank/Institution	Branch
Savings Account:			
Checking Account:			
Money Market or Similar Account:			

Credit Card Accounts

Major Credit Card: ☐ VISA   ☐ MC   ☐ Discover Card   ☐ Am Ex   ☐ Other: _____

Issuer: _____   Account No. _____

Balance: $_____   Average Monthly Payment: $_____

Major Credit Card: ☐ VISA   ☐ MC   ☐ Discover Card   ☐ Am Ex   ☐ Other: _____

Issuer: _____   Account No. _____

Balance: $_____   Average Monthly Payment: $_____

Loans

Type of Loan (mortgage, car, student loan, etc.)	Name of Creditor	Account Number	Amount Owed	Monthly Payment

Other Major Obligations

Type	Payee		Amount Owed	Monthly Payment

Miscellaneous

Describe the number and type of pets you want to have in the rental property: _____

_____

Describe water-filled furniture you want to have in the rental property: _____

_____

Do you smoke?   ☐ yes   ☐ no

Have you ever: Filed for bankruptcy?   ☐ yes   ☐ no   How many times _____

Been sued?   ☐ yes   ☐ no   How many times _____

Sued someone else?   ☐ yes   ☐ no   How many times _____

Been evicted?   ☐ yes   ☐ no   How many times _____

Been convicted of a crime? ☐ yes   ☐ no   How many times _____

Explain any "yes" listed above: _____

_____

_____

_____

_____

References and Emergency Contact

Personal Reference: _____ Relationship: _____

Address: _____

_____ Phone: _____

Personal Reference: _____ Relationship: _____

Address: _____

_____ Phone: _____

Contact in Emergency: _____ Relationship: _____

Address: _____

_____ Phone: _____

Source

Where did you learn of this vacancy? _____

_____

I certify that all the information given above is true and correct and understand that my lease or rental agreement may be terminated if I have made any material false or incomplete statements in this application. I authorize verification of the information provided in this application from my credit sources, credit bureaus, current and previous landlords and employers, and personal references. This permission will survive the expiration of my tenancy.

_____ _____

Applicant   Date

Notes (Landlord/Manager): _____

_____

_____

_____

_____

_____

_____

_____

_____

_____

_____

_____

_____

_____

_____

_____

_____

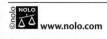

Fixed-Term Residential Lease

Clause 1. Identification of Landlord and Tenant

This Agreement is entered into between _____

_____ ("Tenant") and

_____ ("Landlord"). Each Tenant is

jointly and severally liable for the payment of rent and performance of all other terms of this Agreement.

Clause 2. Identification of Premises

Subject to the terms and conditions in this Agreement, Landlord rents to Tenant, and Tenant rents from

Landlord, for residential purposes only, the premises located at _____

_____ ("the premises"),

together with the following furnishings and appliances: _____

_____.

Rental of the premises also includes _____

_____.

Clause 3. Limits on Use and Occupancy

The premises are to be used only as a private residence for Tenant(s) listed in Clause 1 of this Agreement, and

the following minor children: _____. Occupancy by

guests for more than _____ is prohibited without Landlord's written consent

and will be considered a breach of this Agreement.

Clause 4. Term of the Tenancy

The term of the rental will begin on _____, _____, and end on

_____, _____. If Tenant vacates before the term ends, Tenant will be liable

for the balance of the rent for the remainder of the term.

Clause 5. Payment of Rent

Regular monthly rent.

Tenant will pay to Landlord a monthly rent of $_____, payable in advance on the first day of

each month, except when that day falls on a weekend or legal holiday, in which case rent is due on the next

business day. Rent will be paid to _____ at _____

(or at such other place as Landlord designates) in the following manner unless Landlord designates otherwise:

Delivery of payment.

Rent will be paid:

☐ by mail, to _____

☐ in person, at _____

Form of payment.

Landlord will accept payment in these forms:

☐ personal check made payable to _____

☐ cashier's check made payable to _____

☐ credit card

☐ money order

☐ cash

Prorated first month's rent.

For the period from Tenant's move-in date, _____, _____, through the

end of the month, Tenant will pay to Landlord the prorated monthly rent of $_____.

This amount will be paid on or before the date the Tenant moves in.

Clause 6. Late Charges

If Tenant fails to pay the rent in full before the end of the _____ day after it's due, Tenant will pay

Landlord a late charge of $_____, plus $_____ for each additional day that

the rent remains unpaid. The total late charge for any one month will not exceed $_____.

Landlord does not waive the right to insist on payment of the rent in full on the date it is due.

Clause 7. Returned Check and Other Bank Charges

If any check offered by Tenant to Landlord in payment of rent or any other amount due under this Agreement

is returned for lack of sufficient funds, a "stop payment," or any other reason, Tenant will pay Landlord a

returned check charge of $_____.

Clause 8. Security Deposit

On signing this Agreement, Tenant will pay to Landlord the sum of $_____ as a security deposit.

Tenant may not, without Landlord's prior written consent, apply this security deposit to the last month's rent

or to any other sum due under this Agreement. Within _____ days after Tenant has

vacated the premises, returned keys, and provided Landlord with a forwarding address, Landlord will give

Tenant an itemized written statement of the reasons for, and the dollar amount of, any of the security deposit

retained by Landlord, along with a check for any deposit balance.

Clause 9. Utilities

Tenant will pay all utility charges, except for the following, which will be paid by Landlord:

_____

_____.

Clause 10. Assignment and Subletting

Tenant will not sublet any part of the premises or assign this Agreement without the prior written consent of

Landlord.

Clause 11. Tenant's Maintenance Responsibilities

Tenant will: (1) keep the premises clean, sanitary, and in good condition and, upon termination of the tenancy,

return the premises to Landlord in a condition identical to that which existed when Tenant took occupancy, except for ordinary wear and tear; (2) immediately notify Landlord of any defects or dangerous conditions in and about the premises of which Tenant becomes aware; and (3) reimburse Landlord, on demand by Landlord, for the cost of any repairs to the premises damaged by Tenant or Tenant's guests or business invitees through misuse or neglect.

Tenant has examined the premises, including appliances, fixtures, carpets, drapes, and paint, and has found them to be in good, safe, and clean condition and repair, except as noted in the Landlord-Tenant Checklist.

Clause 12. Repairs and Alterations by Tenant

a. Except as provided by law, or as authorized below, or by the prior written consent of Landlord, Tenant will not make any repairs or alterations to the premises.

b. Tenant will not, without Landlord's prior written consent, alter, rekey, or install any locks to the premises or install or alter any burglar alarm system. Tenant will provide Landlord with a key or keys capable of unlocking all such rekeyed or new locks as well as instructions on how to disarm any altered or new burglar alarm system.

Clause 13. Violating Laws and Causing Disturbances

Tenant is entitled to quiet enjoyment of the premises. Tenant and guests or invitees will not use the premises or adjacent areas in such a way as to: (1) violate any law or ordinance, including laws prohibiting the use, possession, or sale of illegal drugs; (2) commit waste (severe property damage); or (3) create a nuisance by annoying, disturbing, inconveniencing, or interfering with the quiet enjoyment and peace and quiet of any other tenant or nearby resident.

Clause 14. Pets

No animal, bird, or other pet will be kept on the premises, except properly trained service animals needed by blind, deaf, or disabled persons and _____
under the following conditions: _____
_____

Clause 15. Landlord's Right to Access

Landlord or Landlord's agents may enter the premises in the event of an emergency, to make repairs or improvements, or to show the premises to prospective buyers or tenants. Landlord may also enter the premises to conduct an annual inspection to check for safety or maintenance problems. Except in cases of emergency, Tenant's abandonment of the premises, court order, or where it is impractical to do so, Landlord shall give Tenant _____ notice before entering.

Clause 16. Extended Absences by Tenant

Tenant will notify Landlord in advance if Tenant will be away from the premises for _____ or more consecutive days. During such absence, Landlord may enter the premises at times reasonably necessary to maintain the property and inspect it for needed repairs.

Clause 17. Possession of the Premises

a. Tenant's failure to take possession.

If, after signing this Agreement, Tenant fails to take possession of the premises, Tenant will still be responsible for paying rent and complying with all other terms of this Agreement.

b. Landlord's failure to deliver possession.

If Landlord is unable to deliver possession of the premises to Tenant for any reason not within Landlord's control, including, but not limited to, partial or complete destruction of the premises, Tenant will have the right to terminate this Agreement upon proper notice as required by law. In such event, Landlord's liability to Tenant will be limited to the return of all sums previously paid by Tenant to Landlord.

Clause 18. Tenant Rules and Regulations

☐ Tenant acknowledges receipt of, and has read a copy of, the tenant rules and regulations, which are labeled Attachment A and attached to and incorporated into this Agreement by this reference.

Clause 19. Payment of Court Costs and Attorney Fees in a Lawsuit

In any action or legal proceeding to enforce any part of this Agreement, the prevailing party

☐ shall not / ☐ shall recover reasonable attorney fees and court costs.

Clause 20. Disclosures

Tenant acknowledges that Landlord has made the following disclosures regarding the premises:

☐ Disclosure of Information on Lead-Based Paint and/or Lead-Based Paint Hazards

☐ Other disclosures:

_____

_____

_____

Clause 21. Authority to Receive Legal Papers

The Landlord, any person managing the premises, and anyone designated by the Landlord are authorized to accept service of process and receive other notices and demands, which may be delivered to:

☐ The Landlord, at the following address: _____

_____

☐ The manager, at the following address: _____

_____

☐ The following person, at the following address: _____

_____

Clause 22. Additional Provisions

Additional provisions are as follows: _____

_____

_____

_____

_____

_____

_____

Clause 23. Validity of Each Part

If any portion of this Agreement is held to be invalid, its invalidity will not affect the validity or enforceability of any other provision of this Agreement.

Clause 24. Grounds for Termination of Tenancy

The failure of Tenant or Tenant's guests or invitees to comply with any term of this Agreement, or the misrepresentation of any material fact on Tenant's rental application, is grounds for termination of the tenancy, with appropriate notice to Tenant and procedures as required by law.

Clause 25. Entire Agreement

This document constitutes the entire Agreement between the parties, and no promises or representations, other than those contained here and those implied by law, have been made by Landlord or Tenant. Any modifications to this Agreement must be in writing and signed by Landlord and Tenant.

_____   _____   _____
Date   Landlord or Landlord's Agent   Title

_____
Street Address

_____   _____
City, State & Zip   Phone

_____   _____   _____
Date   Tenant   Phone

_____   _____   _____
Date   Tenant   Phone

_____   _____   _____
Date   Tenant   Phone

Month-to-Month Residential Rental Agreement

Clause 1. Identification of Landlord and Tenant

This Agreement is entered into between _____

_____ ("Tenant") and

_____ ("Landlord"). Each Tenant is

jointly and severally liable for the payment of rent and performance of all other terms of this Agreement.

Clause 2. Identification of Premises

Subject to the terms and conditions in this Agreement, Landlord rents to Tenant, and Tenant rents from

Landlord, for residential purposes only, the premises located at _____

_____ ("the premises"),

together with the following furnishings and appliances: _____

_____ .

Rental of the premises also includes _____

_____ .

Clause 3. Limits on Use and Occupancy

The premises are to be used only as a private residence for Tenant(s) listed in Clause 1 of this Agreement, and

their minor children. Occupancy by guests for more than _____

is prohibited without Landlord's written consent and will be considered a breach of this Agreement.

Clause 4. Term of the Tenancy

The rental will begin on _____, _____, and continue on a month-to-month

basis. Landlord may terminate the tenancy or modify the terms of this Agreement by giving the Tenant

_____ days' written notice. Tenant may terminate the tenancy by giving the Landlord

_____ days' written notice.

Clause 5. Payment of Rent

Regular monthly rent.

Tenant will pay to Landlord a monthly rent of $_____, payable in advance on the first day

of each month, except when that day falls on a weekend or legal holiday, in which case rent is due on the

next business day. Rent will be paid to _____ at

_____ or at such other place as Landlord designates in the

following manner unless Landlord designates otherwise:

Delivery of payment.

Rent will be paid:

☐ by mail, to _____

☐ in person, at _____

Form of payment.

Landlord will accept payment in these forms:

☐ personal check made payable to _____

☐ cashier's check made payable to _____

☐ credit card

☐ money order

☐ cash

Prorated first month's rent.

For the period from Tenant's move-in date, _____, _____, through the end of the month, Tenant will pay to Landlord the prorated monthly rent of $_____. This amount will be paid on or before the date the Tenant moves in.

Clause 6. Late Charges

If Tenant fails to pay the rent in full before the end of the _____ day after it's due, Tenant will pay Landlord a late charge of $_____, plus $_____ for each additional day that the rent remains unpaid. The total late charge for any one month will not exceed $_____. Landlord does not waive the right to insist on payment of the rent in full on the date it is due.

Clause 7. Returned Check and Other Bank Charges

If any check offered by Tenant to Landlord in payment of rent or any other amount due under this Agreement is returned for lack of sufficient funds, a "stop payment," or any other reason, Tenant will pay Landlord a returned check charge of $_____.

Clause 8. Security Deposit

On signing this Agreement, Tenant will pay to Landlord the sum of $_____ as a security deposit. Tenant may not, without Landlord's prior written consent, apply this security deposit to the last month's rent or to any other sum due under this Agreement. Within _____ after Tenant has vacated the premises, returned keys, and provided Landlord with a forwarding address, Landlord will return the deposit in full or give Tenant an itemized written statement of the reasons for, and the dollar amount of, any of the security deposit retained by Landlord, along with a check for any deposit balance.

Clause 9. Utilities

Tenant will pay all utility charges, except for the following, which will be paid by Landlord:

_____

_____.

Clause 10. Assignment and Subletting

Tenant will not sublet any part of the premises or assign this Agreement without the prior written consent of Landlord.

Clause 11. Tenant's Maintenance Responsibilities

Tenant will: (1) keep the premises clean, sanitary, and in good condition and, upon termination of the tenancy, return the premises to Landlord in a condition identical to that which existed when Tenant took occupancy, except for ordinary wear and tear; (2) immediately notify Landlord of any defects or dangerous conditions in and about the premises of which Tenant becomes aware; and (3) reimburse Landlord, on demand by Landlord, for the cost of any repairs to the premises damaged by Tenant or Tenant's guests or business invitees through misuse or neglect.

Tenant has examined the premises, including appliances, fixtures, carpets, drapes, and paint, and has found them to be in good, safe, and clean condition and repair, except as noted in the Landlord-Tenant Checklist.

Clause 12. Repairs and Alterations by Tenant

a. Except as provided by law, or as authorized below, or by the prior written consent of Landlord, Tenant will not make any repairs or alterations to the premises, including nailing holes in the walls or painting the rental unit.

b. Tenant will not, without Landlord's prior written consent, alter, rekey, or install any locks to the premises or install or alter any burglar alarm system. Tenant will provide Landlord with a key or keys capable of unlocking all such rekeyed or new locks as well as instructions on how to disarm any altered or new burglar alarm system.

Clause 13. Violating Laws and Causing Disturbances

Tenant is entitled to quiet enjoyment of the premises. Tenant and guests or invitees will not use the premises or adjacent areas in such a way as to: (1) violate any law or ordinance, including laws prohibiting the use, possession, or sale of illegal drugs; (2) commit waste (severe property damage); or (3) create a nuisance by annoying, disturbing, inconveniencing, or interfering with the quiet enjoyment and peace and quiet of any other tenant or nearby resident.

Clause 14. Pets

No animal, bird, or other pet will be kept on the premises, except properly trained service animals needed by blind, deaf, or disabled persons and _____ under the following conditions: _____

_____ .

Clause 15. Landlord's Right to Access

Landlord or Landlord's agents may enter the premises in the event of an emergency, to make repairs or improvements, or to show the premises to prospective buyers or tenants. Landlord may also enter the premises to conduct an annual inspection to check for safety or maintenance problems. Except in cases of emergency, Tenant's abandonment of the premises, court order, or where it is impractical to do so, Landlord shall give Tenant _____ notice before entering.

Clause 16. Extended Absences by Tenant

Tenant will notify Landlord in advance if Tenant will be away from the premises for _____ or more consecutive days. During such absence, Landlord may enter the premises at times reasonably necessary to maintain the property and inspect it for needed repairs.

Clause 17. Possession of the Premises

a. Tenant's failure to take possession.

If, after signing this Agreement, Tenant fails to take possession of the premises, Tenant will still be responsible for paying rent and complying with all other terms of this Agreement.

b. Landlord's failure to deliver possession.

If Landlord is unable to deliver possession of the premises to Tenant for any reason not within Landlord's control, including, but not limited to, partial or complete destruction of the premises, Tenant will have the right to terminate this Agreement upon proper notice as required by law. In such event, Landlord's liability to Tenant will be limited to the return of all sums previously paid by Tenant to Landlord.

Clause 18. Tenant Rules and Regulations

☐ Tenants acknowledges receipt of, and have read a copy of, the tenant rules and regulations, which are attached to and incorporated into this Agreement by this reference.

Clause 19. Payment of Court Costs and Attorney Fees in a Lawsuit

In any action or legal proceeding to enforce any part of this Agreement, the prevailing party

☐ shall not / ☐ shall recover reasonable attorney fees and court costs.

Clause 20. Disclosures

Tenant acknowledges that Landlord has made the following disclosures regarding the premises:

☐ Disclosure of Information on Lead-Based Paint and/or Lead-Based Paint Hazards

☐ Other disclosures:

_____

_____

_____

Clause 21. Authority to Receive Legal Papers

The Landlord, any person managing the premises, and anyone designated by the Landlord are authorized to accept service of process and receive other notices and demands, which may be delivered to:

☐ The Landlord, at the following address: _____

_____

☐ The manager, at the following address: _____

_____

☐ The following person, at the following address: _____

_____

Clause 22. Additional Provisions

Additional provisions are as follows: _____

_____

_____

_____

_____

_____

_____

Clause 23. Validity of Each Part

If any portion of this Agreement is held to be invalid, its invalidity will not affect the validity or enforceability of any other provision of this Agreement.

Clause 24. Grounds for Termination of Tenancy

The failure of Tenant or Tenant's guests or invitees to comply with any term of this Agreement, or the misrepresentation of any material fact on Tenant's rental application, is grounds for termination of the tenancy, with appropriate notice to Tenant and procedures as required by law.

Clause 25. Entire Agreement

This document constitutes the entire Agreement between the parties, and no promises or representations, other than those contained here and those implied by law, have been made by Landlord or Tenant. Any modifications to this Agreement must be in writing and signed by Landlord and Tenant.

_____   _____   _____
Date   Landlord or Landlord's Agent   Title

_____
Street Address

_____   _____
City, State & Zip   Phone

_____   _____   _____
Date   Tenant   Phone

_____   _____   _____
Date   Tenant   Phone

_____   _____   _____
Date   Tenant   Phone

Landlord-Tenant Agreement to Terminate Lease

Landlord: _____ and

Tenant: _____

agree that the lease they entered into for the time period of _____, _____,

to _____, _____, for premises at _____

_____,

will terminate on _____.

Additional conditions for cancellation of lease: _____

_____

_____

_____

_____	_____
Landlord's signature	Date
_____	
Print name	
_____	_____
Tenant 1's signature	Date
_____	
Print name	
_____	_____
Tenant 2's signature	Date
_____	
Print name	
_____	_____
Tenant 3's signature	Date
_____	
Print name	

Consent to Assignment of Lease

Landlord: _____

Tenant: _____

Assignee: _____

Landlord, Tenant, and Assignee agree as follows:

1. Location of Premises

Tenant has leased the premises located at _____

from Landlord.

2. Lease Beginning and Ending Dates

The lease was signed on _____, _____.

It will expire on _____, _____.

3. Assignment

Tenant is assigning the balance of Tenant's lease to Assignee, beginning on _____,

_____. It will end on _____, _____.

4. Tenant's Future Liability

Tenant's financial responsibilities under the terms of the lease are ended by this assignment. Specifically, Tenant's responsibilities for future rent and future damage are ended.

5. Tenant's Right to Occupy

As of the effective date of the assignment, Tenant permanently gives up the right to occupy the premises.

6. Binding Nature of Agreement

Assignee is bound by every term and condition in the lease that is the subject of this assignment.

_____   _____

Landlord's signature   Date

_____   _____

Print name

_____   _____

Tenant's signature   Date

_____   _____

Print name

_____   _____

Assignee's signature   Date

_____   _____

Print name

Landlord-Tenant Checklist
General Condition of Rental Unit and Premises

Street Address _____ Unit Number _____ City _____

	Condition on Arrival	Condition on Initial Move-Out Inspection	Condition on Departure	Actual or Estimated Cost of Cleaning, Repair/Replacement
Living Room				
Floors & Floor Coverings				
Drapes & Window Coverings				
Walls & Ceiling				
Light Fixtures				
Windows, Screens, & Doors				
Front Door & Locks				
Smoke Detector				
Fireplace				
Other				
Kitchen				
Floors & Floor Coverings				
Walls & Ceiling				
Light Fixtures				
Cabinets				
Counters				
Stove/Oven				
Refrigerator				
Dishwasher				
Garbage Disposal				
Sink & Plumbing				
Smoke Detector				
Windows, Screens, & Doors				

	Condition on Arrival	Condition on Initial Move-Out Inspection	Condition on Departure	Actual or Estimated Cost of Cleaning, Repair/Replacement
Dining Room				
Floors & Floor Coverings				
Walls & Ceiling				
Light Fixtures				
Windows, Screens, & Doors				
Smoke Detector				
Other				
Bathroom				
Floors & Floor Coverings				
Walls & Ceiling				
Windows, Screens, & Doors				
Light Fixtures				
Bathtub/Shower				
Sinks & Counters				
Toilet				
Other				
Other				
Bedroom				
Floors & Floor Coverings				
Windows, Screens, & Doors				
Walls & Ceiling				
Light Fixtures				
Smoke Detector				
Other				
Other				
Other				

	Condition on Arrival	Condition on Initial Move-Out Inspection	Condition on Departure	Actual or Estimated Cost of Cleaning, Repair/Replacement
Other Areas				
Heating System				
Air Conditioning				
Lawn/Garden				
Stairs & Hallway				
Patio, Terrace, Deck, etc.				
Basement				
Parking Area				
Other				
Other				
Other				
Other				
Other				

☐ Tenants acknowledge that all smoke detectors and fire extinguishers were tested in their presence and found to be in working order, and that the testing procedure was explained to them. Tenants agree to test all detectors at least once a month and to report any problems to Landlord/Manager in writing. Tenants agree to replace all smoke detector batteries as necesssary.

Notes:

Furnished Property

	Condition on Arrival	Condition on Initial Move-Out Inspection	Condition on Departure	Actual or Estimated Cost of Cleaning, Repair/Replacement
Living Room				
Coffee Table				
End Tables				
Lamps				
Chairs				
Sofa				
Other				
Other				
Kitchen				
Broiler Pan				
Ice Trays				
Other				
Other				
Dining Area				
Chairs				
Stools				
Table				
Other				
Other				
Bathroom				
Mirrors				
Shower Curtain				
Hamper				
Other				

	Condition on Arrival	Condition on Initial Move-Out Inspection	Condition on Departure	Actual or Estimated Cost of Cleaning, Repair/Replacement
Bedroom				
Beds (single)				
Beds (double)				
Chairs				
Chests				
Dressing Tables				
Lamps				
Mirrors				
Night Tables				
Other				
Other				
Other Areas				
Bookcases				
Desks				
Pictures				
Other				
Other				

Use this space to provide any additional explanation:

Landlord-Tenant Checklist completed on moving in on _____, 20____.

_____
Landlord/Manager

and

_____
Tenant

_____
Tenant

_____
Tenant

Landlord-Tenant Checklist completed at Initial Move-Out Inspection on _____, 20____.

_____
Landlord/Manager

and

_____
Tenant

_____
Tenant

_____
Tenant

Landlord-Tenant Checklist completed on moving out on _____, 20____.

_____
Landlord/Manager

and

_____
Tenant

_____
Tenant

_____
Tenant

Notice of Needed Repairs

To: _____ *[name of landlord or manager]*

At: _____ *[address]*

From: _____ *[tenant]*

At: _____ *[address]*

I am writing to inform you of the following problem(s) in my rental unit:

_____

_____

_____

_____

_____

_____

_____.

I would very much appreciate it if you would promptly look into the problem(s). Please contact me so that I'll know when to expect you or a repairperson. You can reach me as follows:

Work (daytime): _____ Home (evenings): _____

Email: _____

Thank you very much for your attention to this problem.

_____   _____
Signature   Date

Tenant's Notice of Intent to Move Out

Date: _____

Landlord/Manager: _____

Street address: _____

City and state: _____

Regarding rental unit address: _____

Dear _____ :

This is to notify you that the undersigned tenant(s) will be moving from the above-noted rental unit on

_____, _____, or _____ days from today.

This notice provides you with at least _____ days' written notice, as required in our rental agreement.

_____
Tenant 1's signature

_____
Print name

_____
Tenant 2's signature

_____
Print name

_____
Tenant 3's signature

_____
Print name

Demand for Return of Security Deposit

Date: _____

_____

_____

_____

_____

[insert landlord's name and address]

Dear _____ *[name of landlord]*:

On _____ *[date]*, we vacated the rental unit at _____
_____ *[address]* and gave you our new address and phone number.
As of today, we haven't received our $_____ *[amount of security deposit owed]* security deposit,
nor any accounting from you for that money. We were entitled to receive our deposit by _____
[date when deposit was due]. You are now _____ *[number of days or weeks]* late.

We left our rental unit clean and undamaged, paid all of our rent, and gave you proper notice of our intention to
move. In these circumstances, it's difficult to understand your oversight in not promptly returning our money.

Perhaps your check is in the mail. If not, please send it promptly. Should we fail to hear from you by
_____ *[date]*, we'll take this matter to small claims court. And please understand that if we
are compelled to do this, we will also sue you for any costs and additional punitive damages allowed by state law.

Please mail our deposit immediately to the above address. If you have any questions, please contact us at the
number below.

Very truly yours,

_____   _____
Signature of tenant   Date

_____   _____
Signature of tenant   Date

_____
Address

_____

_____

_____   _____
Home phone   Cell or other phone

Loan Comparison Worksheet

Purpose of loan: _____

Desired amount of loan: $_____

	Loan 1	Loan 2	Loan 3

General Information

Lender: _____ _____ _____

Contact: _____ _____ _____

Address: _____ _____ _____

_____ _____ _____

_____ _____ _____

Phone: _____ _____ _____

Loan Terms

APR: _____% _____% _____%

Interest rate: _____% _____% _____%

Adjustable? _____ _____ _____

Cap: _____% _____% _____%

No. of months: _____ _____ _____

Monthly payment: $_____ $_____ $_____

Total payments (# of mos.
× monthly payment): $_____ $_____ $_____

Other Costs

Loan application fee: $_____ $_____ $_____

Credit check fee: $_____ $_____ $_____

Credit insurance: $_____ $_____ $_____

Other: $_____ $_____ $_____

Other Features

Collateral required? _____ _____ _____

  If yes, specify: _____ _____ _____

Balloon payment? _____ _____ _____

Prepayment penalty? _____ _____ _____

  If yes, amount: _____ _____ _____

Cosigner required? _____ _____ _____

Payment due date: _____ _____ _____

Grace period? _____ _____ _____

Late fee? _____ _____ _____

Possible loan discounts: _____ _____ _____

Account with lender: _____ _____ _____

Automatic deduction: _____ _____ _____

On-time payments: _____ _____ _____

Authorization to Check Credit and Employment References

I, the undersigned borrower, _____, authorize (name) _____
(address) _____ (phone) _____ to verify my
employment, financial, and credit information provided on this form.

Borrower

Full name—include generations (Jr., Sr., III): _____

Other names used: _____

Street address: _____

Mailing address: _____

City, state, and zip code: _____

Date moved into current address: _____

Home phone: _____

Previous address: _____

City, state, and zip code: _____

Dates there: _____

Date of birth: _____ Social Security number: _____

Driver's license number: _____

Employment History

Name and address of current employer: _____

_____

Position/title: _____

Name of supervisor: _____ Supervisor's phone: _____

Annual gross income: _____

Previous employment (if at current job fewer than 18 months): _____

_____

Credit and Financial Information

Bank/Financial Accounts	Account Number	Bank/Institution	Branch Address
Bank savings account:			
Bank checking account:			
Bank certificate of deposit:			
Mutual fund account:			
Brokerage account:			
Other:			
Other:			
Other:			

Credit accounts & loans	Type of account (auto loan, Visa, etc.)	Account number	Name/address of creditor	Amount owed	Monthly payment
Credit card:					
Credit card:					
Loan (specify type):					
Loan (specify type):					
Loan (specify type):					
Other (specify type):					

I certify that the information given above is true and correct. I authorize the above employers, financial institutions, and creditors to verify my employment, financial, and credit information provided above, and to provide correct information if the above is incorrect. A copy of this signed form is valid for this purpose.

_____   _____
Signature of Borrower   Date

Monthly Payment Record

Name of lender: _____

Name of borrower: _____

Original amount borrowed: _____ Date loan made: _____

Month	(A) Beginning balance (or prior month ending balance)	(B) Annual interest rate divided by 12	(C) Interest due (A) × (B)	(D) Amount of payment made	(E) Principal reduction (D) – (C)	(F) New balance (A) – (E)
1						
2						
3						
4						
5						
6						
7						
8						
9						
10						
11						
12						
13						
14						
15						
16						
17						
18						
19						
20						
21						
22						
23						
24						
25						
26						
27						
28						
29						
30						

Promissory Note

Loan repayable in installments with interest

Name of Borrower 1: _____

Name of Borrower 2: _____

Name of Lender: _____

1. For value received, Borrower promises to pay to Lender the amount of $_____
    on _____ *[due date]* at _____
    _____ *[address where payments are to be sent]* at the rate
    of _____ % per year from the date this note was signed until the date it is *[choose one]*:

    ☐ paid in full (Borrower will receive credits for prepayments, reducing the total amount of interest to be
    repaid).

    ☐ due or paid in full, whichever date occurs last (Borrower will not receive credits for prepayments).

2. Borrower agrees that this note will be paid in installments, which include principal and interest, of not less than
    $_____ per month, due on the first day of each month, until the principal and interest are
    paid in full.

3. If any installment payment due under this note is not received by Lender within _____ days of its due
    date, the entire amount of unpaid principal will become immediately due and payable at the option of Lender
    without prior notice to Borrower.

4. If Lender prevails in a lawsuit to collect on this note, Borrower agrees to pay Lender's attorney fees in an amount
    the court finds to be just and reasonable.

The term Borrower refers to one or more borrowers. If there is more than one borrower, they agree to be jointly and severally liable. The term Lender refers to any person who legally holds this note, including a buyer in due course.

_____   _____
Borrower 1's signature   Date

_____
Print name

_____
Location *[city or county where signed]*

_____
Address

_____   _____
Borrower 2's signature   Date

_____
Print name

_____
Location *[city or county where signed]*

_____
Address

Certificate of Acknowledgment of Notary Public

State of _____

County of _____ } ss

On _____, _____, before me, _____,
a notary public in and for said state, personally appeared _____,
who proved to me on the basis of satisfactory evidence to be the person whose name is subscribed to the within
instrument and acknowledged to me that he or she executed the same in his or her authorized capacity and
that by his or her signature on the instrument, the person, or the entity upon behalf of which the person acted,
executed the instrument.

I certify under PENALTY OF PERJURY under the laws of the State of _____
that the foregoing paragraph is true and correct.

WITNESS my hand and official seal.

_____

Notary Public for the State of _____

My commission expires _____

[NOTARY SEAL]

Promissory Note

Loan repayable in installments with interest and balloon payment

Name of Borrower 1: _____

Name of Borrower 2: _____

Name of Lender: _____

1. For value received, Borrower promises to pay to Lender the amount of $_____
   on _____ *[due date]* at _____
   _____ *[address where payments are to be sent]* at the rate of
   _____% per year from the date this note was signed until the date it is *[choose one]*:

   ☐ paid in full (Borrower will receive credits for prepayments, reducing the total amount of interest to be repaid).

   ☐ due or paid in full, whichever date occurs last (Borrower will not receive credits for prepayments).

2. Borrower agrees that this note will be paid in installments, which include principal and interest, of not less than
   $_____ per month, due on the first day of each month, until the principal and interest
   are paid in full.

3. Borrower agrees to make one final payment for the entire balance owed on or before _____
   [date balloon payment is due].

4. If any installment payment due under this note is not received by Lender within _____ days of
   its due date, the entire amount of unpaid principal will become immediately due and payable at the option of
   Lender without prior notice to Borrower.

5. If Lender prevails in a lawsuit to collect on this note, Borrower agrees to pay Lender's attorney fees in an amount
   the court finds to be just and reasonable.

The term Borrower refers to one or more borrowers. If there is more than one borrower, they agree to be jointly and severally liable. The term Lender refers to any person who legally holds this note, including a buyer in due course.

_____   _____
Borrower 1's signature   Date

_____
Print name

_____
Location *[city or county where signed]*

_____
Address

_____   _____
Borrower 2's signature   Date

_____
Print name

_____
Location *[city or county where signed]*

_____
Address

Certificate of Acknowledgment of Notary Public

State of _____

County of _____ } ss

On _____, _____, before me, _____,
a notary public in and for said state, personally appeared _____,
who proved to me on the basis of satisfactory evidence to be the person whose name is subscribed to the within
instrument and acknowledged to me that he or she executed the same in his or her authorized capacity and
that by his or her signature on the instrument, the person, or the entity upon behalf of which the person acted,
executed the instrument.

I certify under PENALTY OF PERJURY under the laws of the State of _____
that the foregoing paragraph is true and correct.

WITNESS my hand and official seal.

_____

Notary Public for the State of _____

My commission expires _____

[NOTARY SEAL]

Promissory Note

Loan repayable in installments without interest

Name of Borrower 1: _____

Name of Borrower 2: _____

Name of Lender: _____

1. For value received, Borrower promises to pay to Lender the amount of $_____
   on _____ *[due date]* at _____
   _____ *[address where payments are to be sent].*

2. Borrower agrees that this note will be paid in equal installments of $_____ per month,
   due on the first day of each month, until the principal is paid in full.

3. If any installment payment due under this note is not received by Lender within _____ days of
   its due date, the entire amount of unpaid principal will become immediately due and payable at the option of
   Lender without prior notice to Borrower.

4. If Lender prevails in a lawsuit to collect on this note, Borrower agrees to pay Lender's attorney fees in an amount
   the court finds to be just and reasonable.

*The term Borrower refers to one or more borrowers. If there is more than one borrower, they agree to be jointly and severally liable. The
term Lender refers to any person who legally holds this note, including a buyer in due course.*

_____   _____
Borrower 1's signature   Date

_____
Print name

_____
Location *[city or county where signed]*

_____
Address

_____   _____
Borrower 2's signature   Date

_____
Print name

_____
Location *[city or county where signed]*

_____
Address

Certificate of Acknowledgment of Notary Public

State of _____

County of _____ } ss

On _____, _____, before me, _____,
a notary public in and for said state, personally appeared _____,
who proved to me on the basis of satisfactory evidence to be the person whose name is subscribed to the within
instrument and acknowledged to me that he or she executed the same in his or her authorized capacity and
that by his or her signature on the instrument, the person, or the entity upon behalf of which the person acted,
executed the instrument.

I certify under PENALTY OF PERJURY under the laws of the State of _____
that the foregoing paragraph is true and correct.

WITNESS my hand and official seal.

_____

Notary Public for the State of _____

My commission expires _____

[NOTARY SEAL]

Promissory Note

Loan repayable in lump sum with interest

Name of Borrower 1:_____

Name of Borrower 2:_____

Name of Lender: _____

1. For value received, Borrower promises to pay to Lender the amount of $ _____

    on _____ *[due date]* at _____

    _____ *[address where payments are to be sent]*.

2. Simple interest will be charged on the sum specified in Clause 1 at the rate of _____ % per year

    from the date this note was signed until the date it is *[choose one]*:

    ☐ paid in full (Borrower will receive credits for prepayments, reducing the total amount of interest to be
       repaid).

    ☐ due or paid in full, whichever date occurs last (Borrower will not receive credits for making prepayments).

3. If Lender prevails in a lawsuit to collect on this note, Borrower agrees to pay Lender's attorney fees in an amount
    the court finds to be just and reasonable.

The term Borrower refers to one or more borrowers. If there is more than one borrower, they agree to be jointly and severally liable. The term Lender refers to any person who legally holds this note, including a buyer in due course.

_____   _____
Borrower 1's signature   Date

_____
Print name

_____
Location *[city or county where signed]*

_____
Address

_____   _____
Borrower 2's signature   Date

_____
Print name

_____
Location *[city or county where signed]*

_____
Address

Certificate of Acknowledgment of Notary Public

State of _____

County of _____ } ss

On _____, _____, before me, _____,
a notary public in and for said state, personally appeared _____,
who proved to me on the basis of satisfactory evidence to be the person whose name is subscribed to the within
instrument and acknowledged to me that he or she executed the same in his or her authorized capacity and
that by his or her signature on the instrument, the person, or the entity upon behalf of which the person acted,
executed the instrument.

I certify under PENALTY OF PERJURY under the laws of the State of _____
that the foregoing paragraph is true and correct.

WITNESS my hand and official seal.

_____

Notary Public for the State of _____

My commission expires _____

[NOTARY SEAL]

Promissory Note

Loan repayable in lump sum without interest

Name of Borrower 1:_____

Name of Borrower 2:_____

Name of Lender: _____

1. For value received, Borrower promises to pay to Lender the amount of $ _____
    on _____ *[due date]* at _____
    _____ *[address payment is to be sent]*.

2. If Lender prevails in a lawsuit to collect on this note, Borrower agrees to pay Lender's attorney fees in an amount the court finds to be just and reasonable.

The term Borrower refers to one or more borrowers. If there is more than one borrower, they agree to be jointly and severally liable. The term Lender refers to any person who legally holds this note, including a buyer in due course.

_____   _____
Borrower 1's signature   Date

_____
Print name

_____
Location *[city or county where signed]*

_____
Address

_____   _____
Borrower 2's signature   Date

_____
Print name

_____
Location *[city or county where signed]*

_____
Address

Certificate of Acknowledgment of Notary Public

State of _____

County of _____ } ss

On _____, _____, before me, _____,
a notary public in and for said state, personally appeared _____,
who proved to me on the basis of satisfactory evidence to be the person whose name is subscribed to the within
instrument and acknowledged to me that he or she executed the same in his or her authorized capacity and
that by his or her signature on the instrument, the person, or the entity upon behalf of which the person acted,
executed the instrument.

I certify under PENALTY OF PERJURY under the laws of the State of _____
that the foregoing paragraph is true and correct.

WITNESS my hand and official seal.

_____

Notary Public for the State of _____

My commission expires _____

[NOTARY SEAL]

Cosigner Provision

Name of Cosigner 1: _____

Name of Cosigner 2: _____

Name of Borrower 1: _____

Name of Borrower 2: _____

Name of Lender: _____

1. Borrower has agreed to pay Lender the amount indicated in the attached Promissory Note under the terms specified in that Note.

2. Cosigner agrees to guarantee this debt and understands this obligation means the following:

   - If Borrower doesn't pay the debt on time, that fact may become a part of Cosigner's credit record.
   - If Borrower doesn't pay the debt at all, Cosigner will be legally obligated to do so.
   - Cosigner may have to pay late fees or collection costs, which will increase the amount due.
   - Lender can collect this debt from Cosigner without first trying to collect from Borrower.
   - Lender can use the same collection methods against Cosigner that can be used against Borrower, including filing a lawsuit against Cosigner, and if the lawsuit is successful, garnishing Cosigner's wages, seizing other personal property of Cosigner, and putting a lien against Cosigner's house.

The term Cosigner refers to one or more cosigner. If there is more than one cosigner, they agree to be jointly and severally liable.

_____   _____
Cosigner 1's signature   Date

_____
Print name

_____
Location [*city or county where signed*]

_____
Address

_____   _____
Cosigner 2's signature   Date

_____
Print name

_____
Location [*city or county where signed*]

_____
Address

Security Agreement Provision for Promissory Note

Here are some examples of the kind of language to include in the security agreement provision.

If a vehicle is security, use this language:

Borrower agrees that until the principal and interest owed under this note are paid in full, the note is secured by the following security agreement:

Security agreement signed by: _____ [name of owner]

on: _____ [date signed], which gives title to: _____

_____ [date, make, model, and VIN of vehicle].

If other valuable personal property is security, use this language:

Borrower agrees that until the principal and interest owed under this note are paid in full, the note is secured by the following security agreement:

Security agreement signed by: _____ [name of owner]

on: _____ [date signed], which gives a security interest in: _____

_____ [description of the personal property used as collateral].

Security Agreement for Borrowing Money

Name of Borrower: _____

Name of Lender: _____

1. **Grant of Security Interest.** Borrower grants to Lender a continuing security interest in the following personal property: _____

   _____

   (the Secured Property). Borrower grants this security interest to secure performance of the promissory note dated _____ that Borrower executed in favor of Lender (the Note), which obligates Borrower to pay Lender $_____ with interest at the rate of _____% per year, on the terms stated in the Note.

2. **Financing Statement.** Until the amount due under the Note is paid in full, the Note will be further secured by a Uniform Commercial Code (U.C.C.) Financing Statement. Borrower agrees to sign any other documents that Lender reasonably requests to protect Lender's security interest in the Secured Property.

3. **Use and Care of Secured Property.** Until the amount due under the Note is paid in full, Borrower agrees to:

   A. Maintain the Secured Property in good repair.

   B. Refrain from selling, transfering, or releasing the Secured Property without Lender's prior written consent.

   C. Pay all taxes on the Secured Property as they become due.

   D. Allow Lender to inspect the Secured Property at any reasonable time.

4. **Borrower's Default.** If Borrower is more than ____days late in making any payment due under the Note, or if Buyer fails to correct any violations of paragraph 3 within ____ days of receiving written notice from Lender, Borrower will be in default.

5. **Lender's Rights.** If Borrower is in default, Lender may exercise the remedies contained in the U.C.C. for the state of _____ and any other remedies legally available to Lender. Before exercising such remedies, Lender will provide at least ten days advance notice, as provided in paragraph 6. Lender may, for example:

   A. Remove the Secured Property from the place where it is then located.

   B. Require Borrower to make the Secured Property available to Lender at a place designated by Lender that is reasonably convenient to Borrower and Lender.

   C. Sell, lease, or otherwise dispose of the Secured Property.

6. **Notice.** Any notice may be delivered to a party at the address that follows a party's signature below, or to a new address that a party designates in writing. A notice may be delivered in person, by certified mail, or by overnight courier.

7. **Entire Agreement.** This is the entire agreement between the parties. It replaces and supersedes any and all oral agreements between the parties, as well as any prior writings.

8. **Successors and Assigns.** This agreement binds and benefits the parties' heirs, successors, and assigns.

9. **Governing Law.** This agreement will be governed by and construed in accordance with the laws of the state of _____.

10. **Modification.** This agreement may be modified only in writing.

11. **Waiver.** If one party waives any term or provision of this agreement at any time, that waiver will be effective only for the specific instance and specific purpose for which the waiver was given. If either party fails to exercise or delays exercising any rights or remedies under this agreement, that party retains the right to enforce that term or provision at a later time.

12. **Severability.** If any court determines that any provision of this agreement is invalid or unenforceable, any such invalidity or unenforceability will affect only that provision and will not make any other provision of this agreement invalid or unenforceable, and such provision shall be modified, amended, or limited only to the extent necessary to render it valid and enforceable.

_____   _____
Lender's signature   Date

_____
Print name

_____
Address

_____
Address

_____   _____
Borrower's signature   Date

_____
Print name

_____
Address

_____
Address

U.C.C. Financing Statement

This Financing Statement is presented for filing under the Uniform Commercial Code as adopted in

_____ *[name of your state].*

Name of Borrower: _____

Address of Borrower: _____

_____

Name of Lender/Secured party: _____

Address of Lender/Secured party: _____

_____

The term Borrower refers to one or more borrowers. If there is more than one borrower, they agree to be jointly and severally liable. The term Lender refers to any person who legally holds this note, including a buyer in due course.

The property listed as collateral in the security agreement is as follows *[identify or describe]:*

_____

_____

This Financing Statement secures the following debt:

Promissory note dated: _____

Amount of debt: _____

Payback due date: _____

All other terms and conditions are stated in the promissory note, a copy of which is attached.

Borrower's signature: _____

Print name: _____

Date: _____

_____

(For Use of the Filing Officer)

Date of filing: _____ Time of filing: _____

File number and address of filing office: _____

_____

Release of U.C.C. Financing Statement

This Release of Financing Statement is presented for filing under the Uniform Commercial Code as adopted in

_____ [name of your state].

Name of Borrower: _____

Address of Borrower: _____

_____

Name of Lender/Secured party: _____

Address of Lender/Secured party: _____

_____

The term Borrower refers to one or more borrowers. The term Lender refers to any person who legally holds this note, including a buyer in due course.

The property listed as collateral in the security agreement is as follows _[identify or describe]_:

_____

_____

File number of Financing Statement: _____

Date filed: _____

Address of filing office: _____

Borrower's signature: _____

Print name: _____

Date: _____

_____

(For Use of the Filing Officer)

Date of filing: _____ Time of filing: _____

File number and address of filing office: _____

_____

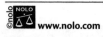

Agreement to Modify Promissory Note

Name of Borrower 1: _____

Name of Borrower 2: _____

Name of Lender: _____

1. This Agreement modifies the original promissory note dated _____, _____,

   under which Borrower promised to pay to Lender the amount of $_____ at the rate of

   _____% per year from the date the note was signed until _____, _____.

2. Lender and Borrower agree to the following modifications [choose all that apply]:

   ☐ Borrower has until _____ to pay the note in full.

   ☐ Borrower will make interest-only payments beginning on _____, _____,

   until _____, _____, at which time the remaining principal balance will

   be reamortized over the remaining months of the note.

   ☐ Beginning on_____, _____, the interest rate will change to

   _____%. The new monthly payments will be in the amount of $_____.

   ☐ Other: _____.

The term Borrower refers to one or more borrowers. If there is more than one borrower, they agree to be jointly and severally liable. The term Lender refers to any person who legally holds this note, including a buyer in due course.

_____   _____
Borrower 1's signature   Date

_____
Print name

_____
Location [city or county where signed]

_____
Address

_____   _____
Borrower 2's signature   Date

_____
Print name

_____
Location [city or county where signed]

_____
Address

_____   _____
Lender's signature   Date

_____
Print name

_____
Location [city or county where signed]

_____
Address

Overdue Payment Demand

Date: _____

To: _____

_____

_____

_____

[insert name and address of person who borrowed money]

Re: Promissory Note dated: _____

Dear: _____

This is to notify you that I have not received the following payment(s) due under the Promissory Note referenced above ("the Note").

Amount:	$ _____	Due date:	_____
Amount:	$ _____	Due date:	_____
Total:	$ _____		

Please let me know at once if there is a problem. If I do not hear from you within 15 days, I will have no choice but to assume that you do not intend to repay the amount that is due under the Note. I will proceed to enforce my rights under the Note, including possibly filing a lawsuit, to collect the entire balance.

Sincerely,

_____
Signature of Lender

_____
Print name of Lender

_____
Address

_____

_____   _____
Home phone   Work phone

Demand to Make Good on Bad Check

Date: _____

To: _____

_____

_____

_____

[insert name and address of check writer]

Re: Check # _____ Dated _____, _____

Issuing financial institution: _____

Dear _____:

Your check was returned to my bank and refused payment for the following reason *[choose one]*:

☐ insufficient funds in the account on which the check was drawn to cover the amount of the check.

☐ the account on which the check was drawn has been closed.

☐ you stopped payment on the check.

Please let me know at once if there is a problem. If I do not hear from you within 30 days, I will have no choice but to assume that you do not intend to make this check good. I will proceed to enforce my rights, which may include filing a lawsuit. I will request that the court award me the maximum monetary damages allowed under state law, as well as:

☐ the amount of the check

☐ the bad check processing fee charged by my bank

☐ the expenses incurred in attempting to collect on the check as allowed under state law

Sincerely,

_____
Signature of check recipient

_____
Print name of check recipient

_____
Address

_____

_____   _____
Home phone   Work phone

Ideal House Profile

Upper price limit: _____

Maximum down payment: _____

Special financing needs: _____

	Must Have	Hope to Have
Neighborhood or location:		
_____	_____	_____
_____	_____	_____
_____	_____	_____
School needs:		
_____	_____	_____
Desired neighborhood features:		
_____	_____	_____
_____	_____	_____
_____	_____	_____
_____	_____	_____
Length of commute:		
_____	_____	_____
Access to public transportation:		
_____	_____	_____
Size of house:		
_____	_____	_____
Number and type of rooms:		
_____	_____	_____
_____	_____	_____
_____	_____	_____
_____	_____	_____
_____	_____	_____
Condition, age, and type of house:		
_____	_____	_____
_____	_____	_____
Type of yard and grounds:		
_____	_____	_____
_____	_____	_____
Other desired features:		
_____	_____	_____
_____	_____	_____
_____	_____	_____
Absolute no ways:		
_____	_____	_____
_____	_____	_____
_____	_____	_____

House Priorities Worksheet

Date visited: _____

Address: _____

Price: $_____

Contact: _____ Phone: _____

Must have:

☐ _____

☐ _____

☐ _____

☐ _____

☐ _____

☐ _____

☐ _____

☐ _____

Hope to have:

☐ _____

☐ _____

☐ _____

☐ _____

☐ _____

☐ _____

☐ _____

☐ _____

Absolutely no way:

☐ _____

☐ _____

☐ _____

☐ _____

Comments about the house:

_____

_____

_____

_____

House Comparison Worksheet

House 1 _____

House 2 _____

House 3 _____

House 4 _____

	1	2	3	4

Must have:

_____

_____

_____

_____

_____

_____

_____

_____

_____

_____

_____

_____

Hope to have:

_____

_____

_____

_____

_____

_____

_____

Absolutely no ways:

_____

_____

_____

_____

Family Financial Statement

	Borrower	Coborrower
Name:	_____	_____
Address:	_____	_____
	_____	_____
Home phone number:	_____	_____
Employer:	_____	_____
Employer's address:	_____	_____
Work phone number:	_____	_____

Worksheet 1: Income and Expenses

I. INCOME	Borrower ($)	Coborrower ($)	Total ($)
A. Monthly gross income			
1. Employment	_____	_____	_____
2. Public benefits	_____	_____	_____
3. Dividends	_____	_____	_____
4. Royalties	_____	_____	_____
5. Interest and other investment income	_____	_____	_____
6. Other (specify):	_____	_____	_____
B. Total monthly gross income	_____	_____	_____

II. MONTHLY EXPENSES	Borrower ($)	Coborrower ($)	Total ($)
A. Nonhousing			
1. Child care	_____	_____	_____
2. Clothing	_____	_____	_____
3. Food	_____	_____	_____
4. Insurance	_____	_____	_____
a. Auto	_____	_____	_____
b. Life	_____	_____	_____
c. Medical & dental	_____	_____	_____
5. Other medical	_____	_____	_____
6. Personal	_____	_____	_____
7. Education	_____	_____	_____
8. Taxes (nonhousing)	_____	_____	_____
9. Transportation	_____	_____	_____
10. Other (specify):	_____	_____	_____
B. Current Housing			
1. Mortgage	_____	_____	_____
2. Taxes	_____	_____	_____
3. Insurance	_____	_____	_____
4. Utilities	_____	_____	_____
5. Rent	_____	_____	_____
6. Other (specify): _____	_____	_____	_____
C. Total monthly expenses	_____	_____	_____

Worksheet 2: Assets and Liabilities

I. ASSETS (Cash or Market Value)	Borrower ($)	Coborrower ($)	Total ($)
A. Cash & cash equivalents			
1. Cash			
2. Deposits (list):			
_____			
_____			
B. Marketable securities			
1. Stocks/bonds (bid price)			
2. Other securities			
3. Mutual funds			
4. Life insurance			
5. Other (specify):			
_____			
_____			
C. Total cash & marketable securities			
D. Nonliquid assets			
1. Real estate			
2. Retirement funds			
3. Business			
4. Motor vehicles			
5. Other (specify):			
_____			
_____			
E. Total nonliquid assets			
F. Total all assets			
II. LIABILITIES			
A. Debts			
1. Real estate loans			
2. Student loans			
3. Motor vehicle loans			
4. Child or spousal support			
5. Personal loans			
6. Credit cards (specify):			
_____			
_____			
_____			
7. Other (specify):			
_____			
_____			
B. Total liabilities			
III. NET WORTH (Total assets minus total liabilities)			

Monthly Carrying Costs Worksheet

1. Estimated purchase price $ _____

2. Down payment $ _____

3. Loan amount: First loan $ _____

    Second loan (if any) $ _____

4. Interest rate: First loan _____ %

    Second loan (if any) _____ %

5. Mortgage payment factor   First loan _____

                                    Second loan _____

6. Monthly mortgage payment
   (divide line 3 by $1,000, then
   multiply by line 5)   First loan $ _____

                                    Second loan $ _____

7. Homeowner's insurance (monthly) $ _____

8. Property taxes (monthly) $ _____

9. Total monthly housing costs (add lines 6–8) $ _____

10. Other monthly debts

    _____ $ _____

    _____ $ _____

    _____ $ _____

    _____ $ _____

    Total monthly debts $ _____

11. Private mortgage insurance (if any) $ _____

12. Homeowners' association fee (if a condo) $ _____

13. Total monthly housing costs and other debts (add lines 9–12) $ _____

14. Lender qualifying ratio (between 28% and 44%)   _____ %

15. Monthly gross income to qualify (divide line 13 by line 14) $ _____

16. Yearly gross income to qualify (multiply line 15 by 12 (months)) $ _____

www.nolo.com

Mortgage Rates and Terms Worksheet

Lender: _____

Loan agent: _____

Phone number: _____

Date: _____

1. General Information

Fixed or adjustable	☐ F ☐ A	☐ F ☐ A	☐ F ☐ A
Fixed interest rate	_____ %	_____ %	_____ %
Government financing	☐ Y ☐ N	☐ Y ☐ N	☐ Y ☐ N
Minimum down payment	_____ %	_____ %	_____ %
PMI required	☐ Y ☐ N	☐ Y ☐ N	☐ Y ☐ N
Impound account	☐ Y ☐ N	☐ Y ☐ N	☐ Y ☐ N
Term of mortgage	_____ Years	_____ Years	_____ Years
Assumable	☐ Y ☐ N	☐ Y ☐ N	☐ Y ☐ N
Prepayment penalty	☐ Y ☐ N	☐ Y ☐ N	☐ Y ☐ N
Negative amortization	☐ Y ☐ N	☐ Y ☐ N	☐ Y ☐ N
Rate lock-in available	☐ Y ☐ N	☐ Y ☐ N	☐ Y ☐ N
Cost to lock in	21 Days $_____	21 Days $_____	21 Days $_____
	30 Days $_____	30 Days $_____	30 Days $_____
	45 Days $_____	45 Days $_____	45 Days $_____

2. Debt-to-Income Ratios Information

Allowable monthly carrying costs as % of income	_____ %	_____ %	_____ %
Allowable monthly carrying costs plus long-term debts as % of monthly income	_____ %	_____ %	_____ %
Maximum loan you qualify for based on debt-to-income ratios	$ _____	$ _____	$ _____

3. Loan Costs

Number of points	$ _____	$ _____	$ _____
Cost of points	$ _____	$ _____	$ _____
PMI	$ _____	$ _____	$ _____

Additional loan fee	$ _____	$ _____	$ _____
Credit report	$ _____	$ _____	$ _____
Application fee	$ _____	$ _____	$ _____
Appraisal fee	$ _____	$ _____	$ _____
Miscellaneous fees	$ _____	$ _____	$ _____
Estimated total loan costs	$ _____	$ _____	$ _____

4. Time Limits

Credit/employment check	_____ Days	_____ Days	_____ Days
Lender appraisal	_____ Days	_____ Days	_____ Days
Loan approval	_____ Days	_____ Days	_____ Days
Loan funding	_____ Days	_____ Days	_____ Days
Loan due date each month	_____	_____	_____
Grace period	_____ Days	_____ Days	_____ Days
Late fee	_____ %	_____ %	_____ %

5. Other Features

[such as a discount for having an account with a certain bank, or a lender discount of interest rate on initial payments]

_____	_____	_____	_____
_____	_____	_____	_____
_____	_____	_____	_____

6. Fixed Rate Two-Step Loans

Initial annual interest rate	_____ %	_____ %	_____ %
Over how many years	_____ Years	_____ Years	_____ Years

7. Fixed Rate Balloon Payment Loans

Interest rate	_____ %	_____ %	_____ %
Monthly payment	$ _____	$ _____	$ _____
Term of loan	_____ Years	_____ Years	_____ Years
Amount of balloon payment	$ _____	$ _____	$ _____

8. Adjustable Rate Mortgages (ARMs)

Index: 11th District COFI	☐ _____ %	☐ _____ %	☐ _____ %
6 Mo. T-Bills	☐ _____ %	☐ _____ %	☐ _____ %
1 Yr. T-Bills	☐ _____ %	☐ _____ %	☐ _____ %
Other _____	☐ _____ %	☐ _____ %	☐ _____ %
Margin	_____ %	_____ %	_____ %
Initial interest rate	_____ %	_____ %	_____ %
How long	____ Mos. ____ Yrs.	____ Mos. ____ Yrs.	____ Mos. ____ Yrs.
Interest rate cap (with negative amortization) or	_____ %	_____ %	_____ %
Interest rate cap (without negative amortization)	_____ %	_____ %	_____ %
Adjustment period	_____ Months	_____ Months	_____ Months
Life-of-loan (overall) cap	_____ %	_____ %	_____ %
Initial payment	_____ Months	_____ Months	_____ Months
Payment cap	_____ %	_____ %	_____ %
Payment cap period	_____ Months	_____ Months	_____ Months

Highest payment or interest rate in:

6 months	____% $ _____	____% $ _____	____% $ _____
12 months	____% $ _____	____% $ _____	____% $ _____
18 months	____% $ _____	____% $ _____	____% $ _____
24 months	____% $ _____	____% $ _____	____% $ _____
30 months	____% $ _____	____% $ _____	____% $ _____
36 months	____% $ _____	____% $ _____	____% $ _____

9. Hybrid Loans

Initial interest rate	_____ %	_____ %	_____ %
Term as a fixed rate loan	_____ Years	_____ Years	_____ Years
Interest rate at first adjustment period	_____ %	_____ %	_____ %

Moving Checklist

[Not all items on this list will apply to you. If you're moving within the same town, you probably won't have to transfer your kids to a new school, get references for a new job, or have your car serviced for travel. So just focus on the applicable items.]

I. Two Weeks Before Moving

☐ Check with your children's new school about what records and transcripts it will need; arrange for their transfer.

☐ Close or transfer bank and safe deposit box accounts.

☐ Cancel deliveries—newspaper, diapers, laundry.

☐ Cancel utilities—gas, electric, cable, phone, water, garbage; transfer services (if possible) or arrange new services; request deposit refunds.

☐ Get recommendations or find in advance (especially if a medical condition needs regular attention) new doctors, dentist, and veterinarian. If possible, photocopy important medical records to have with you.

☐ Get reference letters, if you'll need to find a job.

☐ Cancel membership (or transfer membership, if relevant) in religious, civic, and athletic organizations.

☐ Have car serviced for travel.

☐ Arrange to move pets.

☐ Finalize arrangements with moving company. (You should have gotten bids and made preliminary arrangements weeks earlier.)

☐ Tell close friends and relatives your schedule.

II. Things to Remember While Packing

☐ Before you pack, take the time to do a good inventory and sort through things. This way you can move less and won't end up throwing things away at your new home or needing storage space.

☐ Label boxes on top and side—your name, new city, room of house, and contents.

☐ Pack phone books.

☐ Assemble moving kit—hammer, screwdriver, pliers, tape, nails, tape measure, scissors, flashlight, cleansers, cleaning cloths, rubber gloves, garbage bags, light bulbs, and extension cords. If you're driving to your new home, pack a broom and pail in your car. Larger items that are handy when moving in, such as a step stool or vacuum cleaner, should go in the moving van, unless your new house is nearby and you're moving lots of things by car.

☐ Keep the basics handy—comfortable clothes, toiletries, towels, alarm clock, disposable plates, cups and utensils, can opener, one pot, one pan, sponge, paper towels, toilet paper, plastic containers, and toys for kids.

☐ Consider carrying jewelry, extremely fragile items, currency, and important documents.

☐ Make other arrangements if moving company won't move antiques, art collections, crystal, other valuables, or plants.

III. To Whom to Send Change of Addresses

☐ Friends and relatives

☐ Subscriptions

☐ Government agencies you regularly deal with—Veterans' Administration, IRS, Social Security Administration, etc.

☐ Charge and credit accounts

☐ Installment debt—such as student loan or car loan

☐ Frequent flyer programs

☐ Brokers and mutual funds

☐ Insurance agent/companies

☐ Medical providers—if you'll be able to use them after moving

☐ Catalogs you want to keep receiving

☐ Charities you wish to continue donating to

☐ Post office (If you're trying to get off of catalog and other direct mailing lists, have only first-class mail forwarded. Give your new address to those catalog companies on whose lists you want to remain, and don't forget to tell them not to trade or sell your name.)

IV. Things to Do After Moving In

☐ Open bank accounts.

☐ Open safe deposit box account.

☐ Begin deliveries—oil, newspaper, diapers, laundry.

☐ Register to vote.

☐ Change (or get new) driver's license.

☐ Change auto registration.

☐ Install new batteries in existing smoke detectors (and install any additionally needed smoke detectors); buy fire extinguisher.

☐ Hold party for the people who helped you find your house and your moving helpers, and take yourself out for a congratulatory dinner!

Motor Vehicle Bill of Sale

Seller 1:_____

Address: _____

Seller 2:_____

Address: _____

Buyer 1: _____

Address: _____

Buyer 2: _____

Address: _____

If there is more than one buyer or seller, the use of the singular incorporates the plural.

1. Seller hereby sells the vehicle (Vehicle) described here to Buyer *[specify vehicle year, make, and model]*:

    _____

    Its body type is: _____.

    It carries the following vehicle identification number (VIN): _____.

    Vehicle includes the following personal property items: _____

    _____.

2. The full purchase price for Vehicle is $_____. In exchange for Vehicle, Buyer has paid Seller *[choose one]*:

    ☐ single payment of the full purchase price.

    ☐ $_____ as a down payment, balance of the purchase price due by _____ *[date]*.

    ☐ $_____ as a down payment and has executed a promissory note for the balance of the purchase price.

3. Seller warrants that Seller is the legal owner of Vehicle and that Vehicle is free of all legal claims (liens or encumbrances) by others except: _____

    _____.

    Seller agrees to remove any lien or encumbrance specified in this clause with the proceeds of this sale and other funds if necessary, within _____ days of the date of this bill of sale.

4. Vehicle ☐ has been ☐ has not been inspected by an independent mechanic at Buyer's request. If an inspection has been made, the inspection report ☐ is attached to and made part of this bill of sale ☐ is not attached.

5. Seller believes Vehicle to be in good condition except for the following defects: _____

_____

_____ .

6. To the best of Seller's knowledge, Vehicle:

☐ is ☐ is not a salvage vehicle.

☐ has ☐ has not been declared a total loss by an insurance company.

☐ has ☐ has not been repaired under the terms of a Lemon Law.

7. The odometer reading for Vehicle is: _____ .

8. Additional terms of sale for Vehicle are as follows: _____

_____

_____

_____

Seller 1's signature	Date
Seller 2's signature	Date
Buyer 1's signature	Date
Buyer 2's signature	Date

Certificate of Acknowledgment of Notary Public

State of _____

County of _____ } ss

On _____, _____, before me, _____,

a notary public in and for said state, personally appeared _____,

personally known to me (or proved to me on the basis of satisfactory evidence) to be the person whose name

is subscribed to the within instrument, and acknowledged to me that he or she executed the same in his or her

authorized capacity and that by his or her signature on the instrument, the person, or the entity upon behalf of

which the person acted, executed the instrument.

I certify under PENALTY OF PERJURY under the laws of the State of _____ that

the foregoing paragraph is true and correct.

WITNESS my hand and official seal.

_____

Notary Public for the State of _____

My commission expires _____

[NOTARY SEAL]

Boat Bill of Sale

Seller 1:_____

Address: _____

Seller 2:_____

Address: _____

Buyer 1: _____

Address: _____

Buyer 2: _____

Address: _____

If there is more than one buyer or seller, the use of the singular incorporates the plural.

1. Seller sells the boat (Boat) described here to Buyer:

    Year: _____ Make: _____

    Model: _____ Length: _____

    Serial or hull ID number: _____ General type: _____

    Registration, CF, or document number: _____

2. Boat has the following types of engine(s) (Engines) *[provide details on engines including year, make, type, model, hours, and serial numbers]*:

    _____

    _____

    _____

    _____

    _____

    _____

3. Boat contains the following equipment (Equipment) included in this sale *[list and describe all that apply, including sails and rigging, safety equipment, electronics and navigation equipment, and deck equipment]*:

    _____

    _____

    _____

    _____

    _____

4. Seller believes Boat, Engines, and Equipment to be in good condition except for the following defects:

_____

_____ .

5. Boat and Engines ☐ have been ☐ have not been independently inspected or surveyed at Buyer's request. If an independent inspection or Marine Survey has been made, the inspection report or Marine Survey ☐ is attached to and made part of this bill of sale ☐ is not attached.

6. The full purchase price for Boat, Engines, and Equipment is $_____. In exchange for Boat, Engines, and Equipment, Buyer has paid Seller *[choose one]*:

    ☐ single payment of the full purchase price.

    ☐ $_____ as a down payment, balance of the purchase price due by _____ *[date]*.

    ☐ $_____ as a down payment and has executed a promissory note for the balance of the purchase price.

7. Seller warrants that Seller is the legal owner of Boat, Engines, and Equipment and that Boat, Engines, and Equipment are free of all liens and encumbrances except _____

    _____ .

    Seller agrees to remove any lien or encumbrance specified in this clause with the proceeds of this sale and other funds as necessary within _____ days of the date of this bill of sale.

8. Additional terms of sale for Boat, Engines, and Equipment are as follows: _____

    _____

    _____

_____   _____
Seller 1's signature   Date

_____   _____
Seller 2's signature   Date

_____   _____
Buyer 1's signature   Date

_____   _____
Buyer 2's signature   Date

Certificate of Acknowledgment of Notary Public

State of _____

County of _____ } ss

On _____, _____, before me, _____,
a notary public in and for said state, personally appeared _____,
who proved to me on the basis of satisfactory evidence to be the person whose name is subscribed to the
within instrument and acknowledged to me that he or she executed the same in his or her authorized
capacity and that by his or her signature on the instrument, the person, or the entity upon behalf of which
the person acted, executed the instrument.

I certify under PENALTY OF PERJURY under the laws of the State of _____
that the foregoing paragraph is true and correct.

WITNESS my hand and official seal.

_____

Notary Public for the State of _____

My commission expires _____

[NOTARY SEAL]

Computer System Bill of Sale

Seller 1:_____

Address: _____

Seller 2:_____

Address: _____

Buyer 1: _____

Address: _____

Buyer 2: _____

Address: _____

If there is more than one buyer or seller, the use of the singular incorporates the plural.

1. Seller sells the goods (Goods) described here to Buyer:

   Hardware [*provide the brand name and, wherever possible, the serial number*]:

   ☐ computer (boards, CPU, bus, I/O ports): _____
   _____

   ☐ monitor: _____
   _____
   _____

   ☐ external disk drive: _____
   _____

   ☐ external hard drive: _____
   _____

   ☐ CD-ROM: _____
   _____

   ☐ DVD:_____
   ☐ external mass storage device: _____
   _____

   ☐ printer: _____
   _____

   ☐ modem: _____
   _____

   ☐ multimedia system:_____
   _____

   ☐ furniture or other items as follows: _____
   _____

Software [*provide the titles of the software and, wherever possible, the serial number*]:

_____

_____

_____

_____

_____

2. The full purchase price for Goods is $_____. In exchange for Goods, Buyer has paid Seller [*choose one*]:

   ☐ the single payment of the full purchase price.

   ☐ $_____ as a down payment, balance of the purchase price due by _____ [*date*].

   ☐ $_____ as a down payment and has executed a promissory note for the balance of the purchase price.

3. Seller warrants that Seller is the legal owner of Goods and that Goods are free of all liens and encumbrances except _____

   _____ .

   Seller agrees to remove any lien or encumbrance specified in this clause with the proceeds of this sale and other funds as necessary within _____ days of the date of this bill of sale.

4. Seller believes Goods to be in good condition except for the following defects: _____

   _____ .

5. Additional terms of sale for Goods are as follows:_____

   _____

   _____

_____	_____
Seller 1's signature	Date
_____	_____
Seller 2's signature	Date
_____	_____
Buyer 1's signature	Date
_____	_____
Buyer 2's signature	Date

Certificate of Acknowledgment of Notary Public

State of _____
} ss
County of _____

On _____, _____, before me, _____,
a notary public in and for said state, personally appeared _____,
who proved to me on the basis of satisfactory evidence to be the person whose name is subscribed to the
within instrument and acknowledged to me that he or she executed the same in his or her authorized
capacity and that by his or her signature on the instrument, the person, or the entity upon behalf of which
the person acted, executed the instrument.

I certify under PENALTY OF PERJURY under the laws of the State of _____
that the foregoing paragraph is true and correct.

WITNESS my hand and official seal.

_____

Notary Public for the State of _____

My commission expires _____

[NOTARY SEAL]

General Bill of Sale

Seller 1:_____

Address: _____

Seller 2:_____

Address: _____

Buyer 1: _____

Address: _____

Buyer 2: _____

Address: _____

If there is more than one buyer or seller, the use of the singular incorporates the plural.

1. Seller sells the goods (Goods) described here to Buyer: _____

   _____

   _____

   _____

2. The full purchase price for Goods is $_____. In exchange for Goods, Buyer has paid Seller *[choose one]:*

   ☐ single payment of the full purchase price.

   ☐ $_____ as a down payment, balance of the purchase price due by _____ *[date].*

   ☐ $_____ as a down payment and has executed a promissory note for the balance of the purchase price.

3. Seller warrants that Seller is the legal owner of Goods and that Goods are free of all liens and encumbrances except _____

   _____

   Seller agrees to remove any lien or encumbrance specified in this clause with the proceeds of this sale and other funds as necessary within _____ days of the date of this bill of sale.

4. Seller believes Goods to be in good condition except for the following defects: _____

   _____

   _____

5. Goods will be delivered to Buyer in the following manner *[choose one]:*

   ☐ Buyer will take immediate possession of Goods.

   ☐ Buyer assumes responsibility for picking up Goods from _____

   within _____ days.

---

 www.nolo.com

General Bill of Sale

☐ In exchange for an additional delivery charge of $_____, receipt of which is hereby acknowledged, Seller will deliver Goods within _____ days to the following location:

_____ .

6. Additional terms of sale for Goods are as follows: _____

_____ .

_____   _____
Seller 1's signature   Date

_____   _____
Seller 2's signature   Date

_____   _____
Buyer 1's signature   Date

_____   _____
Buyer 2's signature   Date

Certificate of Acknowledgment of Notary Public

State of _____
                                                                    } ss
County of _____

On _____, _____, before me, _____,
a notary public in and for said state, personally appeared _____,
who proved to me on the basis of satisfactory evidence to be the person whose name is subscribed to the within instrument and acknowledged to me that he or she executed the same in his or her authorized capacity and that by his or her signature on the instrument, the person, or the entity upon behalf of which the person acted, executed the instrument.

I certify under PENALTY OF PERJURY under the laws of the State of _____
that the foregoing paragraph is true and correct.

WITNESS my hand and official seal.

_____

Notary Public for the State of _____

My commission expires _____

[NOTARY SEAL]

Bill of Sale for Dog

Seller 1: _____

Address: _____

Seller 2: _____

Address: _____

Buyer 1: _____

Address: _____

Buyer 2: _____

Address: _____

If there is more than one buyer or seller, the use of the singular incorporates the plural.

1. Seller sells to Buyer the dog (Dog) described as follows:

    Name: _____

    Breed: _____ Sex: _____

    Birth date *[estimate if specific date not known]*: _____

2. The full purchase price for Dog is $_____.

3. Buyer has paid Seller *[choose one]*:

    ☐ single payment of the full purchase price

    ☐ a down payment of $_____ with the balance of $_____ due

    _____ *[date],* or

    ☐ other: _____ *[explain].*

4. Seller warrants that:

    a. Seller is the legal owner of Dog.

    b. Dog has had the following vaccinations *[list all the vaccinations Dog has received, including the date the vaccination was given and the name of the vet who gave it]:* _____

    _____

    _____ .

    c. Dog was *[choose one]:*

        ☐ bred by the Seller

        ☐ bought from a breeder _____ *[name of breeder]*

        on _____ *[date].*

        ☐ acquired from a previous private party owner _____ *[name].*

d. Dog has had the following special training: _____

_____ .

e. Dog ☐ is ☐ is not purebred.

f. Dog is *[check one]*:

☐ registered with the American Kennel Club or another entity *[provide details as appropriate]*

_____ .

☐ not registered with the American Kennel Club or another entity and is not eligible to be registered.

☐ not registered with the American Kennel Club or another entity but is eligible to be registered *[explain]*

_____ .

Seller will provide Buyer with the necessary papers to process registration.

5. Seller believes that Dog is healthy and in good condition, except for the following known problems:

_____ .

6. If a licensed veterinarian certifies, in writing, that Dog has a serious disease or congenital defect that was present when Buyer took possession of Dog, Buyer may, within 14 days of taking possession of Dog *[choose one]*:

☐ return Dog to Seller. In this case, Seller will refund the purchase price plus any sales tax and reimburse Buyer for the cost of reasonable veterinary services directly related to the examination that showed Dog was ill, and emergency treatment to relieve suffering plus any sales tax.

☐ keep Dog. In this case, Seller will reimburse Buyer for the cost of reasonable veterinary services directly related to the examination that showed Dog was ill, and emergency treatment to relieve suffering, up to the amount of the purchase price plus any sales tax.

7. Dog will be delivered to Buyer in the following manner *[choose one]*:

☐ Buyer will take immediate possession of Dog.

☐ Buyer assumes responsibility for picking up Dog from _____

_____ by _____ *[date]*.

☐ In exchange for an additional delivery charge of $_____, Seller will deliver Dog by

_____ *[date]* to the following location: _____

_____ .

8. Additional terms: _____

_____ .

Seller 1's signature _____   Date _____

Seller 2's signature _____   Date _____

Buyer 1's signature _____   Date _____

Buyer 2's signature _____   Date _____

Certificate of Acknowledgment of Notary Public

State of _____

County of _____ } ss

On _____, _____, before me, _____,
a notary public in and for said state, personally appeared _____,
who proved to me on the basis of satisfactory evidence to be the person whose name is subscribed to the
within instrument and acknowledged to me that he or she executed the same in his or her authorized capacity
and that by his or her signature on the instrument, the person, or the entity upon behalf of which the person
acted, executed the instrument.

I certify under PENALTY OF PERJURY under the laws of the State of _____ that
the foregoing paragraph is true and correct.

WITNESS my hand and official seal.

_____

Notary Public for the State of _____

My commission expires _____

[NOTARY SEAL]

Personal Property Rental Agreement

Owner's name: _____ Home phone: _____

Address: _____ Cell phone: _____

Renter's name: _____ Home phone: _____

Address: _____ Cell phone: _____

If there is more than one owner or renter, the use of the singular incorporates the plural.

1. **Property Being Rented; Use**

   Owner agrees to rent to Renter, and Renter agrees to rent from Owner, the following property
   ("the Property"): _____

   _____

   _____.

   Renter will use the Property for the following purpose only: _____

   _____.

   Owner may cancel this agreement and require that Renter return the Property immediately if it is
   used for any other purpose.

2. **Duration of Rental Period**

   This rental will begin at _____ o'clock a.m./p.m. on _____, _____

   and will end at _____ o'clock a.m./p.m. on _____, _____.

3. **Rental Amount**

   The rental amount will be $_____ per _____ *[specify hour, day, week, or month].*

4. **Payment**

   Renter has paid $_____ to Owner to cover the rental period specified in Clause 2.

   ☐ **Security deposit** *[optional].* In addition to the rent, Renter has deposited $_____ with
   Owner. This deposit will be applied toward any additional rent, late return fees, and any amounts
   owed for damage to or loss of the Property, which Owner and Renter agree has the current value
   stated in Clause 8. Owner will return to Renter any unused portion of the deposit within 24 hours
   of the return of the Property. Owner will deposit in the U.S. mail a refund check made out to
   Renter at the address shown above.

5. **Delivery**

   ☐ Renter will pick up the Property from Owner at *[specify address]* _____

   _____.

   ☐ Owner will deliver the Property to Renter ☐ at no charge ☐ for a fee of $_____

   on _____, _____ at: _____

   _____ *[specify address].*

☐ Other delivery arrangements: _____

_____

_____.

6. Late Return

If Renter returns the Property to Owner after the time and date when the rental period ends, Renter will pay Owner a rental charge of $_____ per day for each day or partial day beyond the end of the rental period until the Property is returned. Owner may subtract this charge from the security deposit (if any).

7. Condition of Property

Renter acknowledges receiving the Property in good condition, except for the following defects or damage:

_____

_____.

8. Damage or Loss

Renter will return the Property to Owner in good condition except as noted in Clause 7. If the Property is damaged while in Renter's possession due to Renter's negligent, reckless, or intentional act, Renter will be responsible for the cost of repair, up to the current value of the Property. If the Property is lost while in Renter's possession, Renter will pay Owner its current value. Owner and Renter agree that the current value of the Property is *[list value of items individually as well as total]* $_____.

9. Disputes. (This clause applies only to disputes regarding damage to the property or failure to return it, but not to disputes regarding personal injuries or damage to other property.)

[choose one]:

☐ **Litigation.** If a dispute arises, either Owner or Renter may take the matter to court.

☐ **Mediation and possible litigation.** If a dispute arises, Owner and Renter will try in good faith to settle it through mediation conducted by *[choose one]:*

☐ _____ *[name of mediator].*

☐ a mediator to be mutually selected.

Owner and Renter will share the costs of the mediator equally. If the dispute is not resolved within 30 days after it is referred to the mediator, either Owner or Renter may take the matter to court.

☐ **Mediation and possible arbitration.** If a dispute arises, Owner and Renter will try in good faith to settle it through mediation conducted by *[choose one]:*

☐ _____ *[name of mediator].*

☐ a mediator to be mutually selected.

Owner and Renter will share the costs of the mediator equally. If the dispute is not resolved within 30 days after it is referred to the mediator, it will be arbitrated by *[choose one]:*

☐ _____ *[name of arbitrator].*

☐ an arbitrator to be mutually selected.

Judgment on the arbitration award may be entered in any court that has jurisdiction over the matter. Costs of arbitration, including lawyers' fees, will be allocated by the arbitrator.

_____   _____
Owner's signature   Date

_____   _____
Renter's signature   Date

Notice of Termination of Personal Property Rental Agreement

To [name of person to whom notice is being sent]:

1. **Notice of Termination**

   This is a notice that as of_____, _____,
   I am terminating the following rental agreement:

   Name of Owner: _____

   Name of Renter: _____

   Property covered by agreement: _____

   _____

   Date agreement signed: _____, _____

2. **Reason for Termination**

   The reasons for the termination are as follows [optional, unless a reason to terminate is required by the
   rental agreement]: _____

   _____

   _____

   _____

   _____

3. **Return of Property**

   [choose one]:

   ☐ [for renters] I will return the Property to Owner on or before _____, _____.

   ☐ [for owners] Please return the Property to Owner on or before _____, _____.

4. **Return of Security Deposit**

   ☐ Renter has deposited $_____ with Owner. Owner agrees to inspect the Property for
   damage and refund Renter any unused portion of the security deposit. Within 24 hours of the return
   of the Property, Owner will deposit in the U.S. mail a refund check made out to Renter at the following
   address: _____

   _____

   _____   _____
   Signature   Date

   _____   ☐ Owner ☐ Renter
   Print name

Storage Contract

Property Owner: _____

Address: _____

Property Custodian: _____

Address: _____

If there is more than one owner or custodian, the use of the singular incorporates the plural.

1. Property

Owner desires to store with Custodian, and Custodian agrees to accept and store for Owner, the following property ("the Property"): _____

_____

_____

_____

_____

_____ Photographs of ☐ some ☐ all of the items are attached.

2. Storage Location

The Property will be stored at the following location: _____

_____

Custodian agrees that the Property will not be removed from this location without prior written notice to and written consent of Owner.

3. Storage Term and Payment

[choose one]:

☐ Custodian agrees to store the Property on a _____ *[daily, weekly, or monthly]* basis in exchange for payment of $_____ per _____, payable on the first day of each such period.

☐ Custodian agrees to store the Property for payment of $_____. Payment will be made on or before _____, _____.

4. Beginning and Ending Dates

[choose one]:

☐ Storage will begin on _____, and will continue until Owner claims the Property or Custodian serves Owner with a _____-day written notice terminating this storage agreement.

☐ Storage will begin on _____, _____, and will continue until _____, _____, or until Owner claims the Property, whichever occurs first.

5. Use of Property

Custodian will not use the Property, or permit it to be used by anyone else, without Owner's prior written consent. Notwithstanding Clause 10, Custodian is liable for any damage to the Property during use without Owner's prior written consent.

6. Reclaiming Property

Owner may reclaim the Property at any time, but not later than the date specified in Clause 4, or the date specified in the Custodian's notice of termination under that clause. Custodian will make the Property available to Owner, but may first require Owner to pay Custodian any unpaid charges allowed by Clauses 3 and 7.

Custodian may refuse delivery if Custodian has received any notice of attachment, levy, or similar notice and has given notice to Owner under Clause 12, or is instructed to withhold delivery by a court or law enforcement officer.

7. Failure to Reclaim Property

If Owner fails to reclaim the Property on or before the last day of storage indicated in the Custodian's notice of termination or in Clause 4, Custodian will *[choose one]*:

☐ continue to store the Property at the rate of $_____ per _____ until Owner reclaims the Property. Custodian may require owner to pay accrued storage fees before turning over the Property.

☐ send to Owner's last known address by first-class mail a notice to reclaim the Property, and wait 30 days; if Owner does not make arrangements to reclaim the Property during the 30 days, Custodian may deem the Property abandoned, sell it to pay for outstanding storage fees, and hold the balance (minus reasonable costs of sale) for Owner.

8. Early Reclaiming

If Owner reclaims the Property during a period for which payment has been made, no pro rata refund will be made.

9. Delivery to Someone Other Than Owner

Custodian will not deliver the Property to any person other than Owner without prior written permission from Owner. If Owner dies while this agreement is in effect, Owner instructs Custodian to deliver the Property to _____ upon proper proof of that person's identity and documentation of Owner's death, unless Custodian is instructed otherwise by a court or law enforcement official.

10. More Than One Owner

If more than one Owner is listed at the beginning of this form *[choose one]*:

☐ Custodian may deliver the Property only to all of the Owners.

☐ Custodian may deliver the Property to _____ *[state Owner's name]* rather than all of the Owners.

11. Value of the Property

Owner and Custodian agree that the approximate ☐ replacement value ☐ fair market value of each item of Property on the date this agreement is signed is: *[list items and their value]*

Item	Value
_____	_____
_____	_____
_____	_____

12. Condition of the Property

The Property being stored appears to be in good condition except for the following defects or damage *[provide details on each item of property being stored]*: _____

_____

_____

_____

_____

_____

13. Care During Storage Period

Custodian agrees to exercise reasonable care to protect the Property from loss, theft, or damage. Custodian agrees to be liable for loss, theft, or damage to the Property caused by Custodian's negligent, reckless, or intentional act. Owner agrees to be liable for damage to the Property or the storage location caused by inherent or defective condition of the Property.

☐ Owner will insure the Property. Custodian will insure the Property to the extent allowable under Custodian's homeowners' or other insurance policy.

14. Title to the Property

The title to the Property will remain at all times in Owner.

15. Notice of Attachment

Custodian agrees to notify Owner promptly in writing if Custodian receives any notice of attachment, levy, or similar notice.

16. Disputes

[choose one]:

☐ **Litigation.** If a dispute arises, either Owner or Custodian may take the matter to court.

☐ **Mediation and possible litigation.** If a dispute arises, Owner and Custodian will try in good faith to settle it through mediation conducted by *[choose one]:*

☐ _____ *[name of mediator].*

☐ a mediator to be mutually selected.

Owner and Custodian will share the costs of the mediator equally. If the dispute is not resolved within 30 days after it is referred to the mediator, either Owner or Custodian may take the matter to court.

☐ **Mediation and possible arbitration.** If a dispute arises, Owner and Custodian will try in good faith to settle it through mediation conducted by *[choose one]:*

☐ _____ *[name of mediator].*

☐ a mediator to be mutually selected.

Owner and Custodian will share the costs of the mediator equally. If the dispute is not resolved within 30 days after it is referred to the mediator, it will be arbitrated by *[choose one]:*

☐ _____ *[name of arbitrator].*

☐ an arbitrator to be mutually selected.

Judgment on the arbitration award may be entered in any court that has jurisdiction over the matter. Costs of arbitration, including lawyers' fees, will be allocated by the arbitrator.

17. Modification of This Agreement

All agreements between the parties related to storage of the Property are incorporated in this contract. Any modification to this contract must be in writing signed by Owner and Custodian.

18. Additional Terms

Additional terms for the storage of the Property are as follows: _____

_____

_____

_____.

_____   _____
Owner's signature   Date

_____   _____
Custodian's signature   Date

Home Maintenance Agreement

Homeowner's name: _____

Address: _____

Home phone: _____ Work: _____ Cell: _____

Contractor's name: _____

Address: _____

Business phone: _____ Cell: _____

Contractor's license number (if applicable): _____

Homeowner desires to contract with Contractor to perform certain work on property located at:

_____ .

1. Work to Be Done

The work to be performed under this agreement consists of the following:

_____

_____

_____

_____

_____

_____

_____ .

2. Payment

In exchange for the work specified in Clause 1, Homeowner agrees to pay Contractor as follows [choose one]:

☐ $_____, payable upon completion of the specified work by ☐ cash ☐ check.

☐ $_____, payable one half at the beginning of the specified work and one half at the completion of the specified work by ☐ cash ☐ check.

☐ $_____ per hour for each hour of work performed, up to a maximum of $_____, payable at the following times and in the following manner: _____

_____

_____ .

3. Time

The work specified in this contract shall *[check the boxes and provide dates]*:

☐ begin on _____ , _____ .

☐ be completed on _____ , _____ .

4. Additional Terms

Homeowner and Contractor additionally agree that: _____

_____

_____

_____

_____

_____

_____ .

    All agreements between Homeowner and Contractor related to the specified work are incorporated in this contract. Any modification to the contract must be in writing.

_____   _____
Homeowner's signature   Date

_____   _____
Contractor's signature   Date

Home Repairs Agreement

Homeowner's name: _____

Address: _____

Home phone: _____ Work: _____ Cell: _____

Contractor's name: _____

Address: _____

Business phone: _____ Cell: _____

Homeowner and Contractor agree that contractor will perform certain work on property located at:

_____.

1. Work to Be Done

The work to be performed under this agreement consists of the following:

_____

_____

_____

_____

_____.

2. Payment

In exchange for the work specified in Clause 1, Homeowner agrees to pay Contractor as follows *[choose one]*:

☐ $_____, payable upon completion of the specified work by ☐ cash ☐ check.

☐ $_____, payable by ☐ cash ☐ check as follows:

_____% payable when the following occurs: _____

_____% payable when the following occurs: _____

_____% payable when the following occurs: _____

☐ _____ $per hour for each hour of work performed, up to a maximum of $_____,

payable at the following times and in the following manner: _____

_____

_____.

3. Time

The work specified in Clause 1 will *[check the boxes and provide dates]*:

☐ begin on _____, _____.

☐ be completed on _____, _____.

Time is of the essence.

4. Licensing and Registration Requirements

Contractor will comply with all state and local licensing and registration requirements for type of activity involved in the specified work *[check one box and provide description]*:

☐ Contractor's state license or registration is for the following type of work and carries the following

number: _____

_____.

☐ Contractor's local license or registration is for the following type of work and carries the following

number: _____

_____.

☐ Contractor is not required to have a license or registration for the specified work, for the following

reasons: _____

_____.

5. Permits and Approvals

[check all appropriate boxes]:

☐ Contractor ☐ Homeowner will be responsible for determining which permits are necessary and for obtaining those permits.

☐ Contractor ☐ Homeowner will pay for all state and local permits necessary for performing the specified work.

☐ Contractor ☐ Homeowner will be responsible for obtaining approval from the local homeowner's association, if required.

6. Injury to Contractor

Contractor will carry insurance. If Contractor is injured in the course of performing the specified work, Homeowner will be exempt from liability for those injuries to the fullest extent allowed by law.

7. Additional Terms

Homeowner and Contractor additionally agree that: _____

_____

_____

_____

_____

_____.

All agreements between Homeowner and Contractor related to the specified work are incorporated in this contract. Any modification to the contract must be in writing.

_____   _____
Homeowner's signature   Date

_____   _____
Contractor's signature   Date

Contractor Mid-Job Worksheet

Date	Issue/ Question	Response	Additional cost?	Resolved?	Initials

Daily Expenses

Week of _____

Sunday's Expenses	Cost	Monday's Expenses	Cost	Tuesday's Expenses	Cost	Wednesday's Expenses	Cost
Daily Total: ___		Daily Total: ___		Daily Total: ___		Daily Total: ___	

Thursday's Expenses	Cost	Friday's Expenses	Cost	Saturday's Expenses	Cost	Other Expenses	Cost
Daily Total: ___		Daily Total: ___		Daily Total: ___		Daily Total: ___	

Total for the Week $_____

Monthly Income

Source of Income		Amount of each payment	Time period covered by each payment	Monthly income

A. Wages or Salary

Job 1: _____   Gross pay, including overtime: $ _____ _____

Subtract:

    Federal taxes   _____

    State taxes   _____

    Social Security (FICA)   _____

    Medicare   _____

    Union dues   _____

    Insurance payments   _____

    Child support withholding   _____

    Other deductions
    (specify): _____   _____

    Subtotal Job 1 $ _____ _____ $ _____

Job 2: _____   Gross pay, including overtime: $ _____ _____

Subtract:

    Federal taxes   _____

    State taxes   _____

    Social Security (FICA)   _____

    Medicare   _____

    Union dues   _____

    Insurance payments   _____

    Child support withholding   _____

    Other deductions
    (specify): _____   _____

    Subtotal Job 2 $ _____ _____ $ _____

Job 3: _____   Gross pay, including overtime: $ _____ _____

Subtract:

    Federal taxes   _____

    State taxes   _____

    Social Security (FICA)   _____

    Medicare   _____

    Union dues   _____

    Insurance payments   _____

    Child support withholding   _____

Source of Income		Amount of each payment	Time period covered by each payment	Monthly income
	Other deductions (specify): _____	_____		
	Subtotal Job 3	$ _____	_____	$ _____
	Total Wages or Salary			$ _____

B. Self-Employment Income

Job 1: _____	Gross pay, including overtime:	$ _____	_____	
	Subtract:			
	Federal taxes	_____		
	State taxes	_____		
	Self-employment taxes	_____		
	Other deductions (specify): _____	_____		
	Subtotal Job 1	$ _____	_____	$ _____
Job 2: _____	Gross pay, including overtime:	$ _____	_____	
	Subtract:			
	Federal taxes	_____		
	State taxes	_____		
	Self-employment taxes	_____		
	Other deductions (specify): _____	_____		
	Subtotal Job 2	$ _____	_____	$ _____
	Total Self-Employment Income			$ _____

C. Investment Income

	Dividends	$_____	_____	$ _____
	Interest	$_____	_____	$ _____
	Leases	$_____	_____	$ _____
	Licenses	$_____	_____	$ _____
	Rent	$_____	_____	$ _____
	Royalties	$_____	_____	$ _____
	Other (specify): _____	$_____	_____	$ _____
	_____	$_____	_____	$ _____
	Total Investment Income			$ _____

D. Other Income

	Bonuses	$_____	_____	$ _____
	Note or trust income	$_____	_____	$ _____
	Alimony or child support	$_____	_____	$ _____
	Pension/retirement income	$_____	_____	$ _____
	Social Security	$_____	_____	$ _____
	Other public assistance	$_____	_____	$ _____
	Other (specify): _____	$_____	_____	$ _____
	_____	$_____	_____	$ _____
	Total Other Income			$ _____
	Grand Total Monthly Income			$ _____

Monthly Income

Monthly Budget

	Proj.	Jan.	Feb.	Mar.	April	May	June	July	Aug.	Sept.	Oct.	Nov.	Dec.
Home													
rent/mortgage													
property taxes													
renters' ins.													
homeowners' ins.													
homeowners' association dues													
telephone													
gas & electric													
water & sewer													
cable TV													
Internet access													
garbage													
household supplies													
housewares													
furniture & appliances													
cleaning													
yard or pool care													
maintenance & repairs													
Credit and Loans													
credit card payments													
personal loan payments													
other loan payments													
Food													
groceries													
breakfast out													
lunch out													
dinner out													
coffee/tea													
snacks													
Clothing													
clothing, shoes & accessories													
laundry, dry cleaning & mending													
Self-Care													
toiletries & cosmetics													
haircuts													
massage													
health club membership													
donations													
Health Care													
insurance													
medications													
vitamins													
doctors													

	Proj.	Jan.	Feb.	Mar.	April	May	June	July	Aug.	Sept.	Oct.	Nov.	Dec.
dentist													
eye care													
therapy													

Transportation

car payment													
insurance													
road service club													
registration													
gasoline													
maintenance & repairs													
car wash													
parking & tolls													
public transit & cabs													
parking tickets													

Entertainment

music													
movies & rentals													
concerts, theater, & ballet													
museums													
sporting events													
hobbies & lessons													
club dues or membership													
film development													
books, magazines, & newspapers													
software & games													

Dependent Care

child care													
clothing													
allowance													
school expenses													
toys													
entertainment													

Pet Care

grooming													
vet													
food													
toys & supplies													

Education

tuition or loan payments													
books & supplies													

Travel

	Proj.	Jan.	Feb.	Mar.	April	May	June	July	Aug.	Sept.	Oct.	Nov.	Dec.

Gifts & Cards

holidays

birthdays & anniversaries

weddings & showers

Personal Business

supplies

photocopying

postage

bank & credit card fees

lawyer

accountant

taxes

savings

Savings and Investments

deposit to savings

deposit to retirement account

deposit to annuity

purchase of stock

purchase of mutual funds

other

Total Expenses

Total Income

Difference

Statement of Assets and Liabilities

(as of _____)

Assets	Date of Purchase	Account Number (if relevant)	Current Market Value ($)
Cash and Cash Equivalents			
Cash	_____	_____	_____
Checking accounts	_____	_____	_____
Savings accounts	_____	_____	_____
Money market accounts	_____	_____	_____
Other	_____	_____	_____
Subtotal			_____
Real Estate			
House/condo/co-op	_____	_____	_____
Vacation home	_____	_____	_____
Income properties	_____	_____	_____
Unimproved lot	_____	_____	_____
Other lot	_____	_____	_____
Subtotal			_____
Personal Property			
Motor vehicles	_____	_____	_____
Furniture	_____	_____	_____
Home furnishings	_____	_____	_____
Electronic equipment	_____	_____	_____
Computer system	_____	_____	_____
Jewelry	_____	_____	_____
Clothing	_____	_____	_____
Collections (coin, stamp, etc.)	_____	_____	_____
Animals	_____	_____	_____
Other	_____	_____	_____
Subtotal			_____
Investments and Miscellaneous Assets			
Life insurance (term cash value)	_____	_____	_____
Life insurance (whole policies)	_____	_____	_____
Stocks	_____	_____	_____
Bonds	_____	_____	_____
Mutual funds	_____	_____	_____
Annuities	_____	_____	_____
IRAs	_____	_____	_____
Keoghs	_____	_____	_____
401(k) plans	_____	_____	_____
Other retirement plans	_____	_____	_____
Partnerships	_____	_____	_____
Accounts receivable	_____	_____	_____
Other	_____	_____	_____
Subtotal			_____

Liabilities	Date Incurred	Account Number	Total Balance Due ($)
Secured			
Mortgage	_____	_____	_____
Mortgage	_____	_____	_____
Deeds of trust	_____	_____	_____
Home equity loans	_____	_____	_____
Liens	_____	_____	_____
Motor vehicle loans	_____	_____	_____
Bank loans	_____	_____	_____
Personal loans	_____	_____	_____
Other	_____	_____	_____
Subtotal			_____
Unsecured			
Student loans	_____	_____	_____
Bank loans	_____	_____	_____
Personal loans	_____	_____	_____
Credit card balances	_____	_____	_____
Judgments	_____	_____	_____
Taxes	_____	_____	_____
Support arrears	_____	_____	_____
Other	_____	_____	_____
Subtotal			_____

Net Worth Summary

Total Assets

Cash Subtotal	$ _____	
Real Estate Subtotal	_____	
Personal Property Subtotal	_____	
Investments Subtotal	_____	
Total Assets		$ _____

Total Liabilities

Secured Subtotal	_____	
Unsecured Subtotal	_____	
Total Liabilities		$ _____

Net Worth

(Assets minus liabilities)		$ _____

Assignment of Rights

Assignor 1's name: _____

Address: _____

Assignor 2's name: _____

Address: _____

Assignee 1's name: _____

Address: _____

Assignee 2's name: _____

Address: _____

If there is more than one assignor or assignee, the use of the singular incorporates the plural.

1. Assignor transfers to Assignee all of the following rights of Assignor *[describe the rights you are assigning]*:

   _____

   _____

   _____

   _____ .

2. Evidence of Assignor's rights can be found in the following document *[describe the document, such as a promissory note, providing details of document name, parties, and date]*:

   _____

   _____ .

   Evidence of Assignor's right ☐ is ☐ is not attached to this Assignment of Rights form.

3. This assignment takes effect on: _____ .

4. This assignment lasts until: _____ *[specify date or event that ends assignment]*.

_____   _____
Assignor 1's signature   Date

_____
Print name

_____
Location *[city or county where signed]*

_____
Address

Assignor 2's signature

Date

Print name

Location *[city or county where signed]*

Address

Assignee 1's signature

Date

Print name

Location *[city or county where signed]*

Address

Assignee 2's signature

Date

Print name

Location *[city or county where signed]*

Address

Notice to Terminate Joint Account

Date: _____

_____

_____

_____

_____

[name and address of creditor]

Names on account: _____

Account number: _____

To Whom It May Concern:

With this letter, I am requesting that you close the account referenced above, effective immediately.

I am requesting a "hard close" of the account so that neither party to the account may incur new charges. If you do not hard close the account, please be informed that as of the date of this letter, I will not be responsible for any new charges made to this account.

If my account has an outstanding balance, you may keep the account open for billing purposes only. Nevertheless, I request that you keep the account inactive so that neither party to the account can incur new charges.

Please acknowledge receipt of this notice by signing the duplicate of this letter and returning it to me in the enclosed stamped, self-addressed envelope.

Thank you for your assistance with this matter.

_____   _____
Signature   Date

_____
Printed or typed name

_____
Address

_____

_____   _____
Home phone   Work phone

- -

Receipt acknowledged by:

_____   _____
Signature   Date

_____
Printed or typed name

_____
Title

Outstanding balance: _____ As of: _____

Notice to Stop Payment of Check

Date: _____

_____

_____

_____

_____

[name and address of financial institution]

Re: Stop payment of check

To Whom It May Concern:

This letter is to confirm my telephone request of _____ *[date]* that you stop payment on the following check:

Name(s) on account:_____

Account number: _____ Check number: _____

Payable to:_____

Date written: _____ Amount of check: _____

    Please acknowledge receipt of this notice by signing the duplicate of this letter and returning it to me in the enclosed stamped, self-addressed envelope.

    Thank you for your assistance.

_____   _____
Signature   Date

_____
Printed or typed name

_____
Address

_____

_____ _____
Home phone   Work phone

Receipt acknowledged by:

_____   _____
Signature   Date

_____
Printed or typed name

_____
Title

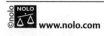

Request for Credit Report

Date: _____

_____

_____

_____

_____

[name and address of credit bureau]

To Whom It May Concern:

Please send me a copy of my credit report.

Full name: _____

Date of birth: _____ Social Security number: _____

Spouse's name: _____

Telephone number: _____

Current address: _____

_____

Previous address: _____

_____

[check one]:

☐ I was denied credit on _____ by _____

_____. Enclosed is a copy of the denial letter.

☐ I hereby swear that I am unemployed and intend to apply for a job within the next 60 days. Enclosed is a copy of a document verifying my unemployment.

☐ I hereby swear that I receive public assistance/welfare. Enclosed is a copy of my most recent public assistance check as verification.

☐ I hereby swear that I believe there is erroneous information in my file due to fraud.

☐ I am requesting my annual free credit report.

☐ I am not entitled to a free copy of my report. Enclosed is a copy of a document identifying me by my name and address and a check for $ _____ .

Thank you for your attention to this matter.

Sincerely,

_____

Signature

Dispute Incorrect Credit Report Entry

Date: _____

_____

_____

_____

_____

[name and address of credit bureau]

This is a request for you to reinvestigate the following items which appear on my credit report:

☐ The following personal information about me is incorrect:

Erroneous Information	Correct Information
_____	_____
_____	_____
_____	_____

☐ The following accounts are not mine:

Creditor's Name	Account Number	Explanation
_____	_____	_____
_____	_____	_____
_____	_____	_____

☐ The account status is incorrect for the following accounts:

Creditor's Name	Account Number	Correct Status
_____	_____	_____
_____	_____	_____
_____	_____	_____

☐ The following information is too old to be included in my report:

Creditor's Name	Account Number	Date of Last Activity
_____	_____	_____
_____	_____	_____
_____	_____	_____

☐ The following inquiries are older than two years:

Creditor's Name	Date of Inquiry
_____	_____
_____	_____
_____	_____

☐ The following inquiries were not authorized:

Creditor's Name	Date of Inquiry	Explanation
_____	_____	_____
_____	_____	_____
_____	_____	_____

☐ The following accounts were closed at my request and should say so:

Creditor's Name	Account number
_____	_____
_____	_____
_____	_____

☐ Other errors:

Explanation

_____

_____

_____

_____

_____

_____

_____

I understand that you will check each specified item, above, with the credit grantor reporting the information, remove any information the credit grantor cannot verify, or modify information that is incorrect or incomplete. I further understand that under 15 U.S.C. § 1681i(a), you must complete your reinvestigation within 30 days of receipt of this letter. Thank you for your attention to this matter.

Sincerely,

_____

Signature

_____

Print name

_____

Address

_____   _____

Home phone   Social Security number

Dispute Credit Card Charge

Date: _____

_____

_____

_____

_____

[name and address of the company or financial institution that issued credit card]

Re: Account number: _____

Names(s) on account: _____

To Whom It May Concern:

I am writing to dispute the following charge that appears on my billing statement dated _____ .

Merchant's name: _____

Amount in dispute: _____ . I am withholding payment of $_____, which represents the unpaid balance on the disputed item.

I am disputing this amount for the following reason(s):

_____

_____

_____

_____

_____ .

As required by law, I have tried in good faith to resolve this dispute with the merchant. *[Describe your efforts]*

_____ .

[For purchases made with a credit card, such as Visa or MasterCard, not issued by the seller]:

☐ This purchase was for more than $50 and was made in the state in which I live or within 100 miles of my home.

Please remove the charge for this item, and all associated late and interest charges from my account.

Sincerely,

_____

Signature

_____

Print name

_____

Address

_____

Home phone

Demand Collection Agency Cease Contact

Date: _____

_____

_____

_____

_____

[name and address of collection agency, including name of individual collector, if known]

Name(s) on account:_____

Account number: _____

Creditor: _____

To _____ :

Since _____ *[date]*, I have received several phone calls and letters from you concerning my account with the above-named creditor.

Under 15 U.S.C. § 1692c, this is my formal notice to you to cease all further communications with me except for the reasons specifically set forth in the federal law.

_____
Signature

_____
Print name

_____
Address

_____

_____
Home phone

Notice to Remove Name From List

Date: _____

_____

_____

_____

_____

[name and address of list maintainer]

To Whom It May Concern:

Please permanently remove all members of this household from all lists you maintain, sell, trade, share, or use in any other capacity for direct marketing, telemarketing, credit card prescreening, or any other promotional purpose.

_____
Name 1

_____
Address

_____
Home phone (with area code)

_____   _____
Date of birth   Social Security number *[provide only when contacting a credit bureau]*

_____
Name 2

_____
Address

_____   _____
Date of birth   Social Security number

_____
Name 3

_____
Address

_____   _____
Date of birth   Social Security number

Sincerely,

_____
Signature

_____
Print name

Notice to Add or Retain Name but Not Sell or Trade It

Date: _____

_____

_____

_____

_____

[name and address of list maintainer]

To Whom It May Concern:

Please ☐ add ☐ retain my name on your mailing list. *Please do not sell, trade, or share my name or address with any other company or business.*

☐ I will accept telemarketing phone calls from your company.

☐ I do not wish to receive telemarketing phone calls from your company. Put me on your "do not call" list.

Sincerely,

_____
Signature

_____
Print name

_____
Address

_____

_____
Home phone

Telemarketing Phone Call Log

Date	Time	Company	Telemarketer's name and phone number	Product	Said "Put me on a 'do not call' list"	Followed up with letter

Notice to Put Name on Company's "Do Not Call" List

Date: _____

_____

_____

_____

_____

[name and address of company on whose behalf call was made]

To Whom It May Concern:

This letter is a follow up to the telemarketing phone call I received from _____
[name of person who placed the call to you] on behalf of your company on _____ *[date]*.

As I stated at that time, I do not wish to receive telemarketing phone calls. Please put me on your "do not call" list immediately.

Sincerely,

_____
Signature

_____
Print name

_____
Address

_____

_____
Home phone

Demand for Damages for Excessive Calls

Date: _____

_____

_____

_____

_____

[name and address of company on whose behalf the calls were made]

To Whom It May Concern:

Since _____ *[date]*, I have received multiple phone calls from telemarketers calling on behalf of your company. I am giving your company the opportunity to settle my claim against you before I sue you in small claims court.

On or about _____ *[date]*, I received a telephone call at my home from a telemarketer by the name of _____, who stated that ☐ he ☐ she was calling on behalf of your company. I told this person that I was not interested in your company's product, and asked that my name be placed on the "do not call" list for calls made on behalf of your company. I was assured that this would be done.

On or about _____ *[date]*, I received a second telephone call at my home from a telemarketer by the name of_____, who stated that ☐ he ☐ she was calling on behalf of your company. I told this person that I was not interested in your company's product, and asked that my name be placed on a "do not call" list for calls made on behalf of your company. Again, I was assured that this would be done.

[Repeat the above paragraph as needed, changing the word "second" to "third," "fourth," etc.]

Section 64.1200(d)(3) of Title 47 of the Code of Federal Regulations states, in pertinent part:

> If a person or entity making a call for telemarketing purposes (or on whose behalf such a call is made) receives a request from a residential telephone subscriber not to receive calls from that person or entity, the person or entity must record the request and place the subscriber's name, if provided, and telephone number on the do-not-call list at the time the request is made. Persons or entities making calls for telemarketing purposes (or on whose behalf such calls are made) must honor a residential subscriber's do-not-call request within a reasonable time from the date such request is made. **If such requests are recorded or maintained by a party other than the person or entity on whose behalf the telemarketing call is made, the person or entity on whose behalf the telemarketing call is made will be liable for any failures to honor the do-not-call request.** [47 CFR § 64.1200(d)(3) as amended 10-1-04.]

A violation of this regulation is actionable under 47 U.S.C. § 227(c)(5). That section provides that:

A person who has received more than one telephone call within any 12-month period by or on behalf of the same entity in violation of the regulations prescribed under this subsection may ... bring in an appropriate court of that state

(A) an action based on a violation of the regulations prescribed under this subsection to enjoin such violation,

(B) an action to recover for actual monetary loss from such a violation, or to receive up to $500 in damages for each such violation, whichever is greater, or

(C) both such actions.

In addition, treble damages may be awarded for knowing and willful violations.

Your company clearly violated the law on _____ separate occasions. I am entitled to $500 for each violation, for a total of $ _____ .

[Optional] Your company also violated state law. I am entitled to damages and/or civil penalties for those violations as well.

I am willing to forego my right to seek an injunction and treble damages against your company if you send me a cashier's check for the amount stated above within the next 30 days. If I do not hear from you within that time, I will seek all appropriate remedies in a court of law.

Sincerely,

_____
Signature

_____
Print name

_____
Address

_____

_____

_____
Home phone

Child Care Agreement

1. Parent or Legal Guardian

Parent(s)' name(s): _____

Address(es): _____

_____

Home phone number(s): _____

Work phone number(s): _____

Cell phone: _____

Email: _____

2. Child Care Provider

Child Care Provider's name: _____

Address: _____

_____ Home phone number: _____

Cell phone: _____

Email: _____

3. Children

Parent(s) desire(s) to contract with Child Care Provider to provide child care for:_____

_____ *[names and birthdates of the children]*.

4. Location and Schedule of Care

Care will be provided at:_____

_____ *[your address or other location where care is to be given]*.

Days and hours of child care will be as follows: _____

_____ .

5. Beginning Date

Employment will begin on _____ *[date]*.

6. Training or Probation Period

There will be a training/probation period during the first _____ *[length of training period]*
of employment.

7. Responsibilities

The care to be provided under this agreement consists of the following responsibilities *[describe and provide*

details]: _____

_____

_____ .

8. Wage or Salary

Child Care Provider will be paid as follows:

☐ $ _____ per hour

☐ $ _____ per month

☐ other: _____

9. Payment Schedule

Child Care Provider will be paid on the following intervals and dates:

☐ once a week on every _____

☐ twice a month on _____

☐ once a month on _____

☐ other: _____

10. Benefits

Parent(s) will provide Child Care Provider with the following benefits *[describe and provide details]*:

_____

_____

_____

_____

11. Termination Policy

Either Parent(s) or Child Care Provider may terminate this agreement at any time, for any reason, without notice.

12. Additional Provisions

Parent(s) and Child Care Provider agree to the following additional terms: _____

_____

_____ .

13. Modifications in Writing

To be binding, any modifications to this contract must be in writing and signed by both parties to the agreement.

Signatures

_____   _____
Parent 1's signature: Date

_____   _____
Parent 2's signature: Date

_____   _____
Child Care Provider's signature   Date

Child Care Instructions

1. Home and Family Information

Parent(s)' name(s) *[list any parents who live at this address; other parents may be listed under Emergency Contacts]*: _____

Names of children: _____

Address: _____

_____ Home phone number: _____

Cell phone: _____

Email: _____

2. Parent(s)' Work Information

[list name and address of employer, work phone number, and regular work hours for each parent]

_____

_____

3. Temporary Contact Information

[specify the address and phone number where you can be reached at a temporary location, such as a restaurant, movie, or friend's house, plus the times you will be at each location]

_____

_____

4. Child's Personal and Care Information

[provide the following information for each child]

Name of child:_____

Date of birth:_____

Allergies and other medical conditions: _____

Medications: _____

Meals, naps, and bedtime schedule:_____

Other comments: _____

5. Child's Health Care Providers

[list names, addresses, and phone numbers]

Doctor: _____

Dentist:_____

Other medical providers:_____

6. Emergency Contacts

[list names, addresses, and phone numbers of people who babysitter can contact if they can't reach you in case of emergency; specify their relationship to your family, such as children's aunt or neighbor]

_____

IN CASE OF EMERGENCY, CALL 911.

7. Other Important Information: _____

Elder Care Agreement

1. Employer

Employer(s)' name(s): _____

Address(es): _____

_____

Home phone number(s): _____

Work phone number(s): _____

Cell phone: _____

Email: _____

2. Elder Care Provider

Elder care provider's name: _____

Address: _____ _____

_____ Home phone number: _____

Cell phone: _____

Email: _____

3. Older Adult(s) to Be Cared For

Employer(s) desire(s) to contract with Elder Care Provider to provide elder care for:_____

_____

_____ *[names and birthdates of person(s) in need of elder care]*.

4. Location and Schedule of Care

Care will be provided at:_____

_____*[your address or other location where care is to be given]*.

Days and hours of elder care will be as follows:_____

_____ .

5. Beginning Date

Employment will begin on _____ *[date]*.

6. Training or Probation Period

There will be a training/probation period during the first_____
[length of training period] of employment, ending on _____ *[date]*.

7. Responsibilities

The care to be provided under this agreement consists of the following responsibilities *[describe and
provide details]*: _____

_____

_____ .

8. **Wage or Salary**

Elder Care Provider will be paid as follows:

☐ $ _____ per hour

☐ $ _____ per month

☐ other: _____

9. **Payment Schedule**

Elder Care Provider will be paid on the following intervals and dates:

☐ once a week on every _____

☐ twice a month on _____

☐ once a month on _____

☐ other: _____

10. **Benefits**

Employer(s) will provide Elder Care Provider with the following benefits [describe and provide details]:

_____

_____

_____ .

11. **Termination Policy**

Either Employer(s) or Elder Care Provider may terminate this agreement at any time, for any reason, without notice.

12. **Additional Provisions**

Employer(s) and Elder Care Provider agree to the following additional terms: _____

_____

_____

_____ .

13. **Modifications in Writing**

To be binding, any modifications to this contract must be in writing and signed by both parties to the agreement.

Signatures

_____   _____

Employer(s)' signature(s):   Date

_____   _____

Elder Care Provider's signature   Date

Housekeeping Services Agreement

1. Employer

Employer(s)' name(s): _____

Address(es): _____

_____

Home phone number(s): _____

Work phone number(s): _____

Cell phone: _____

Email: _____

2. Housekeeper

Housekeeper's name: _____

Address: _____

_____ Home phone number: _____

Cell phone: _____

Email: _____

3. Location and Schedule of Work

Employer desires to contract with Housekeeper to work at: _____

_____ [your address].

Days and hours of cleaning will be as follows: _____

_____ .

4. Beginning Date

Employment will begin on _____ [date].

5. Housecleaning Responsibilities

The services to be provided under this agreement consist of cleaning the following [describe and provide

details]: _____

_____

_____

_____ .

6. Other Responsibilities

Housekeeper also agrees to do the following types of work [describe and provide details regarding

cooking, laundry, and other noncleaning responsibilities]:_____

_____

_____ .

7. Wage or Salary

Housekeeper will be paid as follows:

☐ $ _____ per hour

☐ $ _____ per month

☐ other: _____

8. Payment Schedule

Housekeeper will be paid on the following intervals and dates:

☐ once a week on every _____

☐ twice a month on _____

☐ once a month on _____

☐ other: _____

9. Benefits

Employer(s) will provide Housekeeper with the following benefits *[describe and provide details]*:_____

_____

_____

_____

_____

_____ .

10. Termination Policy

Either Employer(s) or Housekeeper may terminate this agreement at any time, for any reason, without notice.

11. Additional Provisions

Employer(s) and Housekeeper agree to the following additional terms: _____

_____

_____

_____

_____

_____ .

12. Modifications in Writing

To be binding, any modifications to this contract must be in writing and signed by both parties.

Signatures

_____   _____

Employer(s)' signature(s):   Date

_____   _____

Housekeeper's signature   Date

Agreement to Keep Property Separate

Partner 1's name: _____

Partner 2's name: _____

We agree as follows:

1. This contract sets forth our rights and obligations toward each other. We intend to abide by them in a spirit of cooperation and good faith.

2. All property owned by either of us as of the date of this agreement will remain the separate property of its owner and cannot be transferred to the other person except in writing. We have each attached to this contract a list of our major items of separate property.

3. The income each of us earns—as well as any items or investments either of us purchases with our income— belongs absolutely to the person who earns the money unless there is a written joint ownership agreement as provided in Clause 6.

4. We shall each maintain our own separate bank, credit card, investment, and retirement accounts, and neither of us shall in any way be responsible for the debts of the other. If we register legally as domestic partners and, by so doing, the law requires us to be responsible for each other's basic living expenses, we agree to assume no more than the minimum level of reciprocal responsibility required by the law.

5. Expenses for routine household items and services, which include groceries, utilities, rent, and cleaning supplies, shall be shared equally.

6. From time to time, we may decide to keep a joint checking or savings account for a specific purpose (for example, to pay household expenses), or to own some property jointly (for example, to purchase a television). If so, the details of our joint ownership agreement shall be put in writing in a written contract or a deed, title slip, or other joint ownership document.

7. Should either of us receive real or personal property by gift or inheritance, the property belongs absolutely to the person receiving the gift or inheritance and cannot be transferred to the other except in writing.

8. In the event we separate, each of us shall be entitled to immediate possession of our separate property.

9. Any dispute arising out of this contract will be mediated by a third person mutually acceptable to both of us. The mediator's role will be to help us arrive at our solution, not to impose one on us. If good-faith efforts to arrive at our own solution to all issues in dispute with the help of a mediator prove to be fruitless, either of us may pursue other legal remedies.

10. This agreement represents our complete understanding regarding our living together and replaces any and all prior agreements, written or oral. It can be amended, but only in writing, and any amendment must be signed by both of us.

11. If a court finds any portion of this contract to be illegal or otherwise unenforceable, the remainder of the contract is still in full force and effect.

_____   _____
Partner 1's signature   Date

_____   _____
Partner 2's signature   Date

Certificate of Acknowledgment of Notary Public

State of _____

County of _____ } ss

On _____, _____, before me, _____,
a notary public in and for said state, personally appeared _____,
who proved to me on the basis of satisfactory evidence to be the person whose name is subscribed to the within
instrument and acknowledged to me that he or she executed the same in his or her authorized capacity and that by
his or her signature on the instrument, the person, or the entity upon behalf of which the person acted, executed
the instrument.

I certify under PENALTY OF PERJURY under the laws of the State of _____
that the foregoing paragraph is true and correct.

WITNESS my hand and official seal.

_____

Notary Public for the State of _____

My commission expires _____

[NOTARY SEAL]

Attachment A

Separate personal property of _____ :

_____

_____

_____

_____

_____

_____

_____

_____

_____

_____

_____

_____

_____

_____

_____

_____

Separate personal property of _____ :

_____

_____

_____

_____

_____

_____

_____

_____

_____

_____

_____

_____

_____

_____

_____

_____

Agreement for a Joint Purchase

Partner 1's name: _____

Partner 2's name: _____

We agree as follows:

1. We will jointly acquire and own _____

    _____ *[describe the property]* at a cost of $ _____.

2. We will own the Property in the following shares:

    Partner 1 will own _____% of the Property and Partner 2 will own _____% of the Property.

3. If we separate and stop living together, one of the following will occur:

    (a) If one of us wants the Property and the other doesn't, the person who wants the Property will pay the other fair market value (see Clause 4) of the Property.

    (b) If both of us want the Property, the decision will be made in the following way *[choose one]*:

    ☐ Right of First Refusal. _____ *[specify either Partner 1 or 2]* shall have the right of first refusal and may purchase _____ 's *[specify either Partner 1 or 2]* share of the Property for its fair market value (see Clause 4). _____ *[specify either Partner 1 or 2]* will then become sole owner of the Property.

    ☐ Coin Toss Method. We will flip a coin to determine who is entitled to the Property. The winner, upon paying the loser fair market value for the loser's share of ownership, will become the sole owner of the Property.

    ☐ Other: _____ .

4. Should either of us decide to end the relationship, we will do our best to agree on the fair current market value of the Property. If we can't agree on a price, we will jointly choose a neutral appraiser and abide by the appraiser's decision.

5. If we separate and neither of us wants the Property—or if we can't agree on a fair price—we will advertise it to the public, sell it to the highest bidder, and divide the money according to our respective ownership shares as set forth in Clause 2.

6. Should either of us die while we are living together, the Property will belong absolutely to the survivor. If either of us makes a will or other estate plan, this agreement shall be reflected in that document.

7. This agreement can be changed, but only in writing, and any changes must be signed by both of us.

8. Any dispute arising out of this contract will be mediated by a third person mutually acceptable to both of us. The mediator's role will be to help us arrive at our solution, not to impose one on us. If good faith efforts to arrive at our own solution to all issues in dispute with the help of a mediator prove to be fruitless, either of us may pursue other legal remedies.

9. If a court finds any portion of this contract to be illegal or otherwise enforceable, the remainder of the contract is still in full force and effect.

_____   _____
Partner 1's signature   Date

_____   _____
Partner 2's signature   Date

Agreement to Share Property

Partner 1's name: _____

Partner 2's name: _____

We agree as follows:

1. This contract sets forth our rights and obligations toward each other. We intend to abide by them in a spirit of cooperation and good faith.

2. All earned income received by either of us after the date of this contract and all property purchased with this income belongs in equal shares to both of us with the following exceptions: _____

   _____

   _____

   _____ .

3. All real or personal property earned or accumulated by either of us before the date of this agreement (except jointly owned property listed in Attachment C of this agreement), including all future income such property produces, is the separate property of the person who earned or accumulated it and cannot be transferred to the other except in writing. Attached to this agreement in the form of Attachments A, B, and C, respectively, are lists of the major items of property each of us owns separately and both of us own jointly.

4. Should either of us receive real or personal property by gift or inheritance, that property, including all future income it produces, belongs absolutely to the person receiving the gift or inheritance and cannot be transferred to the other except in writing.

5. In the event we separate, all jointly owned property shall be divided equally.

6. Any dispute arising out of this contract will be mediated by a third person mutually acceptable to both of us. The mediator's role will be to help us arrive at our solution, not to impose one on us. If good faith efforts to arrive at our own solution to all issues in dispute with the help of a mediator prove to be fruitless, either of us may pursue other legal remedies.

7. This agreement represents our complete understanding regarding our living together and replaces any and all prior agreements, written or oral. It can be amended, but only in writing, and any amendments must be signed by both of us.

8. If a court finds any portion of this contract to be illegal or otherwise unenforceable, the remainder of the contract is still in full force and effect.

_____   _____
Partner 1's signature   Date

_____   _____
Partner 2's signature   Date

Certificate of Acknowledgment of Notary Public

State of _____

County of _____ } ss

On _____, _____, before me, _____,
a notary public in and for said state, personally appeared _____,
who proved to me on the basis of satisfactory evidence to be the person whose name is subscribed to the
within instrument and acknowledged to me that he or she executed the same in his or her authorized
capacity and that by his or her signature on the instrument, the person, or the entity upon behalf of which
the person acted, executed the instrument.

I certify under PENALTY OF PERJURY under the laws of the State of _____
that the foregoing paragraph is true and correct.

WITNESS my hand and official seal.

_____

Notary Public for the State of _____

My commission expires _____

[NOTARY SEAL]

Attachment A

Separate personal property of _____ :

_____

_____

_____

_____

_____

_____

_____

_____

_____

Attachment B

Separate personal property of _____ :

_____

_____

_____

_____

_____

_____

_____

_____

_____

Attachment C

Jointly owned property acquired prior to _____ *[date of this Agreement]*:

_____

_____

_____

_____

_____

_____

_____

_____

_____

_____

Declaration of Legal Name Change

I, the undersigned, declare that I am 18 years of age or older and further declare:

1. I, _____ [name currently used],

   was born _____ [name on birth certificate]

   in the County of _____ [county where born]

   in the State of _____ [state where born]

   on _____ [birthdate, including year].

2. I HEREBY DECLARE that I have changed my legal name, and from now on will be exclusively known as

   [new name] _____ .

3. My legal name change was completed by order of the _____ County Superior Court in case

   no. _____ on _____ , _____ . A copy of the court order is attached to

   this declaration.

4. NOTICE IS HEREBY GIVEN to all agencies of the State of _____

   [state where you reside], all agencies of the federal government, all creditors, and all private persons, groups,

   businesses, corporations, and associations of said legal name change.

5. Please revise all relevant records accordingly.

   I declare under penalty of perjury under the laws of the State of _____

   [state where you reside] that the foregoing is true and correct.

   _____   _____

   Signature, new name   Date

   _____   _____

   Signature, old name   Date

Demand Letter

Date: _____

_____

_____

_____

_____

[name and address of party with whom you have a dispute]

I am requesting compensation for the following problem:

[Describe in your own words exactly what happened. Specify dates, names of people with whom you dealt, and the damages you have suffered.]

_____

_____

_____

_____

_____

_____

_____

_____

_____

_____

_____

_____

_____

_____ .

Please send me a check or money order in the amount of: $ _____

on or before _____*[specify date].*

If I don't receive payment by this date, I will take this case to court immediately unless you notify me that you are willing to try to resolve this dispute through mediation. In that case, I am willing to meet with a neutral third party agreed to by both of us in a good faith attempt to resolve the dispute without court action.

Thank you for your immediate attention to this matter.

Sincerely,

_____

Signature

_____   _____   _____

Daytime phone   Evening phone   Email

Online Auction Buyer Demand Letter

To: _____ [*name of seller*]

_____ [*address*]

_____

I am writing to you regarding a dispute over _____ [*description of item purchased*] for which I was high bidder on the auction at _____ [*name of auction site*] as Item No. _____ [*number of item at auction site*].

A dispute exists because [*describe the reason you are dissatisfied with your purchase in as much detail as possible*] _____

_____

_____

_____

I would like to resolve the matter as follows [*choose one*]:

☐ I will return the item to you via [*describe the shipping method*] _____
and request compensation from you in the amount of $_____ ,
which includes the following costs [*list all costs for which you are seeking compensation, for example, shipping item to you, shipping item back to seller, amount paid for item, etc.*]_____

_____

☐ I will keep the item, but I request a partial refund of $_____ for the following reasons

_____

[*specify reasons for price reduction, for example, partial damage or not as advertised, and include proof such as photos of item*].

☐ I seek a full refund of all monies paid as I never received the item.

Please make payment by [*specify the method by which payment shall be made to you. For example, if payment to seller was made by credit card, seek a charge back. If payment was made by money order, seek a money order, etc.*] _____ .

If you disagree with my request and would like to resolve the matter through a third-party dispute resolution procedure, I am prepared to use online dispute resolution procedures at:

☐ iCourthouse (www.i-courthouse.com)

☐ myADR (www.namadr.com)

☐ other [*list online dispute resolution website*] _____

If I do not hear back from you by [*date*]_____ I will conclude that you do not wish to resolve the matter and I will [*check as many as apply*]:

☐ [*if payment was made by credit card*] seek a charge back on my credit card.

☐ file an online incident report at the National Consumer League's Fraud Center (www.fraud.org).

☐ post negative feedback at your online auction site.

Signature: _____

Address: _____

Email: _____

Request for Refund or Repair of Goods Under Warranty

Date: _____

_____

_____

_____

_____

[name and address of seller or manufacturer]

ATTN: Customer Service Department

Re: _____ *[description of item purchased, including serial number, if any]*

To Whom It May Concern:

I am writing to request compensation for the item described above, which I purchased for $_____
on_____ *[date]* from _____
[specify place of purchase].

My reason for demanding compensation is as follows *[describe the reason you are dissatisfied with your
purchase, in as much detail as possible. List anything included with this request, such as a copy of the warranty,
purchase receipt, or the item itself]*:_____

_____

_____ .

Specifically, I request the following compensation *[explain what you want, such as a refund of the full purchase
price, a replacement item, or a repair]*: _____

_____

_____ .

Please process this request by _____*[specify a deadline for
processing your request, such as date within 30 days].* If I don't receive compensation by then, I will take further
action, which may include filing a court action.

Thank you for your immediate attention to this matter.

Sincerely,

_____
Signature

_____
Address

_____

_____   _____   _____
Daytime phone   Evening phone   Email

Accident Claim Worksheet

What Happened

Date of accident: _____

Description of accident: _____

_____

Names of parties involved:_____

_____

Names of witnesses: _____

_____

Location of accident:_____

Time of accident:_____

Weather condition (if outside): _____

_____

_____

People Responsible for the Accident

Name: _____

Address: _____

_____

Phone (work): _____ (home): _____ (cell): _____

Insurance company: _____

Policy number: _____Driver's license: _____

What person did: _____

_____

_____

_____

_____

Name: _____

Address: _____

_____

Phone (work): _____ (home): _____ (cell): _____

Insurance company: _____

Policy number: _____Driver's license: _____

What person did: _____

_____

_____

Name: _____

Address: _____

_____

Phone (work): _____ (home): _____ (cell): _____

Insurance company: _____

Policy number: _____ Driver's license: _____

What person did: _____

_____

_____

_____

Witnesses

Name: _____

Address: _____

_____

Phone (work): _____ (home): _____ (cell): _____

Date of first contact: _____

Written statement: ☐ yes ☐ no

What person saw: _____

_____

_____

_____

_____

_____

_____

- -

Name: _____

Address: _____

_____

Phone (work): _____ (home): _____ (cell): _____

Date of first contact: _____

Written statement: ☐ yes ☐ no

What person saw: _____

_____

_____

_____

_____

Name: _____

Address: _____

_____

Phone (work): _____ (home): _____ (cell): _____

Date of first contact: _____

Written statement: ☐ yes ☐ no

What person saw: _____

_____

_____

_____

_____

_____

_____

Medical Treatment Providers

Name: _____

Address: _____

_____Telephone: _____

Date of first visit: _____ Date of most recent or last visit: _____

Person to be contacted for medical records: _____

Date requested: _____ Date received: _____

Person to be contacted for medical billing: _____

Date requested: _____ Date received: _____

Reason for treatment and prognosis: _____

_____

_____

_____

· ·

Name: _____

Address: _____

_____ Telephone: _____

Date of first visit: _____ Date of most recent or last visit: _____

Person to be contacted for medical records: _____

Date requested: _____ Date received: _____

Person to be contacted for medical billing: _____

Date requested: _____ Date received: _____

Reason for treatment and prognosis: _____

_____

Name: _____

Address: _____

_____ Telephone: _____

Date of first visit: _____ Date of most recent or last visit: _____

Person to be contacted for medical records: _____

Date requested: _____ Date received: _____

Person to be contacted for medical billing: _____

Date requested: _____ Date received: _____

Reason for treatment and prognosis: _____

_____

_____

_____

Other Party's Insurance Company (First Party)

Company name: _____

Address: _____

_____

Telephone: _____ Claim number: _____

Insured: _____

Adjuster: _____

Date demand letter was sent: _____

Settlement amount: _____ Date accepted: _____

Other Party's Insurance Company (Second Party)

Company name: _____

Address: _____

_____

Telephone: _____ Claim number: _____

Insured: _____

Adjuster: _____

Date demand letter was sent: _____

Settlement amount: _____ Date accepted: _____

Communications With Insurer

Date: _____ Name of Employee: _____

If oral, what was said: _____

_____

Communications With Insurer

Date: _____ Name of Employee: _____

If oral, what was said:_____

_____

_____

Communications With Insurer

Date: _____ Name of Employee: _____

If oral, what was said:_____

_____

_____

Communications With Insurer

Date: _____ Name of Employee: _____

If oral, what was said:_____

_____

_____

Communications With Insurer

Date: _____ Name of Employee: _____

If oral, what was said:_____

_____

_____

Losses

Describe damage to your property: _____

_____

Do you have photos showing damage? ☐ yes ☐ no

If Repairable

Estimates for repairs (name of repair shop and amounts of estimates):_____

_____

Actual

Repair bills (name of repair shop and amounts of bills): _____

_____

If totaled

Value at the time destroyed: _____

Documentation of value:_____

General Release

Releasor:_____

Address: _____

Releasee:_____

Address: _____

1. Releasor voluntarily and knowingly signs this release with the express intention of canceling Releasee's legal liabilities and obligations as described below.

2. Releasor hereby releases Releasee from all claims, known or unknown, that have arisen or may arise from the following occurrence: _____

   _____

   _____

   Releasor understands that, as to claims that are known to the parties when the release is signed, any statutory provisions that would otherwise apply to limit this general release are hereby waived. Releasor also understands that this release extends to claims arising out of this incident that are *not* known by Releasor at the time this release is signed.

3. In exchange for granting this release, Releasor has received the following payment or other consideration:

   _____

   _____

4. By signing this release, Releasor additionally intends to bind his or her spouse, heirs, legal representatives, assigns, and anyone else claiming under him or her. Releasor has not assigned any claim covered by this release to any other party. Releasor intends that this release apply to the heirs, personal representatives, assigns, insurers, and successors of Releasee as well as to the Releasee.

_____	_____
Releasor's signature	Date
_____	_____
Print name	County of residence
_____	_____
Releasor's spouse's signature	Date
_____	_____
Print name	County of residence
_____	_____
Releasee's signature	Date
_____	_____
Print name	County of residence
_____	_____
Releasee's spouse's signature	Date
_____	_____
Print name	County of residence

Certificate of Acknowledgment of Notary Public

State of _____

County of _____ } ss

On _____, _____, before me, _____,

a notary public in and for said state, personally appeared _____,

who proved to me on the basis of satisfactory evidence to be the person whose name is subscribed to the within instrument and acknowledged to me that he or she executed the same in his or her authorized capacity and that by his or her signature on the instrument, the person, or the entity upon behalf of which the person acted, executed the instrument.

I certify under PENALTY OF PERJURY under the laws of the State of _____
that the foregoing paragraph is true and correct.

WITNESS my hand and official seal.

_____

Notary Public for the State of _____

My commission expires _____

[NOTARY SEAL]

General Mutual Release

Party 1: _____

Address: _____

Party 2: _____

Address: _____

1. We voluntarily and knowingly sign this mutual release with the express intention of eliminating the liabilities and obligations described below.

2. Disputes and differences that we both desire to settle exist between us with respect to the following:

   _____

   _____

   _____

   _____ .

3. The value (consideration) for this mutual release consists of our mutual relinquishment of our respective legal rights involved in the disputes described above.

4. In addition, either party will receive the following payment or other consideration from the other [check and explain any that apply]:

   ☐ Party 1 will receive from Party 2: _____

   _____ .

   ☐ Party 2 will receive from Party 1: _____

   _____ .

5. By signing this release, we both intend to bind our spouses, heirs, legal representatives, assigns, and anyone else claiming under us, in addition to ourselves. Each party understands that, as to claims that are known to that party when the release is signed, any statutory provisions that would otherwise apply to limit this general release are hereby waived. Each party also understands that this release extends to claims arising out of this incident that are *not* known at the time this release is signed.

Party 1's signature _____   Date _____

Print name _____   County of residence _____

Party 1's spouse's signature _____   Date _____

Print name _____   County of residence _____

Party 2's signature _____   Date _____

Print name _____   County of residence _____

Party 2's spouse's signature _____   Date _____

Print name _____   County of residence _____

Certificate of Acknowledgment of Notary Public

State of _____

County of _____ } ss

On _____, _____, before me, _____,
a notary public in and for said state, personally appeared _____,
who proved to me on the basis of satisfactory evidence to be the person whose name is subscribed to the
within instrument and acknowledged to me that he or she executed the same in his or her authorized
capacity and that by his or her signature on the instrument, the person, or the entity upon behalf of which the
person acted, executed the instrument.

I certify under PENALTY OF PERJURY under the laws of the State of _____
that the foregoing paragraph is true and correct.

WITNESS my hand and official seal.

_____

Notary Public for the State of _____

My commission expires _____

[NOTARY SEAL]

Release for Damage to Real Estate

Releasor:_____

Address: _____

Releasee:_____

Address: _____

1. Releasor is the owner of certain property (Property) located at _____
    _____ , which specifically consists of the following:
    _____

2. Releasor voluntarily and knowingly signs this release with the intention of eliminating Releasee's liabilities and obligations as described below.

3. Releasor hereby releases Releasee from all claims, known or unknown, that have arisen or may arise from the occurrence described in Clause 4. Releasor understands that, as to claims that are known to the parties when the release is signed, any statutory provisions that would otherwise apply to limit this general release are hereby waived. Releasor also understands that this release extends to claims arising out of this incident that are *not* known by Releasor at the time this release is signed.

4. Releasor has alleged that Property suffered damage in the approximate amount of $ _____
    as a result of the following activity of Releasee:_____
    _____
    _____

5. By signing this release, Releasor additionally intends to bind his or her spouse, heirs, legal representatives, assigns, and anyone else claiming under him or her. Releasor has not assigned any claim arising from the transaction described in Clause 4 to another party. Releasor intends that this release apply to the heirs, personal representatives, assigns, insurers, and successors of Releasee as well as to the Releasee.

6. Releasor has received good and adequate value (consideration) for this release in the form of:
    _____
    _____

_____   _____
Releasor's signature   Date

_____   _____
Print name   County of residence

_____   _____
Releasor's spouse's signature   Date

_____   _____
Print name   County of residence

_____   _____
Releasee's signature   Date

_____   _____
Print name   County of residence

_____   _____
Releasee's spouse's signature   Date

_____   _____
Print name   County of residence

Certificate of Acknowledgment of Notary Public

State of _____

County of _____ } ss

On _____, _____, before me, _____,
a notary public in and for said state, personally appeared _____,
who proved to me on the basis of satisfactory evidence to be the person whose name is subscribed to the
within instrument and acknowledged to me that he or she executed the same in his or her authorized
capacity and that by his or her signature on the instrument, the person, or the entity upon behalf of which
the person acted, executed the instrument.

I certify under PENALTY OF PERJURY under the laws of the State of _____
that the foregoing paragraph is true and correct.

WITNESS my hand and official seal.

_____

Notary Public for the State of _____

My commission expires _____

[NOTARY SEAL]

Release for Property Damage in Auto Accident

Releasor: _____

Address: _____

Releasee: _____

Address: _____

1. Releasor voluntarily and knowingly signs this release with the express intention of eliminating Releasee's liabilities and obligations as described below.

2. Releasor hereby releases Releasee from all liability for claims, known and unknown, arising from property damage sustained by Releasor in an automobile accident that occurred on _____ *[date]* at_____ *[location]* involving a vehicle owned by Releasee or driven by Releasee or Releasee's agent. Releasor understands that, as to claims that are known to the parties when the release is signed, any statutory provisions that would otherwise apply to limit this general release are hereby waived. Releasor also understands that this release extends to claims arising out of this incident that are *not* known by Releasor at the time this release is signed.

3. By signing this release, Releasor does not give up any claim that he or she may now or hereafter have against any person, firm, or corporation other than Releasee and those persons and entities specified in Clause 6.

4. Releasor understands that Releasee does not, by providing the value described below, admit any liability or responsibility for the accident described in Clause 2 or its consequences.

5. Releasor has received good and adequate value (consideration) for this release in the form of:

   _____

   _____ .

6. By signing this release, Releasor additionally intends to bind his or her spouse, heirs, legal representatives, assigns, and anyone else claiming under him or her. Releasor has not assigned any claim arising from the accident described in Clause 2 to any other party. This release applies to Releasee's heirs, legal representatives, insurers, and successors, as well as to Releasee.

_____   _____
Releasor's signature   Date

_____   _____
Print name   County of residence

_____   _____
Releasor's spouse's signature   Date

_____   _____
Print name   County of residence

_____   _____
Releasee's signature   Date

_____   _____
Print name   County of residence

_____   _____
Releasee's spouse's signature   Date

_____   _____
Print name   County of residence

Certificate of Acknowledgment of Notary Public

State of _____

County of _____ } ss

On _____, _____, before me, _____,
a notary public in and for said state, personally appeared _____,
who proved to me on the basis of satisfactory evidence to be the person whose name is subscribed to the
within instrument and acknowledged to me that he or she executed the same in his or her authorized
capacity and that by his or her signature on the instrument, the person, or the entity upon behalf of which the
person acted, executed the instrument.

I certify under PENALTY OF PERJURY under the laws of the State of _____
that the foregoing paragraph is true and correct.

WITNESS my hand and official seal.

_____

Notary Public for the State of _____

My commission expires _____

[NOTARY SEAL]

Release for Personal Injury

Releasor:_____

Address: _____

Releasee:_____

Address: _____

1. Releasor voluntarily and knowingly executes this release with the intention of eliminating Releasee's liabilities and obligations as described below.

2. Releasor hereby releases Releasee from all liability for claims, known and unknown, arising from injuries, mental and/or physical, sustained by Releasor as follows: _____

   _____

   _____ .

   Releasor understands that, as to claims that are known to the parties when this release is signed, any statutory provisions that would otherwise apply to limit this general release are hereby waived. Releasor also understands that this release extends to claims arising out of this incident that are *not* known by Releasor at the time this release is signed.

3. Releasor has been examined by a licensed physician or other health care professional competent to diagnose *[choose one or both]*:

   ☐ physical injuries and disabilities.

   ☐ mental and emotional injuries and disabilities.

   Releasor has been informed by this physician or health care professional that the injury described in Clause 2 has completely healed without causing permanent damage.

4. By executing this release Releasor does not give up any claim that he or she may now or hereafter have against any person, firm, or corporation other than Releasee and those persons specified in Clause 7.

5. Releasor understands that Releasee does not, by providing the value described in Clause 6 below, admit any liability or responsibility for the above described injury or its consequences.

6. Releasor has received good and adequate value (consideration) for this release in the form of:

   _____

   _____ .

7. By signing this release, Releasor additionally intends to bind his or her spouse, heirs, legal representatives, assigns, and anyone else claiming under him or her. Releasor has not assigned any claim arising from the accident described in Clause 2 to any other party. This release applies to Releasee's heirs, legal representatives, insurers, and successors, as well as to Releasee.

_____	_____
Releasor's signature	Date
_____	_____
Print name	County of residence
_____	_____
Releasor's spouse's signature	Date
_____	_____
Print name	County of residence
_____	_____
Releasee's signature	Date

Print name _____

County of residence _____

Releasee's spouse's signature _____

Date _____

Print name _____

County of residence _____

Certificate of Acknowledgment of Notary Public

State of _____

County of _____ } ss

On _____, _____, before me, _____,

a notary public in and for said state, personally appeared _____,

who proved to me on the basis of satisfactory evidence to be the person whose name is subscribed to the

within instrument and acknowledged to me that he or she executed the same in his or her authorized

capacity and that by his or her signature on the instrument, the person, or the entity upon behalf of which the

person acted, executed the instrument.

I certify under PENALTY OF PERJURY under the laws of the State of _____

that the foregoing paragraph is true and correct.

WITNESS my hand and official seal.

_____

Notary Public for the State of _____

My commission expires _____

[NOTARY SEAL]

Mutual Release of Contract Claims

Party 1: _____

Address: _____

Party 2: _____

Address: _____

1. We voluntarily and knowingly sign this mutual release with the intention of eliminating the liabilities and obligations described below.

2. Disputes and differences have arisen between us with respect to an agreement entered into between us on _____ *[date]* _____, under which we agreed to the following:

    _____

    _____

    _____

    This agreement is hereby made a part of this release and incorporated by reference. A copy of the agreement (if written) is attached to this release.

3. We each hereby expressly release the other from all claims and demands, known and unknown, arising out of the agreement specified in Clause 2. Each party understands that, as to claims that are known to that party when the release is signed, any statutory provisions that would otherwise apply to limit this general release are hereby waived. Each party also understands that this release extends to claims arising out of this incident that are *not* known at the time this release is signed.

4. This release additionally applies to our heirs, legal representatives, and successors and is binding on our spouses, heirs, legal representatives, assigns, and anyone else claiming under us. Neither of us has assigned to another party any claim arising under or out of the contract specified in Clause 2.

5. The value (consideration) for this mutual release binds our mutual agreement to forgo our respective legal rights with reference to the disputes and differences described above.

6. We also agree that the contract specified in Clause 2 shall be and is hereby rescinded, terminated, and canceled as of _____ *[date]*.

_____   _____
Party 1's signature   Date

_____   _____
Print name   County of residence

_____   _____
Party 1's spouse's signature   Date

_____   _____
Print name   County of residence

_____   _____
Party 2's signature   Date

_____   _____
Print name   County of residence

_____   _____
Party 2's spouse's signature   Date

_____   _____
Print name   County of residence

Certificate of Acknowledgment of Notary Public

State of _____

                                          } ss

County of _____

On _____, _____, before me, _____,
a notary public in and for said state, personally appeared _____,
who proved to me on the basis of satisfactory evidence to be the person whose name is subscribed to the
within instrument and acknowledged to me that he or she executed the same in his or her authorized
capacity and that by his or her signature on the instrument, the person, or the entity upon behalf of which the
person acted, executed the instrument.

I certify under PENALTY OF PERJURY under the laws of the State of _____
that the foregoing paragraph is true and correct.

WITNESS my hand and official seal.

_____

Notary Public for the State of _____

My commission expires _____

[NOTARY SEAL]

Complaint Letter

Date: _____

_____

_____

_____

_____

[name and address of consumer protection office]

To Whom It May Concern:

I wish to lodge a complaint about the following company:

Name: _____

Address: _____

_____

Phone number: _____

Name of person with whom I dealt: _____

The details of my complaint are as follows *[attach additional sheets if necessary]*:

_____

_____

_____

_____

_____ .

Please investigate this matter and inform me of the results.

Sincerely,

_____
Signature

_____
Printed name

_____
Address

_____
Email

_____
Daytime phone   Evening phone   Cell phone

cc: _____

_____

_____

Notice of Insurance Claim

Date: _____

_____

_____

_____

_____

[name and address of insurance company]

Name of your insured: _____

Policy number: _____

To Whom It May Concern:

Please be advised that ☐ I received injuries ☐ I sustained property damage in an accident on

_____, _____, at the following location: _____

_____ .

The accident involved:

☐ two or more motor vehicles

☐ motor vehicle and pedestrian

☐ motor vehicle and bicycle

☐ motor vehicle and property

[for all motor vehicles involved other than your own, give]:

Make, model, year, and color of vehicle: _____

License plate number and state of issuance: _____

Vehicle identification number: _____

Name of driver (if different from name of insured above): _____

Driver's license number and state of issuance: _____

☐ slip and fall

☐ animal bite, claw, knockdown, etc.

☐ dangerous or defective product

☐ other (specify): _____

The person named above was involved in the incident. Please confirm in writing to the address below your liability coverage of the insured identified above. Please also advise whether your insured contends that anyone other than your insured may be in whole or in part legally responsible for accidents on or near the premises or for this accident.

As requested, please respond in writing. If necessary, I may be reached by telephone at the number below.

Thank you for your prompt attention to this matter.

Sincerely,

_____   _____
Signature   Date

_____
Printed name

_____
Address

_____   _____
                                                                    Phone

Notice to Cancel Certain Contracts

To Whom It May Concern:

This letter constitutes written notice to you that I am canceling the following contract:

Seller: _____

Address: _____

Buyer: _____

Address: _____

Contract pertains to the following goods/services purchased: _____

_____ .

Date contract signed for these goods/services:_____, _____.

Please acknowledge receipt of this letter by signing below and returning the acknowledgment to me in the enclosed envelope. I understand that under the law, you must refund my money within _____ days. Furthermore, if applicable, I understand that you must either pick up the items purchased, or reimburse me within _____ days for my expense of mailing the goods back to you. If you do not pick up the goods within that time, I am entitled to keep them.

_____   _____
Buyer's signature   Date

_____
Print name

....

Acknowledgment

_____   _____
Seller's signature   Date

_____
Print name

Cancel Membership or Subscription Notice

Date: _____

_____

_____

_____

_____

[name and address of publication or organization; include name of department if available]

Re: _____ *[subscription or membership number]*

This letter is to notify you that I would like to cancel my _____

_____ *[specify what you are canceling, such as a subscription to publication or*

membership in organization] effective _____ *[date of cancellation].*

The reason for this cancellation is _____

_____ *[specify reason for cancellation].*

Thank you for your prompt assistance.

_____
Signature

_____
Address

_____
Subscription or account number

Request to Begin Special Education Process

Date: _____

_____

_____

_____

_____

[name and address of special education administrator]

Re: _____ *[name of child]*

Child's school: _____

Child's teacher: _____ Child's grade: _____

I am writing because my child is experiencing difficulties in school, including *[describe difficulties]*:

_____

_____

_____

I am formally requesting that the school immediately begin its special education process, including initial assessment for eligibility. I understand that you will send me an assessment plan explaining the tests that may be given to my child. Because I realize the assessment can take some time, I would appreciate receiving the assessment plan within ten days. I would also appreciate any other information you have regarding assessments, how eligibility is determined, and the general IEP process.

I am also requesting that you make available to me a complete copy of my child's school file, including all tests, reports, assessments, grades, notes by teachers or other staff members, and any other information contained in the file. I understand that I am entitled to these records under the Family Educational Rights and Privacy Act (FERPA) (20 U.S.C. Section 1232 [g]). I would greatly appreciate having these files within the next five days. I will call you to discuss how and when I will get the copies.

Thank you very much for your assistance. I look forward to working with you and your staff.

Sincerely,

_____
Signature of parent

_____
Printed name

_____
Address

_____ _____
                                    Email

_____ _____ _____
Daytime phone Evening phone Cell phone

Identity Theft Worksheet

Credit Bureaus

☐ Experian: 888-397-3742

Date of Contact	Contact Person	Comments

☐ Equifax: 800-525-6285

Date of Contact	Contact Person	Comments

☐ TransUnion: 800-680-7289

Date of Contact	Contact Person	Comments

Financial Institutions

Credit Card Companies

Name of Company	Phone Number	Date of Contact	Contact Person	Comments

Banks

Name of Bank	Phone Number	Date of Contact	Contact Person	Comments

Other Service Providers

Name of Institution	Phone Number	Date of Contact	Contact Person	Comments

Law Enforcement Agencies

Local Police Department

Name of Department	Phone Number	Date of Contact	Name of Person/Officer Contacted	Comments

Federal Trade Commission: 877-438-4338

Date of Contact	Contact Person	Comments

Other Law Enforcement Agencies

Name of Agency	Phone Number	Date of Contact	Contact Person	Comments

Other Contacts

Local Postal Inspector: Call 800-275-8777 for the phone number of your local inspector

Phone Number	Date of Contact	Contact Person	Comments

Social Security Administration: 800-269-0271

Date of Contact	Contact Person	Comments

Debt Collectors

Name of Collection Agency	Phone Number	Date of Contact	Contact Person	Comments

U.S. State Department: 202-955-0430

Date of Contact	Contact Person	Comments

Department of Motor Vehicles

DMV Location	Phone Number	Date of Contact	Contact Person	Comments

Additional Conversations/Correspondence

Name of Institution	Phone Number	Date of Contact	Contact Person	Comments

Expenses Incurred

Date Expense Incurred	Reason for Expense	Cost
	Total Costs:	

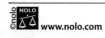

Index

A

Acceleration clause, promissory notes, 61
Accidents
    accident claim worksheet, 134
    notice of insurance claim, 141–142
    See also Releases
Adjustable interest rates, 57
    adjustable rate mortgages (ARMs), 78, 79
Amending forms, 4–5
Amortization calculators, 61
Amortization chart, mortgage payments, 76
Amortization, negative, 79
Apartment-finding service checklist, 46–47
Arbitration, 9–10
ARMs (adjustable rate mortgages), 78, 79
Assets
    assets and liabilities statement, 100
    on family financial statement, 74–75
    See also Property; *specific types*
Assignment of lease, consent to, 51
Assignment of rights form, 100–101
ATM cards, stolen, 146
Attachment pages, 6
Attorney fees and court costs, identity theft-related, 146
Attorney fees clause
    lease or rental agreement, 48–49
    promissory notes, 61
Attorney-in-fact
    power of attorney for finances, 19–20, 21
    power of attorney for real estate, 24, 25, 26
Auctions, online, 131–132, 140
Authorization agreements
    authorization to check credit and employment
      references, 58
    children's carpool agreement, 17–18
    to drive a motor vehicle, 18–19
    foreign travel with a minor, 16
    housesitting instructions, 16–17
    minor's medical treatment, 14–15, 16, 121
    pet care agreement, 18
    power of attorney for finances (limited), 19–23
    power of attorney for real estate, 23–27
    power of attorney notice of revocation, 27
    temporary guardianship of a minor, 14–15
Autos. *See* Vehicle *entries*

B

Babysitting. *See* Child care
Bad checks, demand to make good on, 67–68
Balloon payments, 57
    mortgages, 78, 79
    promissory note with, 61–62
Bank accounts
    beneficiary designations, 31
    identity theft and, 146–147
    notice to terminate joint account, 101–102
    See also Checks
Banks. *See* Financial institutions
Beneficiary designations and worksheet, 30, 31
Bills of sale, 82–85
    basics, 82
    for boats, 83–84
    for computer system, 84
    for dog, 85
    general, 82, 84
    for motor vehicles, 82–83
Boat bill of sale, 83–84
Borrowing money. *See* Loans; Mortgages; Promissory
    notes
Breach of contract, 138
Budgets, 98
    daily expenses form, 98–99
    monthly budget form, 99–100
    monthly income form, 99
    See also Finances
Buyer in due course (promissory notes), 61, 66

C

Cancellation rights, consumer contracts, 142–144
Care agreements
    child care instructions form, 120–121
    in-home child care, 118–120
    in-home elder care, 121
    pet care, 18
    shared care arrangements, 120, 121
    See also Temporary guardianship authorization
Carpool agreement, 17–18
Carrying costs (home purchases), 75–77, 79
Cars. *See* Vehicle *entries*

CD-ROM
   form completion tips, 3–6, 151–152
   form numbers and titles listed, 153–155
   how to use, 150–152
Cease contact demand, collection agencies, 106
Certificate of Acknowledgment of Notary Public, 8
Changing forms, 4–5
Checks
   bad check demand letter, 67–68
   check cashing time limits, 102–103
   stopping payment on, 102–103, 146–147
Child care, 116
   agreement for in-home child care, 118–120
   child care instructions form, 120–125
   shared care arrangements, 120
Children
   carpool agreement, 17–18
   foreign travel authorization, 16
   leaving property to, 35–36
   medical treatment authorization, 14–15, 16, 121
   mentioning in will, 34
   naming guardian in will, 35
   request to begin special education process, 144–145
   temporary guardianship authorization, 14–15
   trusts for, 32, 36
   See also Child care; Estate planning
Closing credit card accounts, 102
Codicil (basic will), 36
Collateral, 57, 59
   homes as, 64, 65, 143
   security agreements, 63–66
Collection agencies
   cease contact demand, 106
   identity theft and, 147
Community property law
   joint assignments of rights, 101
   spousal debt liability, 59, 60, 136
Complaint letters, 140–141
Computer system bill of sale, 84
Consent to assignment of lease, 51
Contractors, 92–93
   contractor mid-job worksheet, 94–95
   home maintenance agreement, 93–94
   home repairs agreement, 94
   independent contractors vs. employees, 93
   insurance issues, 92–93, 94
Contracts, 124
   assignments of rights under, 100–101
   cancellation rights and notice, 142–144
   legal validity, 2–3, 136

   mutual release of contract claims (breach of contract disputes), 138
   oral vs. written, 2
   See also Forms; *specific types*
Conventional power of attorney, 21, 23. *See also* Power of attorney
Cosigners, 57, 63
   promissory note provision, 63
County offices
   death certificate requests, 38–39
   recording documents, 26–27
Couples
   joint assignments of rights, 101
   notice to terminate joint account, 101–102
   See also Living together; Spouses
Court costs and attorney fees
   lease or rental agreement, 48–49
   promissory notes, 61
Credit bureaus, 103
   placing a fraud alert, 146
   reporting unauthorized credit card charges, 105
   sending notice to remove name from mailing lists, 109–110
Credit cards
   closing accounts after identity theft, 146
   disputing charges, 105
   notice to terminate joint accounts, 101–102
   notifying issuer of accountholder's death, 39–40
   unauthorized charges, 105
Credit checks, 57
   authorization for, 56, 58
Credit insurance, 57
Creditors
   closing accounts after identity theft, 146
   notice to terminate joint account, 101–102
   notifying of death, 39–40
   See also Debts
Credit reports
   disputing incorrect entries, 104–105
   if you are a victim of identity theft, 146
   requesting, 103–104
Custodianships, UTMA custodianships for gifts to minors, 35

D

Daily expenses form, 98–99
Damages
   bad checks, 67, 68
   describing in demand letter, 131
   for excessive telemarketing calls, 111, 113

Death
    documents for executors, 38–43
    power of attorney for finances and, 20
    See also Estate planning
Death certificate request form, 38–39
Death notifications
    to creditors, 39–40
    general notice, 40–41
    to insurance companies, 41–43
Debit cards, stolen, 146
Debt collectors
    collection agency cease contact demand, 106
    identity theft and, 147
Debt liability
    joint and several liability, 61
    notice of, to cosigners, 63
    of spouses, 59, 60, 136
    unmarried partners, 127
Debts
    assets and liabilities statement, 100
    on family financial statement, 75
    forgiving, 31
    leaving encumbered property, 33
    See also Loans; Mortgages
Debt-to-income ratios, 76–77, 79
Declaration of legal name change, 127–128
Deeds of trust, 64. *See also* Mortgages
Defective goods, 133
    refund/repair requests, 6, 132–134
Demand letters
    basics, 130, 131
    collection agency cease contact demand, 106
    for damages for excessive telemarketing calls, 113
    general demand letter, 130–131
    to make good on bad check, 67–68
    for overdue payment under promissory note, 67
    for return of security deposit, 53–54
Direct Marketing Association, 110
Disabilities, children with, 32, 144–145
Discrimination, caution for landlords, 47
Disputes, dispute resolution, 130–138
    accident claim worksheet, 134
    agreement clause, 9, 10
    arbitration, 9–10
    attorney fees and court costs, 48–49
    basics, 8–10, 130
    demand letter form, 130–131
    demand letter for online auction buyers, 131–132
    home repair/maintenance agreements, 93
    landlord-tenant disputes, 51–52, 54

mediation, 9, 10, 130
    purchases made with credit cards, 105
    refund/repair request for goods under warranty, 132–134
    release forms, 134–138
    unmarried couples, 125, 126
    See also Lawsuits
Disputing credit card charges, 105
Divorce/separation
    notice to terminate joint account, 101–102
    power of attorney for finances and, 20
    unmarried couples, 124, 126
DMV
    checking vehicle registration, 83
    reporting stolen driver's license, 148
Dogs, bill of sale for, 85
Domestic partners, 34, 125
"Do not call" lists, 108–109, 111–113
Door-to-door sales contracts, 142–143
Driver's license, stolen, 148
Driving. *See* Vehicle *entries*
Durable power of attorney, 21, 23

E

eBay. *See* Online auctions
Editing forms, 4–5
EIN (employer identification number), 117
Elder care agreement, 121
Employees, 116–122
    employer legal obligations, 116–118
    for home repairs/maintenance, 93
    housekeepers/housecleaners, 121–122
    vs. independent contractors, 93, 116
    in-home child care, 118–121
    in-home elder care, 121
Employer identification number, 117
Employment references, authorization to check, 56, 58
Encumbered property, leaving by will, 33
Estate planning, 30–43
    basic wills, 30, 32–36
    beneficiary designations and worksheet, 30, 31
    books and software for, 32
    documents for executors, 38–43
    property worksheet, 30
    will codicil, 36
Events, describing, 6
Executor
    documents for, 38–43
    duties, 38, 40
    naming, 33–34

providing proof of executor status, 43
See also Wills
Executor's checklist, 40
Expenses
   agreement to share (unmarried couples), 125
   daily expenses form, 98–99
   on family financial statement, 73–74
   in monthly budget, 99–100

F

Fair Credit Reporting Act (FCRA), 103–104
Fair Debt Collection Practices Act, 106
Family Education Rights and Privacy Act (FERPA),
   144
Family financial statement, 72–75
Family pot trusts, 36
Farm machinery, 82
FCC. *See* Federal Communications Commission
FCRA (Fair Credit Reporting Act), 103–104
Federal Communications Commission (FCC), 109,
   141
Federal law
   Fair Credit Reporting Act, 103–104
   Fair Debt Collection Practices Act, 106
   Family Education Rights and Privacy Act (FERPA),
      144
   hazard disclosures to tenants, 49
   Individuals with Disabilities Education Act (IDEA),
      144
   lease termination for servicemembers, 50
   minimum wage and overtime, 117
   Telemarketing and Consumer Fraud and Abuse
      Prevention Act, 108
   Telephone Consumer Protection Act, 108, 111, 112
   Truth in Lending Act, 143
Federal Trade Commission (FTC), 105, 109, 140, 141
   cooling-off rule, 142–143
   identity theft resources, 147, 148
Fees, notarization, 7
FERPA (Family Education Rights and Privacy Act),
   144
FICA taxes, 116, 118
Final arrangements, 21
Finances, 98–106
   assets and liabilities statement (net worth), 100
   assignment of rights form, 100–101
   collection agency cease contact demand, 106
   credit report requests and corrections, 103–105
   disputing credit card charges, 105

family financial statement, 72–75
monthly budget, 99–100
monthly income, 99
notice to terminate joint account, 101–102
notifying creditors of death, 39–40
power of attorney for finances, 19–23, 27
See also Loans; Mortgages; Promissory notes
Financial institutions
   closing accounts after identity theft, 146
   notifying of death, 39–40
   powers of attorney and, 21, 24
   See also Bank accounts; Credit cards
Fixed rate mortgages, 78, 79. *See also* Mortgages
Fixed-term residential lease, 48–49. *See also* Leases;
   Renting
Foreign travel authorization, 16
Forms, 2–11
   attachment pages, 6
   basics, 2–4
   dispute resolution clause, 8–10
   form numbers and titles listed, 153–155
   how to use the CD-ROM, 150–152
   lawyer review, 10–11
   signatures and notarization, 7–8
   tips for completing, 3–6, 151–152
Fraud, 104
   complaint letters, 140–141
   identity theft, 104, 145–148
   Internet Fraud Watch, 131
   reporting unauthorized credit card charges, 105
Fraud alerts, 146
FTC. *See* Federal Trade Commission

G

General bill of sale, 82, 84
General mutual release form, 137
General notice of death, 40–41
General release form, 136
Goods. *See* Personal property; Purchases
Government agencies
   complaint letters, 140–141
   notifying of death, 40, 41
   reporting identity theft, 147, 148
   telemarketing and junk mail complaints, 109
Grace periods, loan payments, 57, 78
Guardianships
   formal vs. informal, 14
   naming children's guardian in will, 35
   property guardians for minors, 35
   temporary guardianship authorization, 14–15

H

Hard closes, credit card accounts, 102
Hazard disclosures, to tenants, 49
Health care directives, 21
Health club memberships, right to cancel, 143
Hiring. *See* Employees
Home equity lines of credit, 102
Home-finding services, 46–47
Homeowner's associations, 93
Homeowner's insurance
  estimating cost, 76
  identity theft coverage3, 146
  impound accounts, 79
  notification of insured's death, 41–42
  personal property storage contracts and, 90
  vehicles and, 42–43
Home purchases, 70–80
  family financial statement, 72–75
  house comparison worksheet, 72
  house priorities worksheet, 71–72
  ideal house profile, 70–71
  monthly carrying costs, 75–77, 79
  mortgage rates and terms worksheet, 77–78
  moving checklist, 80
  online resources, 70
  unmarried couples, 126
Home repairs and maintenance, 92–95
  contract cancellation rights and, 142
  contractor mid-job worksheet, 94–95
  home maintenance agreement, 93–94
  home repairs agreement, 94
  housekeeping services agreement, 121–122
  independent contractors vs. employees, 93
  local permits, 93
  notice to landlord of needed repairs, 52–53
  state licensing requirements, 92–93, 94
Homes
  as loan collateral, 64, 65, 143
  See also Home purchases; Home repairs; Mortgages; Renting
House comparison worksheet, 72
Household employees. *See* Employees
Housekeepers/housecleaners, 121–122
House priorities worksheet, 71–72
Housesitting instructions, 16–17
Housing discrimination, 47

I

IDEA (Individuals with Disabilities Education Act), 144
Ideal house profile, 70–71
Identity theft, 104, 145–148
IEPs (Individualized Education Programs), 144
Impound accounts, 79
Imputed interest, 62, 63
Incapacity, power of attorney for finances and, 20, 21
Income
  on family financial statement, 73
  in monthly budget, 99
  monthly income form, 99
Income taxes, household employees, 116
Indemnification clause, power of attorney for finances and, 20
Independent contractors, vs. employees, 93, 116
Individualized Education Programs (IEPs), 144
Individuals with Disabilities Education Act (IDEA), 144
Informal dispute resolution, 9
Informal guardianship, 14–15
Inheritance rights
  of children, 34
  of spouses and domestic partners, 34
Inspections
  landlord-tenant checklist, 51–52, 53
  vehicle sales/purchases, 83
Installment loans
  monthly payment record, 58
  promissory notes for, 60–62
Insurance
  credit insurance, 57
  home repair contractors, 92–93, 94
  notice of insurance claim, 141–142
  notifying insurers of death, 41–43
  private mortgage insurance (PMI), 76, 79
  workers' compensation, 117, 118
  See also Homeowner's insurance
Intangible property, 64, 75
Intellectual property, 75
  as loan collateral, 64
Interest, 56, 57, 60–61, 62–63
  estimating mortgage interest, 75
  imputed interest, 62, 63
  mortgage rates and terms, 77–78, 79–80
  See also Promissory notes
Interest-free loans, 60
  promissory notes for, 62, 63

Internet Fraud Watch, 131
Intestacy, 30
IRS
  assignments of rights as taxable transactions, 101
  employer resources, 117
  failure to meet employer obligations, 118
  imputed interest rules, 62, 63
  worker classification information, 93
  See also Taxes

J

Joint accounts, notice to terminate, 101–102
Joint and several liability, 61
Joint tenancy property, 30
Junk mail, 108
  notice to add or retain name but not sell or trade it, 111
  notice to remove name from list, 109–111

L

Landlord-tenant agreements. *See* Renting
Landlord-tenant checklist, 51–52, 53
Lawsuits, 8, 10
  attorney fees and court costs, 48–49, 61
  over bad checks, 67, 68
  suing for return of security deposit, 54
  suing telemarketers, 111
Lawyers, 10–11
  debt collections and, 106
  for help with executor's duties, 40
Leases
  agreement to terminate, 50–51
  consent to assignment, 51
  fixed-term residential lease, 48–49
  See also Renting
Lending money. *See* Loans; Mortgages; Promissory notes
Letters testamentary, letters of administration, 43
Liabilities. *See* Debts
Liability
  release forms, 134–138
  See also Debt liability; Insurance
Licensing, contractor license requirements, 92–93
Life insurance, beneficiary designations, 31
Limited power of attorney for finances, 19–23
Living together, 124–128
  agreement for a joint purchase, 125–126
  agreement to keep property separate, 124–125
  agreement to share property, 126–127

declaration of legal name change, 127–128
Living trusts, 21
Loans, 56–68
  agreement to modify promissory note, 66–67
  authorization to check credit and employment references, 56, 58
  balloon payments, 57, 61–62
  basic loan terms, 56, 57
  calculating payment amounts, 61, 62
  collateral, 57, 59
  cosigners, 57, 63
  forgiving loans on death, 31
  home equity lines of credit, 102
  interest, 56, 57, 60–61, 62–63
  loan comparison worksheet, 56
  monthly payment record, 58
  overdue payment demand, 67
  points and fees, 57
  prepayment penalties, 57
  promissory notes, 58–63
  release of U.C.C. Financing Statement after payoff, 66
  security agreements, 59, 63–66
  shopping for, 56
  vehicle loans, 83, 84
  See also Mortgages; Promissory notes
Louisiana residents, will forms and, 32, 34
Lump-sum loan repayment
  balloon payments, 57, 61–62
  promissory notes for, 62–63

M

Mail fraud, 147
Mailing lists, 108
  notice to add or retain name but not sell or trade it, 111
  notice to remove name from, 109–111
Maintenance agreements. *See* Home repairs and maintenance
Marital property. *See* Community property law
Married couples, 124. *See also* Divorce/separation; Spouses
Mediation, 9, 10, 130
Medical treatment authorization, 14–15, 16, 121
Membership contracts, right to cancel, 143–144
Mental competence, 33. *See also* Incapacity
Merchandise. *See* Purchases
Military personnel. *See* Servicemembers
Minimum wage law, 117
Minors. *See* Children

Mobile homes, 82
Monthly budget, 99–100
Monthly carrying costs (home purchases), 75–77, 79
Monthly income form, 99
Monthly payment record (loan payments), 58
Month-to-month residential rental agreement, 48–49.
  See also Renting
Mortgages, 56, 64
  basic loan terms, 57
  key terms, 79–80
  leaving encumbered property, 33
  monthly carrying costs, 75–77, 79
  mortgage rates and terms worksheet, 77–78
  points and fees, 77–78, 80
  powers of attorney and, 24
  shopping for, 77–78
Motor vehicles. *See* Vehicle *entries*
Moving checklist, 80
Mutual release form, general, 137
Mutual release of contract claims, 138

N

Name changes, 127–128
Names, on forms, 5–6
National Do Not Call Registry, 108, 109, 113
Negative amortization, 79
Neighbor disputes, 137
Net worth statement, 100
New hire reporting, household employees, 117
Newspaper obituaries, 41
Notarization, 7–8. *See also specific forms*
Notice of intent to move out, 53
Notice of needed repairs (to landlord), 52–53
Notice of revocation (of power of attorney), 27
Notice of termination of personal property rental
  agreement, 89

O

Obituary information fact sheet, 41
Online auctions, 131, 140
  buyer demand letter, 131–132
Online resources
  amortization calculators, 61
  birth, death, and marriage records, 39
  complaints to government agencies, 140, 141
  contractor license information, 92
  county websites, 38
  credit bureaus and credit report requests, 103
  credit card problems, 105
  home purchases, 70
  lawyer directory, 40
  legal research, 85
  online fraud, 131
  reporting identity theft, 147
  statutory damages, 67
  telemarketing and junk mail, 108, 109, 110
  vehicle sales/purchases, 83
  wage and hour law, 117
Oral agreements, 2
Oral notice of intent to move, 53
Overdue payment demand (promissory notes), 67
Overtime pay, household employees, 117

P

Passports, stolen, 148
Payment arrangements
  home repair contracts, 94
  See also Promissory notes
Pay-on-death accounts, 31
Payroll taxes, household and maintenance employees,
  93, 116–118
People, naming on forms, 5–6
Permits, for home repairs, 93, 94
Personal finances. *See* Finances
Personal guardians for children, naming in will, 35
Personal information, organizing, 30
Personal injury
  notice of insurance claim, 141–142
  release for, 137
  See also Accidents
Personal property
  agreement to keep property separate (unmarried
    couples), 124–125
  agreement to share (unmarried couples), 126–127
  bills of sale for, 82–85
  identifying, 6
  identifying in will, 33
  as loan collateral, 64, 65
  personal property rental agreement, 88–89
  property worksheet, 30
  storage space rental contract, 88, 89–90
  See also Pets; Property; Purchases; Vehicles
Personal representative. *See* Executor
Pets
  bill of sale for dog, 85
  pet care agreement, 18
Pet stores, 85
PMI (private mortgage insurance), 76, 79
Police reports, identity theft, 147

Postal inspector, reporting identity theft to, 147
Power of attorney
   for finances (limited), 19–23
   notice of revocation, 27
   for real estate, 19, 23–27
   revoking, 20, 23, 26, 27
   witness requirements, 21, 22, 26
Prepayment penalties, 57, 79
Privacy Rights Clearinghouse, 108
Private mortgage insurance (PMI), 76, 79
Probate, 33, 38, 39
Probate avoidance, 30, 32
Product registration cards, 110
Promissory notes, 56, 58–63
   acceleration clause, 61
   agreement to modify, 66–67
   assignments of rights under, 100–101
   basics, 58–59
   cosigners, 57, 63
   installment payments with interest, 60–61
   installment payments with interest and balloon
      payments, 61–62
   installment payments without interest, 62
   legal terms, 61
   lump sum payment with interest, 62–63
   overdue payment demand, 67
   sale of, 61, 66
   security agreements, 59, 63–66
   signatures, 8, 59
Property
   beneficiary designations and worksheet, 30, 31
   identifying in forms, 6
   identifying in will, 33
   leaving to minor children, 35–36
   property worksheet, 30
   See also Personal property; Purchases; Real estate;
     specific types
Property damage
   notice of insurance claim, 141–142
   releases for, 137
   See also Accidents
Property taxes, 76, 79
Purchases
   contract cancellation rights and notices, 142–144
   defective items, 105
   disputing credit card charges, 105
   joint, agreement for (unmarried couples), 125–126
   online auction buyer demand letter, 131–132
   refund/repair requests, 6, 132–134
   See also Home purchases; Warranties

R

Real estate
   describing on power of attorney form, 24–25
   on family financial statement, 74
   identifying in will, 33
   joint ownership, 30, 31, 59
   joint ownership (unmarried couples), 126
   as loan collateral, 64, 65
   mobile homes, 82
   online resources, 70
   power of attorney for, 19, 23–27
   property worksheet, 30
   release for damage to, 137
   See also Home purchases; Home repairs; Property
Real estate taxes, 76, 79
Recording documents, 26–27
Reference checks, authorization for, 56, 58
Refund/repair requests, 6
   cancellation of purchase contracts, 142–144
   disputing credit card charges, 105
   for goods under warranty, 132–134
Registered domestic partners, 34, 125
Release of U.C.C. Financing Statement, 66
Releases (from liability), 134–138
   basics, 134–136, 138
   for contract claims, 138
   for damage to real estate, 137
   general mutual release, 137
   general release, 136
   for personal injury, 137
   for property damage in auto accident, 137
Rental agreements
   month-to-month residential rental agreement, 48–49
   for personal property, 88–89

   storage space rental, 89–90
Rental application, 47, 50
Rental listing services, 46–47
Rental unit inspection checklist, 51–52, 53
Rent control ordinances, 49
Renting, 46–54
   apartment-finding service checklist, 46–47
   books and software, 46
   demand for return of security deposit, 53–54
   fixed-term residential lease, 48–49
   landlord-tenant checklist, 51–52, 53
   lease assignment consent, 51
   lease termination agreement, 50–51
   month-to-month residential rental agreement, 48–49

notice of needed repairs, 52–53
rental application, 47, 50
renting personal property, 88–89
storage space rental contract, 88, 89–90
tenant's notice of intent to move out, 53
Repairs. *See* Defective goods; Home repairs and maintenance; Refund/repair requests
Repairs, notice to landlord of needed repairs, 52–53
Request for Refund or Repair of Goods Under Warranty (Form 93), 6
Residuary beneficiaries, residuary estate, 31, 33
Retirement accounts
beneficiary designations, 31
on family financial statement, 74

S

Sales contracts, cancellation rights and notices, 142–143
Same-sex couples, 124. *See also* Domestic partners; Living together
Schools
request to begin special education process, 144–145
school-related authorizations, 14
Securities, beneficiary designations, 31
Security agreements, 59, 63–66
Security deposits, 48, 49, 51–52, 53–54
Selling property. *See* Bills of sale
Separate property of spouses, 60
Separation. *See* Divorce/separation
Servicemembers, lease termination rights, 50
Signatures, 7–8
of spouses, 8, 59, 136
See also specific forms
Small claims court
getting release agreements enforced, 138
suing for return of security deposit, 54
suing telemarketers, 111
Social Security Administration
notifying of death, 40, 41
reporting identity theft, 147
Social Security taxes, 116, 118
Special education process, request to begin, 144–145
Special needs trusts, 32
Spouses, 124
debt liability of, 59, 60, 136
inheritance rights, 34
signatures on forms and contracts, 8, 59, 136
See also Divorce

State agencies
checking vehicle registration, 83
complaint letters, 140–141
filing U.C.C. Financing Statement with, 64, 65–66
reporting stolen driver's license, 148
telemarketing and junk mail complaints, 109
State contractor licensing, 92–93
State "do not call" registries, 108–109
State law
community property law, 59, 60
contract cancellation rights, 143
death certificate access, 38
inheritance rights of spouses and domestic partners, 34
interest rates, 60
landlord-tenant laws, 48, 49, 50, 54
monetary damage amounts, 67, 68
notarization language, 7
pet purchases, 85
powers of attorney, 20, 21, 22, 26
property ownership by minors, 35
telemarketing laws, 112
UTMA custodianships, 35
wage and hour law, 117
Statement of assets and liabilities, 100
Stepparents, 14
Stopping payment of checks, 102–103, 146–147
Storage space rental contract, 88, 89–90
Subscriptions, right to cancel, 143–144
Successors, assigns, and heirs, 136

T

Taxes
employer tax obligations, 116–118
real estate taxes, 76, 79
See also IRS
Taxpayer ID number, 117
Tear-out forms
attachment pages, 6
wills, 3, 33
Telemarketing, 108–109
demand for damages for excessive calls, 113
"do not call" lists, 108–109, 111–113
phone call log, 111–112
Telephone Consumer Protection Act, 108, 111, 112
Temporary guardianship authorization for minors, 14–15

Tenants
   notice of intent to move out, 53
   See also Renting
Terminating joint credit accounts, 101–102
Termination agreements
   fixed-term residential lease, 50–51
   personal property rental agreement, 89
Transfer-on-death registration, 31
Travel
   authorization for foreign travel with minor, 16
   housesitting instructions, 16–17
   pet care agreement, 18
   temporary guardianship authorization for minors,
     14–15
Trucks. *See* Vehicle *entries*
Trusts, 21, 32
   for children, 32, 36
Truth in Lending Act, 143

U

U.C.C. Financing Statement, 64, 65–66
Unemployment taxes, household employees, 117
Unmarried couples. *See* Domestic partners; Living
   together
U.S. Postal Service, reporting identity theft, 147
U.S. State Departmen, reporting stolen passport, 148
Usury, 60
UTMA (Uniform Transfers to Minors Act)
   custodianships, 35

V

Vehicle accidents
   accident claim worksheet, 134
   notice of insurance claim, 141–142
   release for property damage, 137
Vehicle insurance, notifying carrier of insured's death,
   42–43
Vehicle loans, 83, 84

Vehicles
   authorization to drive a motor vehicle, 18–90
   boat bill of sale, 83–84
   carpool agreement, 17–18
   checking registration, 83
   joint ownership, 126
   motor vehicle bill of sale, 82–83
   online resources, 83
   reporting stolen driver's license, 148
   vehicles as loan collateral, 64, 65
   vehicles on family financial statement, 74
   See also Personal property

W

Warranties, 132
   refund/repair request for goods under warranty,
     132–134
   refund/repair requests, 6
   sales of personal property, 82, 83
Warranty cards, 110
Wills, 21, 30, 32–36
   beneficiary worksheet, 31
   books and software for, 32
   documents for executors, 38–43
   legal requirements, 33, 34
   naming guardians for children, 35
   property worksheet, 30
   revoking or making changes, 36
   tear-out will cautions, 3, 33
   will codicil, 36
   witnesses, 34
   See also Probate
Witnesses, 7
   accident witness statements, 134
   notarization and, 7
   power of attorney for finances, 21, 22
   wills, 34
Workers' compensation insurance, 117, 118
Written agreements, 2

NOLO ®   *Keep Up to Date*

 Go to **Nolo.com/newsletters/index.html** to sign up for free newsletters and discounts on Nolo products.

- **Nolo Briefs.** Our monthly email newsletter with great deals and free information.

- **BizBriefs.** Tips and discounts on Nolo products for business owners and managers.

- **Landlord's Quarterly.** Deals and free tips just for landlords and property managers, too.

- **Nolo's Special Offer.** A monthly newsletter with the biggest Nolo discounts around.

 Don't forget to check for updates at **Nolo.com**. Under "Products," find this book and click "Legal Updates."

Let Us Hear From You

 Comments on this book? We want to hear 'em. Email us at feedback@nolo.com.

SPOT7

NOLO® *Online Legal Forms*

Nolo offers a large library of legal solutions and forms, created by Nolo's in-house legal staff. These reliable documents can be prepared in minutes.

Online Legal Solutions

- **Incorporation.** Incorporate your business in any state.
- **LLC Formations.** Gain asset protection and pass-through tax status in any state.
- **Wills.** Nolo has helped people make over 2 million wills. Is it time to make or revise yours?
- **Living Trust (avoid probate).** Plan now to save your family the cost, delays, and hassle of probate.
- **Trademark.** Protect the name of your business or product.
- **Provisional Patent.** Preserve your rights under patent law and claim "patent pending" status.

Online Legal Forms

Nolo.com has hundreds of top quality legal forms available for download—bills of sale, promissory notes, nondisclosure agreements, LLC operating agreements, corporate minutes, commercial lease and sublease, motor vehicle bill of sale, consignment agreements and many, many more.

Review Your Documents

Many lawyers in Nolo's consumer-friendly lawyer directory will review Nolo documents for a very reasonable fee. Check their detailed profiles at **www.nolo.com/lawyers/index.html**.

Lawyer Directory

Find a Quality Attorney

- *Qualified lawyers*
- *In-depth profiles*
- *Respectful service*

When you want help with a serious legal problem, you don't want just any lawyer—you want an expert in the field who can provide up-to-the-minute advice to help you protect your loved ones. You need a lawyer who has the experience and knowledge to answer your questions about personal injury, wills, family law, child custody, drafting a patent application or any other specialized legal area you are concerned with.

Nolo's Lawyer Directory is unique because it provides an extensive profile of every lawyer. You'll learn about not only each lawyer's education, professional history, legal specialties, credentials and fees, but also about their philosophy of practicing law and how they like to work with clients. It's all crucial information when you're looking for someone to trust with an important personal or business matter.

All lawyers listed in Nolo's directory are in good standing with their state bar association. They all pledge to work diligently and respectfully with clients—communicating regularly, providing a written agreement about how legal matters will be handled, sending clear and detailed bills and more. And many directory lawyers will review Nolo documents, such as a will or living trust, for a fixed fee, to help you get the advice you need.

WWW.NOLO.COM